The A

The Actress

Hollywood Acting and the Female Star

Karen Hollinger

Routledge
Taylor & Francis Group
New York   London

Routledge is an imprint of the
Taylor & Francis Group, an informa business

Published in 2006 by
Routledge
Taylor & Francis Group
270 Madison Avenue
New York, NY 10016

Published in Great Britain by
Routledge
Taylor & Francis Group
2 Park Square
Milton Park, Abingdon
Oxon OX14 4RN

Printed in the United States of America
10 9 8 7 6 5 4 3 2 1

International Standard Book Number-10: 0-415-97792-4 (Softcover)
International Standard Book Number-13: 978-0-415-97792-0 (Softcover)
Library of Congress Card Number 2005031057

Library of Congress Cataloging-in-Publication Data

Hollinger, Karen.
The actress : Hollywood acting and the female star / by Karen Hollinger.
p. cm.
Includes bibliographical references and index.
ISBN 0-415-97791-6 (hb) -- ISBN 0-415-97792-4 (pb) 1. Motion picture actors and actresses--United States--Biography. 2. Actresses--United States--Biography. 3. Motion picture acting. I. Title.

PN1998.2.H627 2006
791.4302'8092273--dc22   2005031057

Taylor & Francis Group
is the Academic Division of Informa plc.

Visit the Taylor & Francis Web site at
http://www.taylorandfrancis.com

and the Routledge Web site at
http://www.routledge-ny.com

Contents

List of Illustrations

Preface

The Actress: Hollywood Acting and the Female Star investigates the contemporary film actress as an artist and an ideological construct. The book is divided into two sections: Part I looks at the major issues involved in the study of film acting, stardom, and the Hollywood actress. My intention is to point to the problematic nature of this study and to move the analysis of the images and careers of major female Hollywood stars in a new direction. My study of the star–actress breaks new ground by bringing together theories of screen acting and film stardom. The first section of the book fully discusses how these two areas of inquiry might be combined.

Of particular usefulness to the study of screen acting is the intertextual approach so often advocated in star studies. According to this paradigm, the star–actor is seen as an amalgam of complementary texts, including performance, promotion, publicity, criticism, and commentaries. The intertextual case studies of Meryl Streep, Susan Sarandon, Jodie Foster, Angela Bassett, and Gwyneth Paltrow that compose Part II of the book involve an analysis of the interaction among these stars' career trajectories, the elements of their star images, their comments on their acting craft, and the ideological significance of their star personas. In this way, many of the insights of star studies can be brought to the study of star acting and vice versa, and some light can be shed on the much neglected craft of the Hollywood film actress.

Before we turn to that study, however, a few acknowledgments of the people and institutions that helped to bring this project to fruition are in order. First of all, I would like to thank Judith Simon of Taylor & Francis, William Germano and Frederick Veith of Routledge, the copy editing and production staff, and the anonymous outside reader, who offered extremely insightful suggestions for revision. I would also like to express my gratitude to Armstrong Atlantic State University for two research and scholarship grants that helped me to conduct my research. My thanks also extend to my film students at Armstrong for sharing, stimulating, and critiquing my ideas. The Margaret Herrick Library of the Academy of Motion Picture Arts and Sciences in Beverly Hills and the Billy Rose Theater Collection of the New York Public Library were absolutely essential to the completion of this book, and Corbis was useful in providing the book's illustrations. Finally, I would like to thank my husband and sons, who are always supportive of and inspirational to me.

The Author

Karen Hollinger is professor of film and literature at Armstrong Atlantic State University in Savannah, Georgia. She is the author of *In the Company of Women: Contemporary Female Friendship Films* (1998) and coeditor of *Letter from an Unknown Woman* (1986). She has also published numerous articles about women in film.

PART I

Acting, Stardom, and the Hollywood Actress

CHAPTER **1**

The Hollywood Star–Actress
and Studies of Acting

Scholarly considerations of film acting invariably begin by asserting that screen acting has been and still remains a neglected area of film scholarship, but this is really not the case anymore. There have been several book-length considerations of film acting,[1] some important anthologies,[2] a significant number of journal articles on film acting, and an abundance of collections of actor interviews.[3] I would still agree with Scott McDonald, however, who asserts that "film studies has yet to provide any sustained inquiry into film acting,"[4] and I would add that the work of the film actress has been particularly ignored. This chapter considers at some length why this is the case. It seeks to move beyond the mere assertion that screen acting, and in particular the study of the film actress, is neglected, to examine a number of problems involved in the study of acting in film and the screen actress in particular.

As Alan Lovell and Peter Krämer have suggested, the problems that plague investigations of film acting stem from practical issues and unfavorable theoretical paradigms in film scholarship.[5] As critic after critic has pointed out, acting is a crucial aspect of the filmmaking process, yet even with a recent revival of interest in the subject, screen performance inexplicably remains one of the most undertheorized areas in film study. There are several reasons for this scholarly failure to interrogate successfully the complexities of the phenomenon of screen acting. First of all, it is exactly this view of acting as a phenomenon and a mystical art beyond the scope of methodical investigation that has prevented scholarly analysis. Early considerations of screen acting and even those currently found in the popular press approach film acting from what can be called the reverie approach, which sees performance as ineffable and seeks to discuss it through "adulation, anecdote, and reminiscence."[6]

This approach led to the foregrounding of actor interviews in studies of film acting, which in turn resulted in acting being understood not as a "systematic or standardized process" that can be carefully examined with some objectivity by scholars, but instead as an intuitive, quasimystical, elusive art that is the particular individualized practice of particularly gifted individuals who consider it an almost religious experience.[7] This reverie approach has been applied extensively to actresses, who are most often characterized not as skilled craftswomen, but rather as screen goddesses naturally gifted with the beauty and charisma that has made them stars.

A quote from Meryl Streep, who has even been referred to as "Magic Meryl" by journalists attempting to praise her acting talent, exemplifies this attitude perfectly. When asked by that guru of the reverie approach to screen acting, James Lipton, to describe her acting process on Bravo's popular television interview program *Inside the Actor's Studio*, she demurred:

> I'm not really articulate about this subject because it is like church to me. I mean it's like approaching the altar. I feel like the more I talk about whatever it is, the less … something will go away. I mean there is a lot of superstition in it. But I do know that I feel freer, less in control, more susceptible. I don't know. I'm always accused of being a technical actress, and I am, I think, probably the least technical—what people think of as technical—actress in the world because I have really no way to talk about what we are talking about. I mean honestly.

She went on to claim that, when acting, she enters a "zone" in which she feels "really happy, somewhere deep, deep inside…and transported on some level to a place that [is] really like being in love."[8] One can see how difficult it is to enter into a methodical inquiry into acting described as such.

In fact, actor interviews are notoriously unreliable as sources for the methods used by screen actors. When actors talk about acting, they often do so in ways that are anecdotal, elliptical, mystifying, and indirect. No single approach seems to suit all actors, so reading actor interviews reveals startling disagreements. For instance, early movie actors repeatedly proposed that one of the major difficulties they had in acclimating to working in film, as opposed to acting in the theater, was getting used to the camera's intrusive presence. They insisted that, to work effectively in film, it is necessary to disregard the camera entirely, pretend it is not there, and never under any circumstances play to the camera. Then, one comes across the words of Lillian Gish (not exactly a minor figure in the silent period), who insisted that she played directly to the camera and even had a mirror attached to its side so that she could see herself as she acted.[9] What is one to make of that? Is she lying to tell a good story or are there really no consistent rules for effective screen acting?

Actors' attitudes to the presence of the camera actually range from those who regard it as a foreign presence that must be ignored to those who see it as a friendly eye that must be acknowledged, cultivated, and even wooed as if it were a substitute for a live audience. Actors will also disagree considerably about the influence of film technology on screen acting, what they want from a director, whether they prefer to feel that they are working in an ensemble or alone, and how they prepare for a part. Really, actor interviews reveal disagreements about almost every aspect of film acting.

Film and Stage Acting: A Troubled Relationship

One aspect of film acting that often takes center stage in actor interviews is its troubled relationship to stage acting. One reason for film acting's long history of critical neglect is film scholars' tendency simply to follow the lead of many actors, who in interviews have compared, and still continue to compare, film acting unfavorably with stage acting. One can point to what amounts to a long crusade by stage actors to denigrate film acting as an unsophisticated amateurish second cousin to theater acting; this is portrayed, even by film actors, as the more sustained exercise in acting skills and commitment, the place where live performance offers the actor the ideal environment for perfecting his or her craft.

Yet, many scholars have pointed out that this bias against film acting is founded primarily on an antipathy to the technological aspects of filmmaking and that the characterization of stage acting as so much more liberating and enriching is really based only on anecdotal evidence from actors and on a long-standing denigration of film acting by actors dating back to the silent-film period. Others believe the compulsion actors seem to feel to compare film to stage acting could be the result of their difficulty in describing their acting process at all; therefore, they resort to saying what it is not.[10] Unfortunately, the film- vs. stage-acting debate has spawned only impressionistic comparisons between the two acting forms, rather than the formulation of a consistent methodology to discuss film acting in ways that move beyond subjective description.

This is not to say that considerations of the differences between stage and film acting have not led to some useful analysis. One issue that has been discussed extensively involves exactly what defines acting in each medium. Scholars of acting have, however, found the matter of how exactly the work of the actor should be defined to be a rather thorny problem. For instance, acting has been described as having what Julia Kristeva termed an "anaphoric function," which involves the construction of "a physical arrangement that arrays spectacle for persons in an audience role." James Naremore added that it involves not only this high degree of ostentation or visibility by actors, but also the requirement that they must become an agent in a narrative.[11] As Paul McDonald has suggested, the actor must come together with a dramatic character to construct a believable, truthful, realistic performance (1998, 30). The task of the actor is thus to construct an inner model of a character and then convert that model into a believable enactment that gives the illusion of spontaneity for an audience, yet also allows for the creation of a repeatable performance.[12]

Building on this general definition of acting, critics have teased out numerous differences between acting for the stage and screen. They have argued, for instance, that the differences between acting for the two media are more quantitative than qualitative. The actor is said to do more on stage and less in film, adjusting vocally, expressively, and in use of gestures to the film medium by creating what some have called a narrower performance on film as opposed to the wider acting associated with theater. The prominence of the close-up in film is said to necessitate the actor's greater concentration on facial expressions and acting with the eyes. The actor's bond with the audience is also reputed to be different in film because the screen serves as an impenetrable barrier to actor–audience interaction, thus making the actor's job of establishing some connection with the audience more difficult.

Yet, at the same time, the use of the close-up in film allows for a greater sense of audience–actor intimacy, creating what John Ellis has called the film medium's "photo effect."[13] Because film actors have the appearance of being there and not being there, Ellis believes their fetishistic quality is heightened. As a result, their acting is transformed from the stage actor's impersonation, attempting to become the character played, into the film star's personification, seemingly playing oneself repeatedly in each performance (Naremore, 30). Even more negatively, other critics have proposed that because screen acting is so shaped by editing, technology, typecasting, and the star system, it is not acting at all, but merely the actor's repeated presentation of a star image on the screen.

Clearly, the technical characteristics of the film medium do shape the contours of film acting. Because film scenes are customarily shot out of order so that scenes that take place in the same setting can be shot together, film performance is unquestionably more fragmented, discontinuous, and disunified than stage performance. Many critics have argued, however, that these characteristics actually make film acting more difficult than stage acting because it is hard to build a performance and maintain expressive coherence (i.e., create a unified character) on screen, where the actor performing in a particular scene has less sense of the work as a whole. It is difficult for an actor to live in story time, given the extremely fragmented nature of plot time during shooting, and the technical requirements of film acting also require specific acting skills.

In spite of the notion that film actors are just playing themselves, there is nothing more natural about acting in film than on stage, except that actors do not need to accentuate their performances vocally and with gestures as they must do in theater because of the audience's distance from the stage. At the same time, however, the camera in many ways calls for acting that is not only technically informed, but also quite unnatural, counterintuitive, and artificial. Film actors must learn how to adapt their acting techniques and adjust the scale of their performance to variously angled shooting, blocked movements, and changes in shot distance and framing. For instance, tight framing requires that actors show unnatural stillness and restraint, act in close proximity to each other, and stifle their automatic reactions to stay in frame (Naremore, 40). All of this is far from what might be considered natural, yet the myth still persists that film acting simply involves "making it real." For example, in his manual of screen acting, Tony Barr recommends, "On stage you can give a performance. In front of a camera, you'd better have an experience."[14]

Technical aspects of filmmaking, especially the importance of editing in film, also give much more creative control to the director, who is often credited with almost single handedly constructing actors' film performances. Theater actors are purported to have a greater opportunity to mold a part to their own designs because they are freer from directorial control. Film actors' performances are often considered so "muddied" by technology and so controlled by the director that actors are said to become almost part of a film's mise-en-scene, like visual props or puppets.[15]

Significant in this regard is the early influence of the Soviet silent filmmaker Lev Kuleshov's famous experiment in editing. Kuleshov reputedly juxtaposed identical images of an actor's expressionless face with various shots that would be expected to evoke very different emotions, such as sadness, joy, and hunger. He claimed that audiences believed that the actor actually changed expressions. Although the exact footage that Kuleshov shot has been lost and no one has been able to replicate his findings,[16] his experiment was extremely influential in propagating the notion that, in film, acting is largely passive, if not completely insignificant. At best, film acting was seen as a war pitting the actor against the film apparatus and director. At worst, it was believed to fall into the realm of "received acting" (Naremore, 24), in which the actors perform totally under the instruction of the director without even knowing the significance of their actions.

The Dominance of the Realist Aesthetic

Clearly, this comparative approach has led more to the denigration of the work of the film actor than to a methodological analysis of the craft of film acting. Attempts to develop this type of analysis have been plagued not only by this constant comparison of film and theater acting, but also by a long tradition of subjective evaluations of film acting stemming from what Virginia Wright Wexman has called the dominance of the realist aesthetic in evaluations of film acting.[17] Because film acting has traditionally been viewed as an intuitive, almost instinctive, activity described in acting manuals as "whatever works," critics have in turn responded by evaluating good acting as whatever moves them emotionally and describing it in what James Naremore calls "fuzzy adjectival language" (Naremore, 2). As Wexman suggests, realist theories of acting, which look for its true-to-life quality, fail as critical tools because they "disallow consideration of specific acting techniques in favor of a rhetoric that valorizes the actor's inner feelings and their putative authenticity" (1993, 20).

Yet the realist aesthetic has been extremely influential in thinking about film acting because of the reputed prominence of Method acting in film. There is, however, significant disagreement about the exact influence The Method has had on screen acting, and this issue has become a major area of scholarly dispute (more on this later). Nevertheless, terms like "a believable performance" or "a true-to-life portrayal" are too often used to praise a film performance with little sense of their lack of specificity and methodological rigor.

As Wexman points out, The Method's conception of realistic acting, privileging as it does the actor's internal acting process, makes it extremely difficult to study this process systematically (1993, 20). What often happens is that discussions of film acting employing the realist aesthetic tend to merge actor and character, as Method acting advocates, resulting in plot summaries of the actions of fictional characters, rather than analyses of how those characters are embodied by actors. Also troubling is the fact that Method acting has been strongly identified with male actors and used as a means of validating the superiority of their acting methods to those of actresses, who are seen as incapable of the emotional intensity and philosophical depth said to characterize the performances of male Method actors.

Typologies of Acting Styles

Closely allied to this use of the realist aesthetic as a criterion of evaluation are attempts to study acting by establishing a typology of acting styles or traditions. Examples of this approach are often historical in orientation and include arguments for the evolution from melodramatic to naturalistic acting styles in the silent era, the development of a Hollywood studio style in the 1930s and 1940s, the reputed dominance of Method acting in film beginning in the 1950s, and the influence of antirealist techniques on contemporary Hollywood acting. The idea of film acting as tied to a naturalist aesthetic has a long history that can be traced back to the silent-film era, when film acting reputedly underwent a major transformation from a melodramatic, declamatory, gestural mode, which Roberta Pearson has dubbed the histrionic acting code, to a more muted naturalism, called the verisimilar code by Pearson.[18]

How, when, and why this development of naturalistic silent film acting occurred has been a matter of considerable scholarly perplexity. Pearson proposes that the change took place between 1908 and 1913, as naturalism gradually overtook an exhausted, inferior melodramatic style inherited from nineteenth-century popular theater (24). On the other hand, David Meyer maintains that the silent period actually was characterized by a range of styles derived from a variety of sources, such as popular dance, ballet, and vaudeville performance, not just from theater, and that the melodramatic mode of acting actually coincided with naturalistic acting well after 1913.[19]

The silent period is not the only era under dispute in the examination of acting traditions. Debates have also surfaced concerning the nature of acting in the studio era. Richard Dyer's description of what he calls the Hollywood studio style perhaps best represents conventional views of what acting was like in the 1930s and 1940s. Dyer traces the heritage of the studio acting style back to radio performance and distinguishes it sharply from what he terms the Broadway repertory style, where actors are said to transform themselves into the characters they play and never seem to be merely playing themselves (impersonation). The studio style, on the other hand, was said to encourage actors to repeat idiosyncratic behavior so that the audience would come to feel that they really knew the actors on the screen as they would real people (personification).[20] Studio promotion and publicity worked to reinforce this acting style of personification by promoting stars as regular people just playing themselves on the screen, rather than as artists or professionals.[21]

Cynthia Baron and Scott McDonald have challenged this traditional view of studio acting and have characterized it instead as promoting a very script-based acting process that emphasizes the actor's training, craft, and technique. Baron points to the studios' founding of drama schools, development of acting manuals, and hiring of drama and dialogue coaches, elocution teachers, and other "experts," all charged with the task of educating contract players in the craft of acting (33–35). McDonald argues that the studios developed a systematic process of actor training that began with the screen test, moved through an apprentice period, and finally culminated in a long-term studio contract and film stardom.[22] Baron characterizes studio acting as an eclectic mix of pragmatic acting strategies and guidelines that centered around three major concerns: the actor's adjustment from stage to screen, the development of "silent thinking" as a way to help formulate appropriate reactions during shooting, and the building of a character through careful script analysis, extensive preparation, and dispassionate execution. She proposes that Studio actors developed their craft, not by using a single method, but rather by drawing on a complex integration of techniques taken from silent films, theater, dance, modeling, vaudeville, and the theories of Constantin Stanislavski (31–32).

Stanislavski or Strasberg?

The relative influence on film acting of Stanislavski's System, as opposed to Lee Strasberg's Method, has been an area of considerable dispute, and even more contentious is the debate over the merits of this influence. This is especially true in regard to Strasberg, who has been characterized, on one hand, as the genius who almost single handedly transferred Stanislavski's ideas to film, and on the other, as the demon who forever impoverished screen acting by bringing to it only a corrupted version of the original Stanislavski System. A great deal of critical energy has been expended on this issue, producing little or no consensus. Particularly ignored is the influence of Stanislavski's System and Strasberg's Method on actresses. Stanislavskian and Method acting techniques have always been more strongly connected with male stars, but their influence on female stars has yet to be explored fully.

Constantin Stanislavski, the eminent director and acting theorist who worked in the Moscow Art Theater in the 1880s, certainly did not intend for his ideas to be applied beyond stage acting; in fact, he did not even like film. According to Jay Leyda, Stanislavski's personal feelings about film "began in contempt, warmed to antagonism and never went beyond tolerance in later years" (quoted in Wexman 1993, 240, n. 3). However, as the single most important exponent of nineteenth-century naturalistic acting, Stanislavski's influence on film acting has been immense. Stanislavski advocated a style of acting that has become so commonplace in thinking about acting in film that its influence is now almost invisible.

Crucial to what became known as the Stanislavski System are certain key ideas about acting technique. First is the conception that the actor must live the part, rather than merely imitating someone else's model of the character. Stanislavski took the stance that the actor must perform a double function of becoming emotionally and psychologically involved with the character, while at the same time always maintaining conscious control of the acting performance. He developed specific exercises, termed his "psychotechnique," for cultivating this involvement.[23] The most important is "emotion-memory," "a technique allowing the actor to suffuse his acting with genuine emotions of his own which are analogous to the emotions the character is supposed to experience" (Meyer–Dinkgrafe, 40). Secondly, Stanislavski advocated scene analysis as a way to break down the play into units and discover each unit's "creative objective" or "subtext," as well as the "superobjective" for the actor's character (39, 42).

These terms have been defined variously, but the creative objective or subtext seems to refer quite simply to the theme of the play as a whole and the individual underlying meanings of its particular scenes. The character's superobjective is the logical progression of a character's actions throughout a play and the motivations for this progression. Stanislavski also advocated spontaneity, improvisation, and introspection in actor training and performance. In fact, his later writings show a shift from his earlier emphasis on psychotechnique to what he called "the method of physical actions," which advocated physical training for actors to enable them to choose just the right actions appropriate to the characters that they play (Meyer–Dinkgrafe, 45).

Stanislavski's naturalistic acting methods were particularly applicable to film acting, and they early found translation to the screen through the work of his disciple V. I. Pudovkin, who in the 1920s wrote the first book to address specifically the issue of film acting, *Film Technique and Film Acting*.[24] Pudovkin proposed that Stanislavski's conception of the actor living the part provided the ideal way for the actor to stay in character and overcome other acting difficulties associated with the discontinuous nature of filmmaking. Although there is evidence that Stanislavski's ideas were already influential in Hollywood during the studio era, Lee Strasberg has traditionally been credited with bringing The Method, his version of Stanislavski's ideas, to the American theater and film world. There have been extensive discussions of the distinctions between the theories of the two men, as well as arguments about whether Strasberg further refined Stanislavski's ideas or actually corrupted them. Essentially, the defining difference between Stanislavski's System and Strasberg's Method is that, for Stanislavski, the actor is guided by close script analysis and should live the part by internalizing the character's emotions; for Strasberg, actors should substitute emotions drawn from their past experiences for those of the character (Meyer–Dinkgrafe, 50).

Building upon, reshaping, or corrupting Stanislavski's theories, depending upon one's view, Strasberg developed his "psychotheatrical exercises" for actor training and rehearsal that involve the actors' "manipulating their own psychological histories to identify with the character in creating the performance" (Maltby, 394). By coming to understand their deepest motivations, drives, and anxieties through these exercises, actors can produce appropriate surface behavior and convince the audience of their characters' psychological complexity. Primary among these exercises are techniques associated with the concepts of affective memory, motivation and substitution, improvisation, "the through-line of action," "the private moment," and "The Method ensemble."

Affective memory builds on Stanislavski's emotion-memory, but places more emphasis on the actor delving into past personal experiences to find the emotions needed to construct a role. It encompasses two separate but interrelated techniques: sense memory (training one's analytical memory through exercises with imaginary objects) and emotional memory (re-experiencing past emotions through the memory of thoughts and sensations associated with them). The two are connected in that the actor is only able to stimulate past emotions (emotional memory) by reliving the "sensory concreteness" of a particular moment from the past (sense memory).[25]

Expanding on affective memory, Strasberg's related concepts of motivation and substitution require actors to substitute their past emotions for those of the character. Strasberg built upon Stanislavski's idea of "the magic if," which instructed actors to imagine, given the circumstances of the play, how they would behave, react, or feel if they were in their character's situation. Strasberg adopted this concept, but with a subtle change. The "magic if" became the notion of motivation, which asks the actors

to determine what would motivate them to behave, react, or feel as the character does. Then, they are instructed to engage in substitution, which involves using affective memory to substitute their past emotions for the character's (Meyer–Dinkgrafe, 48).

Connected to these techniques is Strasberg's notion of "the private moment," which involves actors reliving through a staged re-enactment a very private scene from their life. This was Strasberg's version of Stanislavski's exercise in "public solitude," but again with more emphasis on the actors' substituting their emotions for those of the character. Stanislavski's conception of public solitude called for an actor to construct an imaginary circle around himself or herself and then create an imagined environment inside that circle to which the actor would react. The desired result was the elimination of the actor's self-consciousness on stage. Similarly, the private moment is a way for actors to lose self-consciousness by displaying deeply personal aspects of their lives in a classroom exercise; however, it also crucially involves reliving past experiences and emotions on stage, whereas public solitude is concerned only with the imaginative creation of a character's emotions.[26]

Another major technique that Strasberg advocated is improvisation, but he did not define the term as it is commonly defined. Strasberg's notion of improvisation is not the changing of dialogue during performance; instead, it calls for verbal innovation in rehearsal that leads to an exploration of the character's thoughts and feelings. In this way, it is hoped that the actor will be able to play the scene in performance as if he or she does not know what will happen next. This principle, termed "the illusion of the first time," was advocated as a way to solve the problem of "anticipation" in acting — the loss of spontaneity and verisimilitude due to the actor's knowledge of the play's conclusion (Strasberg, 44–45). Somewhat paradoxically, Strasberg also advocated that the actor must strive to understand "the through-line of action" of the character by determining "a subtextual line that runs through the work and gives logical order and perspective to the various roles, while organically uniting them."[27] According to Strasberg, all of these various techniques would allow actors to come together to form "The Method ensemble" in which they would be "creating together through careful listening, rhythmical delivery of syncopated lines, and respectful understanding of each other's body language" (Larue and Zucker, 314).

As noted earlier, film scholars have hotly contested the importance and value of Strasberg's influence on film acting. For some, he distorted Stanislavski's ideas, converting them into an "introspective neurotic acting style" that came to dominate Hollywood film acting in the 1950s because it fit well with the current cultural obsession with psychoanalysis and suited recent technical innovations in filmmaking (Naremore, 19). The Method provided exactly the type of big emotional acting called for by developments in sound technology and widescreen cinematography. It also arguably created an acting style that "largely celebrated the neuroses of the individual performer" (Wexman 1993, 166), reduced the social progressivism of Stanislavski's politically committed theater to a conventional Hollywood realism, fed the star system by its strong emphasis on the actor's personality, and created a cultlike atmosphere of director worship by its idolization of Strasberg (Naremore, 199).

In spite of these strong criticisms, The Method's influence on Hollywood acting should not be minimized. From Stanislavski's ideas, which were intended strictly for the theater, Strasberg developed an acting theory well suited to film, and especially to the Hollywood system. The Method provided actors with "concrete tools" to deal with "the practical problems of film acting" (Carnicke, 76). It offered techniques for constructing emotionally fresh and varied performances despite film's lack of rehearsal time; fragmented, multiple-take shooting schedule; extraordinary attention to detail through the extensive use of the close-up; lack of a live audience; and dictatorial control by the film director. In calling for an acting style that prioritized character psychology, "emotional truth," and the actor's substitution of personal feelings for character emotions, Strasberg renovated the Hollywood studio style from actors simply playing roles tailored to their star images to the cultivation of performances that rendered complex, emotionally rich characterizations. As Richard Maltby points out, by the 1970s, mainstream Hollywood had so absorbed the tenets of The Method that it became dominant as well as invisible as the accepted acting practice (394).

As noted earlier, another issue in regard to The Method that has received some critical attention is the strong association it has had with male actors. As it became integrated into Hollywood acting in the 1950s, The Method distinctly became the province of male stars, such as Marlon Brando, James Dean, Rod Steiger, Montgomery Clift, Lee J. Cobb, and Karl Malden, even though many of these actors never studied at Strasberg's famous Actors' Studio. There were also notable female Method performers. Joanne Woodward, Shelley Winters, Ruby Dee, Estelle Parsons, Anne Jackson, and Julie Harris come to mind immediately. Yet, the exemplars of Method acting were men, with Marlon Brando becoming The Method poster boy, even though he studied under Stella Adler, rather than Strasberg.

One explanation for this male association holds that The Method is well suited to the traditional conception of masculinity. Method acting always has a type of expressive incoherence, a tension between an outer mask of stoic strength and self-control and an inner emotional core constantly on the verge of breaking through in the form of a violent outburst (Maltby, 398). Thus, as Virginia Wexman points out, The Method early became associated with male rebel heroes whose antisocial behavior, inner disturbance, emotional repression, and personal anguish came to be seen as authentic and distinctly masculine (1993, 167). Richard Maltby suggests that in this way The Method gave male performers an emotional expressiveness they had not been able to achieve since the silent-film era. At the same time, however, it associated good acting with the expression of masculine emotion (398), and actresses in female-oriented genres like the "woman's film" became increasingly connected with the emotionally excessive acting of the tearjerker.

Wexman also suggests that, whereas 1950s Method acting originally associated masculinity with self-absorbed and neurotic behavior, it has served to connect contemporary male stars, like Robert De Niro and Al Pacino, with a "cold narcissism that suggests that they are beyond romance" and "a truculent incommunicativeness that pointedly excludes the audience" (1993, 179). Yet, The Method's initial effect of strongly connecting good acting with male actors has indisputably denigrated the actress as an artist and exacerbated what feminist critics have since characterized as The Method's "inherently patriarchal and misogynist" characteristics. Feminist objections to The Method include its "mistrustful attitude toward feeling and the biological body in general" and promotion of "a naive, anti-intellectual investment in narrative closure, 'realistic' mimesis, and continuity that erases difference and ignores social critique."[28]

The Method's benefits to film acting have not only been disputed, but the extent of that influence has also been challenged, most recently by Elly A. Konijn's concept of task emotion theory. Konijn categorizes Stanislavski's and Strasberg's ideas as propagating an acting "style of involvement"; their goal is the illusion of truthfulness through the actor's presentation of character-emotions that render the actor's personality invisible behind the character portrayed (158). Konijn, who undertook an extensive ethnographic study of contemporary European and American stage actors, concluded from her results that actors, in fact, neither experience the emotions of the characters they portray, as Stanislavski suggested, nor use their past emotions to make character emotions believable, as Strasberg indicated. What they do, according to Konijn, is imitate the emotions of characters and use what she calls task-emotions to make this imitation seem spontaneous and believable.

Task-emotions are generated by the actor's emotional response to the challenges of acting, such as the need to appear competent, present a positive self-image, and create an aesthetically pleasing performance, as well as the risk, excitement, and stress of the performance situation. The emotions generated by these acting tasks are then used to create "the illusion of spontaneous character-emotions for the audience ... lending to the external form of emotions the aspect of real emotions" (Konijn, 152). She claims that when actors discuss acting they often confuse task-emotions with character-emotions because their training in the acting style of involvement leads them to believe that good acting means expressing the emotions of the character they are portraying. Studies of the emotions experienced by actors when on stage, however, do not support this belief. Recent studies of actors' physiological responses during performance indicate no correlation between actors' real emotions and those of their characters. According to Konijn, actors experience an increased level of excitement when on stage that is associated more with the experience of acting than with the emotions of their characters (107–108).

The extent of The Method's influence has been challenged in other ways. The overwhelming adoption of Method acting in Hollywood has traditionally been seen as leading to a rejection of modernist antirealist acting styles in film. However, Virginia Wright Wexman has pointed out that progressive acting theories have, in fact, influenced the work of such prominent contemporary Hollywood directors as Robert Altman, David Mamet, and Spike Lee. She sees Altman as influenced by Viola Spolin's theories of improvisation, Mamet by the semiparodic acting style of absurdist drama, and Spike Lee by Brechtian theories of distanciation and politicized performance. Wexman proposes that contemporary directors combine antirealist techniques with realistic portrayals in an eclectic blending of acting styles that work to promote spectator involvement in the film's diegesis (1993, 184).

Other Typologies of Film Acting

Other critics tend to be less concerned with identifying the influence of established acting traditions on film acting and more conceptual in their typologies of film acting. Richard Dyer in *Stars,* for instance, early argued that Hollywood acting could be classified as falling into one of five styles: vaudeville or music hall, melodramatic, Hollywood studio, Broadway repertory, and Method (1979, 154–162):

> The vaudeville or music-hall style, prominent in musicals and comedy films, involves the antirealist, distancing devices, and presentational

direct address to the audience associated with musical numbers and comic gags and routines.

The melodramatic style, characteristic of silent films and largely abandoned with the introduction of sound, advocates an ostensive acting style inherited from nineteenth-century theater and relies on a formalized repertoire of expressions and gestures.

The Hollywood studio style, associated with sound films and, according to Dyer, inherited from radio performance, encourages personification; the actors seem to just play themselves.

In contrast is the Broadway repertory style, taken from theater acting and demanding impersonation, in which the actor plays a different character in each role.

Dyer's final category is The Method, which he defines as the actor temporarily identifying with the character.

Other attempts to categorize acting include some of the designations used earlier:

presentational (with direct address to the audience) vs. representational (acting as if the audience were not there) (Naremore, 28–30)

impersonation (attempting to create a different character in each film) vs. personification (playing the same character, generally assumed to be oneself, in repeated performances) (King, 130)

ostensive (stylized, mannered) acting (Naremore, 34) vs. invisible (naturalistic) acting (Maltby, 382)

outside–in (basing one's performance on imitation and traditional acting skills without ever losing oneself in the role) vs. inside–out (basing one's performance on deeply felt inner emotions, living the role) (Dyer 1979, 150)

The outside–in/inside–out distinction is the result of a longstanding dispute in the field of acting theory that has encompassed theatrical and film acting: the emotionalist/antiemotionalist debate. It is a controversy that has raged for centuries over the value of technique as opposed to emotional involvement with a character. Nineteenth-century stage acting techniques were associated with the rhetorical theories of Francois Delsarte, a Parisian elocutionist, who developed "signal acting," an ostensive declamatory acting style somewhat similar to pantomime. Accompanied by a "vocabulary" of gestures and stances appropriate to certain actions and emotional expressions, this antiemotionalist style was extremely influential on silent film acting (Maltby, 400).

Antiemotionalism is in many ways an extension of the eighteenth-century theories of Denis Diderot. Diderot proposed what he called the "paradox of the actor": the best actor expresses emotion on stage by actually feeling absolutely nothing in common with the character. For Diderot, the actor engages in what later would be termed outside–in acting, perfecting his or her technique in order to reproduce the external signs of character emotions without ever experiencing those emotions himself or herself. This is done by creating an "ideal model" of the character that can then be enacted in repeated stage performances (Konijn, 22–24). Diderot's extreme antiemotionalism was countered by emotionalists who believed the actor must experience the character's emotions on stage in order to give an authentic performance; this was later termed inside–out acting. The debate led in 1888 to William Archer's "Paradox of Double Consciousness," a compromise theory arguing against Diderot that what an effective actor really needed to do in order to keep control of the performance was to experience and to stand apart from the character's emotions (Konijn, 30–31).

Although influential, Archer's compromise did not resolve the debate. Although current acting theory no longer calls for the actor's complete absence of emotion, as did Diderot, it still continues to debate, for stage as well as screen, the proper balance between emotionality and technique in performance and the efficacy of naturalistic invisible acting vs. more mannered ostensiveness (Konijn, 30). Currently, the consensus seems to be that although invisible acting has come to dominate, especially in film, ostensiveness has never really disappeared. One might even propose that there is always a degree of obviousness in acting and that this ostensive quality is essential, after all, for acting even to be identified as acting. Great acting can perhaps be best characterized as the perfect blend of the ostensive and the verisimilar.

Another typological approach investigates acting in relation to film genres. This approach attempts to demonstrate how acting manifests itself in certain generic contexts, especially those involving an unusual mode of performance. Even in looking at specific genres, however, studies of film acting have been more suggestive than exhaustive, focusing on how genre shapes performance and how actors serve as iconic figures within certain genres. For example, Richard de Cordova has looked at performance within four genres: the musical, film noir, the historical film, and melodrama. He concludes that each genre is notable for the unique performance qualities with which it is associated. The musical, for instance, is characterized by the "syntagmatic specificity" of its performance modes, a shifting between narrative and musical performances, with each associated respectively with a representational or a presentational acting style. The musical also contains an unusually high level of symbolic or ritualizing performance, with actors taking on iconic significance as embodying the myth of personal discovery through performance or the conflict between high and popular art.[29]

Similarly, de Cordova points out that other genres also have their distinct acting modes. In the historical film, for example, a particularly strong distinction always exists between actor and character because an actor can never be seen as fully embodying an historical figure, whose real identity remains a constant presence in the film (de Cordova, 119). Film noir, on the other hand, is a genre that seems distinctive in its problematization of the actor's relationship to the body in terms of the split between body and voice. Film noir's use of voice-over narration, chiaroscuro lighting, multiangled and close-up framing, and pronounced camera movement problematizes the relation of the actor's body to the technological aspects of filmmaking. Particularly in terms of the acting style of actresses, film noir affords an interesting contrast with melodrama. In film noir, the acting mode for the actress is primarily one of dissimulation, whereas in melodrama, the mode involves emotional excess, even hysteria (de Cordova, 120–121). The two genres are similar, however, in that they present showcases for the acting talent of the female star as she enacts the machinations of the *noir* femme fatale or the victimization of the melodramatic heroine.

As intriguing as these attempts to categorize and describe acting modes and subtypes are, acting performances tend to blend and transcend types rather than fit neatly into given categories, thus making the applications of film acting typologies less than completely satisfying. Again, these typologies have too often been used to denigrate the work of actresses, associating their acting styles with what have been seen as less prestigious categories, such as melodramatic, Hollywood studio, presentational, personificational, and ostensive acting.

Semiotics and Kinesics

Another theoretical paradigm somewhat widely applied to the study of film acting is semiotics. Many critics have attempted to formulate structuralist analyses of acting signs or codes, and this approach has been devoted in particular to formulating a critical vocabulary for the study of screen acting. An early example of this tradition, as noted earlier, is Barry King's classification of acting into personification (where the actor seems to be playing himself or herself), impersonation (where the actor's personality seemingly disappears into the part), and hypersemioticization (the tendency of film performance to create star actors who are bigger than life supersigns, invested with an exaggerated level of meaning) (King, 142).

In a similar vein, Richard Dyer and Andrew Higson attempted to break acting down into a series of discrete performance signs related to different areas of the body, such as facial features, gestures, and body movement (Dyer 1979, 120–132).[30] The semiotic approach led John O. Thompson to develop "the commutation test," which he hoped would prove to be a major tool in the methodical scientific analysis of acting. His idea was to substitute one actor for another in order to observe the difference it makes to a performance, break the performance down into a bundle of distinctive features, and investigate how change in one feature alters others.[31] Unfortunately, his procedure turned out to be rather imprecise in its methodology and did not result in any really startling revelations about the craft of acting. More recently, Roberta Pearson has combined historical and semiotic approaches to formulate the idea of acting codes rather than of acting signs. As noted earlier, she uses these codes to distinguish between acting styles and to argue for the development from a histrionic to a verisimilar acting code over the course of the silent-film period.

Another approach closely related to semiotics is kinesics, which also attempts to break an acting performance into its component features of voice, appearance, gesture, and expression in order to examine the overall effect produced. The most notable application of this approach to film acting is Virginia Wright Wexman's study of Humphrey Bogart's performances in *The Maltese Falcon* and *The Big Sleep*.[32] Using kinesics, Wexman examines how Bogart used his appearance, gestures, mannerisms, and interaction with other actors to create characters that fit with the vision of different directors, subtly shaping his tough guy image to different roles.

However, as Paul McDonald has pointed out, the semiotic approach (and I would suggest kinesics as well) is plagued by the difficulty involved in breaking an acting performance down into its individual components (1998, 30). A performance is, after all, analogical — a continuous stream of interconnected aspects — and not digital (Naremore, 2). It is not an easily discernable sequence of discrete steps; thus, it does not lend itself to semiotic or kinesic analysis, which always seems in the final analysis essentially reductive. Semiotics and kinesics also tend to treat acting merely as a sign system, part of a "performance text" representing a cluster of signifiers decoded as a sort of performance language by the spectator. Their concentration on the visual rather than the dramatic aspect of acting has the unfortunate effect of de-emphasizing acting as a craft and reducing the actor to an aspect of the film's mise-en-scene.

Gender Studies and Acting

Although one might expect that gender studies would provide interesting insights into the art of acting, especially as it relates to the actress, feminist analyses have actually approached acting in very limited ways. One reason for this limitation seems to be the importance of psychoanalytic theory in the development of feminist film criticism. Laura Mulvey's germinal 1975 essay "Visual Pleasure and Narrative Cinema" was extremely influential in establishing the theories of Freud and Lacan as central to feminist film analysis. Within this paradigm, the actress is characterized by what Mulvey calls her "to-be-looked-at-ness."[33] She is merely a fetishistic object of spectacle and of the voyeuristic male gaze, and the male actor serves only as the gazer, an identification figure for the spectator.

Study of acting technique is pushed to the side by these considerations, and early feminist film theory came to view the film actress as merely a construction, a product of culture industrially manufactured and prefabricated by patriarchy as a signifier of sexuality and nothing more. As interesting as Mulvey's conceptions are, and I do not mean in any way to denigrate feminist theory's many contributions to film scholarship, her ideas did not easily lend themselves to the serious study of acting.

In fact, even before Mulvey precipitated the turn to psychoanalysis in feminist film theory, earlier pioneering feminist film critics, like Molly Haskell and Marjorie Rosen,[34] using what has been termed "reflection theory,"[35] considered actresses merely as embodiments of social stereotypes that control definitions of femininity in a male-dominated culture. As will be discussed in the next chapter, their typologies of actresses have been much more useful for star studies than for considerations of acting. Haskell, for instance, divides actresses into categories of roles played or images projected, such as the pin-up, passive love object, treacherous woman, superfemale (too intelligent and ambitious for the docile feminine role allotted to her), superwoman (adopting "male characteristics" to enjoy male prerogatives and survive in a male-dominated world), and sweet, innocent female helpmate (always standing by, and just a few steps behind, her man).

As we shall see in the next chapter, actresses are also often discussed in terms of their association with celebrity, consumption, and fashion; as victims of Hollywood exploitation; and, on occasion, as symbols of female resistance and rebellion against patriarchy. These categories suggest that analyses of actresses using reflection theory really study star images, characters portrayed, and women's narrative treatment in films, rather than actresses as actors.

Concluding Comments

I am not going to try to conclude this chapter, or this book really, by providing the definitive answer to the myriad problems involved in the study of film acting and the film actress. My intention is rather to point to the problematic nature of this study. I do believe, however, that one direction that does hold particular promise for the study of acting is to draw more heavily than has been the case in the past on the important work that has been done in the study of film stardom, work that will be discussed more fully in the next chapter. Curiously, the study of stars has received more attention than as well as largely been divorced from the study of acting. Some scholars of acting have even argued that work in the area of star studies has hindered the study of film acting. It has tended to view stars as separated from regular actors by their star quality and charisma, which is seen as distinct from, and in many cases even antithetical to, the development of acting ability. As a result, studies of stars have not viewed them as having the same concerns and cultivating the same skills as other actors. Stars have been studied for their ideological effects as social texts to be analyzed through publicity and advertising, rather than through the study of performance.

Yet, I think that the study of screen acting, and particularly of the film actress, desperately needs to be integrated with star studies; star–actresses, about whom after all we have the most information, need to be studied for their projection of star images and as craftspersons skilled in the art of acting. Of particular usefulness to the study of acting, I would argue, is the intertextual approach so often advocated in star studies. According to this paradigm, the star actor is seen as an amalgam of complementary texts, including performance, promotion, publicity, criticism, and commentaries.

Thus, the intertextual case studies of Meryl Streep, Susan Sarandon, Jodie Foster, Angela Bassett, and Gwyneth Paltrow that compose the second section of this book include the interaction among their career trajectories, the elements of their star images, their comments on their acting craft, and the social significance of their star personas. In this way, many of the insights of star studies can be brought to the study of star acting and vice versa, and some light can be shed on the much neglected craft of the Hollywood actress. Before we undertake this project, however, it is necessary to examine the contributions of star studies to the discourse on film acting and the Hollywood actress.

References

1. Affron, Charles. 1977. *Star Acting: Gish, Garbo, Davis*. New York: Dutton; Naremore, James. 1988. *Acting in the Cinema*. Berkeley: University

of California Press; Pearson, Roberta E. 1992. *Eloquent Gestures: the Transformation of Performance Style in the Griffith Biograph Films*. Berkeley, University of California Press; and Wexman, Virginia Wright. 1993. *Creating the Couple: Love, Marriage, and Hollywood Performance*. Princeton, N.J.: Princeton University Press.

2. Butler, Jeremy, ed. 1991. *Star Texts: Image and Performance in Film and Television*. Detroit: Wayne State University Press; Zucker, Carole, ed. 1990. *Making Visible the Invisible*. Metuchen, N.J.: Scarecrow Press; Lovell, Alan and Peter Kramer, eds. 1999. *Screen Acting*. New York: Routledge; and Wojcik, Pamela Robertson, ed. 2004. *Movie Acting, The Film Reader*. New York: Routledge.

3. Vilga, Edward. 1997. *Acting Now: Conversations on Craft and Career*. New Brunswick, N.J.: Rutgers University Press; Cardillo, Burt et al. 1998. *Playing to the Camera: Film Actors Discuss Their Craft*. New Haven, Conn.: Yale University Press; Zucker, Carole. 1999. *In the Company of Actors: Reflections on the Craft of Acting*. New York: Routledge; and Zucker, Carole. 2002. *Conversations with Actors on Film, Television, and Stage Performance*. Portsmouth, N.H.: Heinemann.

4. McDonald, Paul. 1998. "Film Acting." p. 30 in *The Oxford Guide to Film Studies*, ed. J. Hill and P. C. Gibson. Oxford: Oxford University Press; hereafter cited in text.

5. Lovell, Alan and Peter Krämer. 1999. "Introduction." p. 4 in *Screen Acting*, eds. A. Lovell and P. Kramer. New York: Routledge.

6. King, Barry. 1991. "Articulating Stardom." p. 126 in *Star Texts: Image and Performance in Film and Television*, ed. J. Butler. Detroit: Wayne State University Press; hereafter cited in text.

7. Maltby, Richard. 2003. *Hollywood Cinema*, 2d ed. Malden, Mass.: Blackwell, p. 370; hereafter cited in text.

8. Lipton, James. Nov. 22, 1998. Interview with Meryl Streep, *Inside the Actor's Studio*, Bravo Television; hereafter cited in text.

9. Gish, Lillian. 1998. "The Movies, Mr. Griffith, and Me." p. 43 in *Playing to the Camera: Film Actors Discuss Their Craft*, eds. Cardillo, Burt et al. New Haven, Conn.: Yale University Press.

10. Woods, Leigh. 1998. "Introduction." p. 7 in *Playing to the Camera: Film Actors Discuss Their Craft*, eds. B. Cardillo et al. New Haven, Conn.: Yale University Press.

11. Naremore, James. 1988. *Acting in the Cinema*, Berkeley: University of California Press, p. 23; hereafter cited in text.

12. Konijn, Elly A. 2000. *Acting Emotions*. Amsterdam: Amsterdam University Press, p. 51; hereafter cited in text.

13. Ellis, John. 1991. "Stars as a Cinematic Phenomenon." p. 308 in *Star Texts: Image and Performance in Film and Television*. ed. J. Butler. Detroit: Wayne State University Press.

14. Carnicke, Sharon Marie. 1999. "Lee Strasberg's Paradox of the Actor." p. 78 in *Screen Acting*, eds. A. Lovell and P. Kramer. New York: Routledge.

15. Zucker, Carole. 1990. "Preface." p. viii in *Making Visible the Invisible*, ed. C. Zucker. Metuchen, N.J.: Scarecrow Press.

16. Prince, Stephen and Wayne Hensley. 1992. "The Kuleshov Effect: Recreating the Classic Experiment."*Cinema Journal*, 3(2) (Winter): 59–75.

17. Wexman, Virginia Wright. 1993. *Creating the Couple: Love, Marriage, and Hollywood Performance*. Princeton, N.J.: Princeton University Press, p. 20; hereafter cited in text.

18. Pearson, Roberta E. 1990. "O'er Step not the Modesty of Nature: A Semiotic Approach to Acting in the Griffith Biographs." p. 8 in *Making Visible the Invisible*, ed. C. Zucker. Metuchen, N.J.: Scarecrow Press; hereafter cited in text.

19. Meyer, David. 1999. "Acting in Silent Film: Which Legacy of the Theater?" p. 12 in *Screen Acting*, eds. A. Lovell and P. Kramer. New York: Routledge.

20. Dyer, Richard. 1979. *Stars*. London: British Film Institute, pp. 156–160; hereafter cited in text.

21. Baron, Cynthia. 1999. "Crafting Film Performances: Acting in the Hollywood Studio Era." p. 31 in *Screen Acting*, eds. A. Lovell and P. Kramer. New York: Routledge; hereafter cited in text.

22. McDonald, Paul. 2000. *The Star System: Hollywood's Production of Popular Identities*. London: Wallflower Press, pp. 43–45; hereafter cited in text.

23. Meyer–Dinkgrafe, Daniel. 2001. *Approaches to Acting Past and Present*. London: Continuum, p. 45; hereafter cited in text.

24. Pudovkin, V. I. 1970. *Film Technique and Film Acting*. New York: Grove.

25. Strasberg, Lee. 1991. "A Dream of Passion: The Development of the Method." p. 49 in *Star Texts: Image and Performance in Film and Television*. ed. J. Butler. Detroit: Wayne State University Press; hereafter cited in text.

26. Gordon, Marc. 2000. "Salvaging Strasberg at the Fin de Siecle." p. 54 in *Method Acting Reconsidered: Theory, Practice, Future*, ed. D. Krasner. New York: St. Martin's Press.

27. Larue, Johanne and Carole Zucker. 1990. "James Dean: The Pose of Reality? *East of Eden* and the Method Performance." pp. 310–311 in *Making Visible the Invisible*, ed. C. Zucker. Metuchen, N.J.: Scarecrow Press; hereafter cited in text.

28. Blair, Rhonda. 2002. "Reconsidering Stanislavsky: Feeling, Feminism, and the Actor." *Theatre Topics* 12(2) (Sept.): 177, 179.

29. de Cordova, Richard. 1991. "Genre and Performance: An Overview." pp. 117–118 in *Star Texts: Image and Performance in Film and Television*. ed. J. Butler. Detroit: Wayne State University Press; hereafter cited in text.

30. Higson, Andrew. 1991. "Film Acting and Independent Cinema." pp. 158–159 in *Star Texts: Image and Performance in Film and Television*. ed. J. Butler. Detroit: Wayne State University Press.

31. Thompson, John O. 1991. "Screen Acting and the Commutation Test." pp. 183, 185–186 in *Stardom: Industry of Desire*, ed. C. Gledhill. London: Routledge.

32. Wexman, Virginia Wright. 1991. "Kenesics and Film Acting: Humphrey Bogart in *The Maltese Falcon* and *The Big Sleep*." pp. 203–213 in *Star Texts: Image and Performance in Film and Television*. ed. J. Butler. Detroit: Wayne State University Press.

33. Mulvey, Laura. 1989. "Visual Pleasure and Narrative Cinema." p. 19 in *Visual and Other Pleasures* Bloomington, Ind.: Indiana University Press; hereafter cited in text.
34. Haskell, Molly. 1974. *From Reverence to Rape: The Treatment of Women in the Movies.* New York: Penguin; Rosen, Marjorie. 1973. *Popcorn Venus: Women, Movies, and the American Dream.* New York: Coward, McCann, and Geoghegen.
35. White, Patricia. 1998. "Feminism and Film." p. 118 in *The Oxford Guide to Film Studies*, eds. J. Hill and P. C. Gibson. Oxford: Oxford University Press.

CHAPTER 2

The Hollywood Star–Actress and Studies of Stardom

Performance has been neglected in the study of Hollywood stars— particularly the star–actress; stardom, on the other hand, has received considerable attention. As Alan Lovell points out, star studies originated not as a way "to develop a richer account of performance,"[1] but as a means of uncovering the ideological meaning of the star phenomenon. The result has been that stardom has been extensively investigated for its social significance at the expense of star acting. One reason for the fascination with the star phenomenon is its complex nature. Produced by a star system that attempts to create many "popular identities" suitable for consumption by a wide range of audience members rather than a uniform category of stardom,[2] Hollywood stardom presents seemingly endless possibilities for investigation.

The Concept of Stardom

Even the concept of stardom has provoked intense debate. It is generally agreed that stardom involves not only a real-life person, the star, but also a "construction," an image that has an ideological or totemic function for the star's fans and is attached to the star as a type of cover (Naremore, 157).

This "fixed image [is] largely circulated by the media" as a "fictive personality," corresponding to a social stereotype.[3] Created with almost novelistic precision, according to Richard Dyer, the star image contains qualities also found in fictional characters, such as particularity, interest, autonomy, roundness, development, intertextuality, motivation, discrete identity, and consistency (Dyer 1979, 104).

Additionally, stars represent figures of audience identification, articulating aspects of contemporary life and offering themselves as role models of appropriate social behavior.[4] In this way, they can be said to serve as totems or gods and goddesses in a pseudoreligion of fandom. As Charles Affron and Edgar Morin have suggested, fans often venerate stars as idols, elevated above the level of common humanity, marked with an aura of impenetrable mystery, and endowed with extraordinary gifts and superhuman powers. Morin, whose ideas would later be expanded and reshaped by Richard Dyer, was particularly influential in developing the conception of stars as mythological, heroic cult figures and items of merchandise shaped and promoted by the film industry.

Morin's thesis is that early film stars in particular were perceived as heroes, role models, and embodiments of ideal ways of behaving (Dyer 1979, 24). As the star system developed, however, stars were no longer regarded as gods above humanity, but were seen somewhat paradoxically as totemic figures representing the "audience's indefinite spiritual longings and aspirations"[5] and as figures of identification expressing "how we are human now."[6] As a result of this shift, stardom became indelibly attached to questions of personal identity or, as Dyer phrases it, stars became for their fans "one of the most significant ways we have for making sense of it all" (1979, 2).

Thus, the star system came to promote the cult of the individual. Christine Gledhill has described it as working in ways very similar to those associated with the genre of melodrama. Both melodramatic characters and stars function as emblematic types that render as individual and personal what is really social and as exciting and extraordinary what is really ordinary. In so doing, they personalize contemporary social issues, embodying current ideological contradictions, social conflicts, and ethical struggles. Participating in what Peter Brooks has called "the moral occult," they offer their decentered fans, lost in the modern world, a unified identity, a sense of wholeness, and a feeling of coherence.[7]

Cultural studies scholars have argued that fans construct from the constellation of the star's image different contested meanings based on their varied and contradictory knowledge about the star and their own social identities and experience. For instance, stars appear to be objects of intense identification for marginalized social groups, such as gays, women, and adolescents, all of whom are characterized as suffering from intense identity/role conflicts and a sense of exclusion from the dominant adult male heterosexual culture.[8] Barry King has proposed that contemporary stardom, which he terms "autographic," creates stars with "increased plasticity," who change with their different film roles and according to the trends in current gossip about their personal lives. They can become whatever their fans want them to be. They are "individuals engaged in constantly renegotiating the terms of their engagement with public life" and "permanently resetting the terms of their representation." Fans, therefore, see the star not as "a definite kind of individual … [but as] the essential glue that holds together a series of approximate stabs at self-realization."[9]

What King calls plasticity, other critics have termed instability or duality. For instance, Judith Mayne sees star images as essentially unstable, characterized by "inconsistency, change, fluctuation." Their appeal is based on "constant reinvention, the dissolution of contraries, the embrace of widely opposing terms" (Geraghty 2000, 185). Similarly, John Ellis characterizes stars as unstable accumulations of paradoxical attributes that find "stable points of identity" only in the characters they play on the screen (310). For Ellis, the star image, as gleaned from promotion and publicity, is always incomplete; thus, it functions as "an invitation to cinema" (304). It is only in movie-going that the fan can find a temporary and rare moment of completion.

The attraction of the star is this appeal to the fan's desire for the fulfillment embodied in the film performance; however, after leaving the theater, the fan is left with a renewed sense of emptiness, exacerbated by his or her return to the consumption of publicity material on the star. This consumption, in turn, creates the need for renewed completion through watching the star perform yet again on screen (Ellis, 302–304). Richard Dyer points out that, in their attempts to describe this cyclical process, early theorists of stardom employed what Dyer calls the "fashion thesis" of stardom, regarding stars as novelty items achieving the temporary popularity of fads and then quickly becoming has-beens (1979, 15–16).

Other critics have pointed to a sense of duality that pervades all star images. First of all, film stardom can be said to involve a mixture of fiction and reality, in the public spectacle of the on-screen performance and the private self of the off-screen image. Even star performance encompasses an uneasy relationship between the star's portrayal of the character and a sense of the star's personality hidden behind the role. John Ellis has proposed what he calls the "photo effect" of the filmed image, with the actor being seen as *there,* in the sense of the image on the screen, and not *there,* in a real sense (307).

The star's off-screen image can also be seen as partaking in this duality. As Dyer has pointed out, the star image can best be described as a "structured polysemy" (1979, 3), an "infinite multiplicity of [possible] meanings and affects" (1979, 72), holding in an uneasy tension discordant elements, temporarily foregrounding some, while masking and displacing others through an ongoing process of negotiation, reconciliation, condensation, oscillation, and fragmentation (1979, 77). This polysemic effect involves the combination of seemingly contradictory qualities, such as the extraordinary (great beauty, glamour, strength, skill, success) and the ordinary (marriage, family, personal problems). As simultaneously irresistible and impossible objects of desire, stars exhibit yet another sense of duality; they are highly desirable, yet ultimately unattainable (1979, 50).

Much of the instability associated with the star image stems from stardom's intertextual nature. As Dyer has suggested, a star's image is derived from a multitude of texts, including

promotional material (the deliberate creation of the star's image by the studio or the star's publicity agents)

publicity (promotional material that seems to have resulted from media interest in the star's films and personal life, rather than from deliberate studio promotion)

overall filmic presentation of the star throughout his or her career

criticism/commentaries (ranging from film reviews to academic scholarship) (Dyer 1979, 69–72)

Sources of information on contemporary stars have increased exponentially as the Internet, book tie-ins with films, star biographies, DVD commentaries, and TV interview and gossip shows have created an explosion of readily available star information.[10] As Alan Lovell points out, this wealth of material makes it extremely difficult for the researcher to know exactly how much of this wide array of star information is known by an individual viewer and exactly what effect it has on the filmgoer's reaction to a particular star (2003, 365–366). Barry King argues, for instance, that the commonness of star promotion and publicity has led to a "dissipation of [star] persona." Now, in order to distinguish themselves from the multitude of other stars, actors must continually strive to be "sensational in word and deed" (2003, 50). The proliferation of celebrity gossip, constantly providing new revelations about stars' personal lives, reinforces the idea that star information can ultimately reveal an authentic self behind the star image and increases the fictional character of stars as they become "characters in the drama of their own biographies" (2003, 51).

The sense of duality surrounding the star image is also created by the relationship of that image to the star's filmic representation. For Dyer, there are several ways that the star image can function in regard to the star's film appearances. Whereas star image and film performance most often match and serve to reinforce each other, at other times they can conflict. When this happens, the star image, as Dyer says, "partly cracks open [the film's] mythology" by exposing its underlying contradictions.[11] At other times, however, the image of the star can hold together contradictory elements within a film that would otherwise split it asunder. Additionally, film performance can have reciprocal effect on the star image, celebrating, scrutinizing, exposing, or problematizing it. By echoing or reflecting upon the star's personal life, film performances can play a role in the process of image manufacture or even expose that manufacture as a fraud (Dyer 1991, 216).

Film performance can also give the star a sense of charisma, an aura of exceptionality that sets the star apart from the ordinary person. This charismatic quality is connected, first of all, to the star's larger than life quality on the screen, termed by Barry King "hypersemiotization"—the sense that stars are cinematic supersigns invested with profound significance (1991, 142). Charisma also relates to other qualities of the star phenomenon, such as the mystification of stars as extraordinarily gifted screen idols endowed with exceptional even magical talent or as heroic protagonists in the mythical success stories of their private lives. Their charisma comes from being seen as just ordinary people who have been made extraordinary by talent, luck, and specialness. As Charles Eckert has suggested, stars are rendered charismatic by their aura of "numinosity," their status as "highly overdetermined objects" with a "sense of transcendental and irrational significance."[12]

This charismatic quality is not only connected to the magical quality of stars but also to "the rhetoric of authenticity" that surrounds the concept of stardom (Dyer, 1979, 138). Stars must be what they seem to be—thus the notion of true or proven stars, whose stardom has been legitimized by the "truthfulness of their performances" (1979, 133–134). This sense of true star quality does not mean that the star must actually be a good actor, but merely that his or her performances are seen as expressing a true self, whatever that might be. This expression of authentic selfhood might take place through a seemingly unpremeditated effect or by the screen revelation of what is taken to be the star's intimate private self. In a larger sense, star charisma comes from the star "authenticating authenticity," conveying to fans that even in a postmodern world there still exists a unified coherent sense of self hidden under masks of falsehood and that this authentic sense of self is manifest in the star's persona.[13]

Perhaps the question of stars' authenticity is so prominent because they are so strongly identified with commodification and so obviously marketable entities. From the early days of the star system, stars have been used to sell films as well as related products through synergy, the connection made between films and other commercial goods by means of film tie-ups or tie-ins. Daniel Boorstin's manipulation thesis of stardom even proposes that stars are examples of pure industry manipulation. Lacking real substance, they are merely "pseudoevents" that appear meaningful, although really being empty individuals who are famous just for being famous, celebrities marketed on the basis of appearance, trademarks used to market goods, and ultimately representations of "a new category of human emptiness" (Dyer 1979, 14).

Although Boorstin's manipulation thesis may be rather extreme, his point that stardom serves to support consumerism, conspicuous consumption, Hollywood commercialism, capitalism, and social stratification is well taken. At the same time, however, there is also much more to stardom than simple manipulation. Star images are complex and contradictory entities, not empty products constructed entirely by the entertainment industry. If stars are commodities, they are certainly unpredictable ones whose promotion in no way assures their acceptance by fans or the popularity of their films (Dyer 1979, 15). Although much can be said for the manipulation thesis, it seems too simple and extreme in its cynical assumption that fans are passive dupes controlled and exploited by a malicious, capitalistic film industry.

Stars have been seen as products not only of industry manipulation, but also of the film apparatus, the audience's whims and desires, and society's stereotypes and mores. For instance, theorists have speculated about what aspects of film help to create the phenomenon of stardom. Some candidates include film's sense of intimacy, its realism, and the use of the close-up, which Bela Belazs early theorized created stardom by providing an unmediated glimpse of the star's true personality (Dyer 1979, 16). Stars have also been seen as products or expressions of fans' dreams, desires, and needs. The compensation thesis of stardom argues that stars compensate the audience for what they feel they lack in their own lives (Dyer 1979, 32). The industry nominates candidates for stardom, but only the fans elect who will be elevated to the exalted position of the star (Dyer 1979, 22). As Richard Dyer points out, the audience can even "sabotage" a star's proffered image by rejecting industry promotion and creating their own conception of a star's persona. Yet, the power of fans to shape the star phenomenon is decidedly limited. They cannot designate their candidates for stardom, but can only choose from among those nominated by the industry (Dyer 1986, 5; 1979, 20).

Stars can also be connected to social types. For instance, Dyer proposes that stars often fall into social categories, such as the pin-up, the tough guy, and the "good Joe." He believes one reason stars are famous is because of their typicality, representability, and individuation of social types, characteristics that render them more human and thus more acceptable to the average fan. The star can be seen as "an idealized concept of how people are supposed to be or act" (Dyer 1979, 53). Although most stars represent types that support the status quo, Dyer contends that some stars get their star quality from their symbolic representation of resistance to social conformity and accepted values. These anomic stars—James Dean, Marlon Brando, and Jane Fonda immediately come to mind—are rebels expressing social dissent and angst (Dyer 1979, 59).

The idea of the anomic star has been and remains a subject of considerable controversy. In first proposing the idea, even Dyer questioned whether stars could really represent a challenge to the established order or whether they merely act as safety valves that allow for the expression of a certain amount of generalized discontent and alienation, while lacking a specific social goal that would really make them socially challenging. They might even be regressive figures, recuperating rebellion for the status quo by labeling it an inadequate and irresponsible reaction to social problems, a passing phase of socially acceptable youth rebellion, or merely the effect of personal psychological problems (Dyer 1979, 60–61). As will be discussed later, the idea of the anomic star has been particularly vexed when applied to female stars. Whereas some critics see certain actresses, like Bette Davis and Katherine Hepburn, as resisting traditional women's roles, others believe their nonconformity was always recuperated for the status quo and never represented a significant challenge to patriarchal norms.[14]

Although star studies have investigated many areas of stardom, two important dimensions have been neglected: stars as auteurs and stars as workers within the film industry. The idea of the star as auteur is perhaps not discussed as much as it should be because it remains a rather controversial assertion. The movie-going public seems early to have identified stars, rightly or wrongly, as the authors of their films and of the characters they play, yet film scholars have been reluctant to do so. For example, Allen Lovell maintains that stars cannot be auteurs, a term originated primarily to denote directors, because they lack the kind of control of the film's overall design that directors have (264).

Richard Dyer proposes, however, that although most stars remain "semipassive icons" manipulated to serve the designs of the director, others can establish themselves as actor–auteurs in three ways: through performance, by constructing their image, and by influencing the overall design of their films. For instance, stars can gain auteurist status by demanding that a film accommodate their screen persona in terms of character presentation or script development and by influencing the narrative content or style of a film in terms of line changes, improvisation, or subtly shifting the significance of scenes. They can also signify meanings through their characterization that were never intended by the director or writer (Dyer 1979, 179).

In addition, stars have always had considerable auteurist influence on one major type of Hollywood production—the star vehicle—because, as I will discuss later when we examine star acting, the whole reason for existence of this type of film is to showcase the qualities of its star. Stars can also be actor–auteurs in terms of engineering the construction of their image by careful role choice and by taking an active part in the development of their publicity campaigns. As Barry King points out, contemporary stars are now much more likely to take on the role of "self-contained auteurs pursuing a personal vision" because they have become individual entrepreneurs rather than contract players under the control of a studio (2003, 50).

Stars have been neglected not only as auteurs but also as workers within the film industry. This neglect can to a large extent be attributed to the mystification of acting and stardom that surrounds the discussion of stars. As I will discuss more fully later, it also has resulted from star studies' failure to adopt a political economy approach to stardom, which would place it within an industrial context, and study stardom as a job among others within the Hollywood film labor system. As Paul McDonald points out, stardom needs to be studied as a relationship between labor and capital. For instance, stars have always functioned for producers as a means of assuring product differentiation and demand elasticity (2000, 11). The star's ability to attract audiences to films by supplying a unique personality that makes one film stand out from its competitors was early perceived as a way for studios to increase film demand and box office prices.

Stars need to be studied not just as images or performance specialists but also as multitasking professionals whose job involves working within every area of filmmaking, including preproduction (reading scripts, choosing parts, learning lines), production (rehearsal, shooting on location and in the studio), and postproduction (postdubbing, promotional interviews, premiers) (McDonald 2000, 9–10). Stars need to be studied as workers, and the roles of agents, publicists, casting agents, studio executives, and studio publicity departments also need to be examined to better understand the marketing and promotion of stars.

Danae Clark has contributed significantly to the study of acting as work by looking at what she calls the screen "actors' subjectivity" as it is shaped materially by "labor power practices."[15] In *Negotiating Hollywood: The Cultural Politics of Actor's Labor*, Clark examines how the star system has structured labor power differences between actors and producers and between different levels of actors, ranging from stars to supporting players, extras, stunt people, and body doubles. Confining her analysis to labor–management relations in the 1930s and touching only briefly on contemporary actors' labor, she concentrates on the struggle of screen actors to achieve self-representation through the formation of the Screen Actors Guild against studio attempts to undercut their efforts. Interestingly, according to Clark, the special relationship that stars have with management actually impeded the efforts of actors as a whole to negotiate for equitable working conditions (26–27).

Major Approaches to the Study of Stars

Star studies have always been a poor second cousin within the family of film studies, never seen as a truly respectable area of concentration. This attitude no doubt stems from the 1960s, when the field of film studies was in its infancy and the study of stars was the domain of popular star biographies and textual analysis of star performances. Charles Affron's *Star Acting*, which contains close readings of the film performances of Lillian Gish, Bette Davis, and Greta Garbo, is often credited with moving star studies out of the realm of anecdotal and impressionistic star adoration into the more exacting study of performance.[16] What Affron actually does, however, involves simply describing the characters portrayed by the stars, contextualizing them within the stars' careers as a whole, and attributing most of the stars' accomplishments to their directors. By designating the actresses he studies as screen goddesses, taking an evaluative stance to their performances, and adopting what Jeremy Butler has called an untheorized, strongly "value-laden aesthetics" (Butler, 90–91), Affron does not really move very far from earlier star hagiography.

Richard Dyer's *Stars* did precipitate a seismic shift in the way in which star studies were perceived. Dyer's sociosemiotic approach still investigated issues of performance, but it viewed them in a new way. Coming out of the British cultural studies movement of the 1970s, which sought to understand the ideological functions of the media by examining production and reception in a cultural and historical context, Dyer developed the concept of the "star text," "an intertextual construct produced across a range of media and cultural practices, capable of intervening in the working of particular films, but also demanding analysis as a text in its own right."[17]

Dyer saw stars not as gods, biographical curiosities, or sources of anecdotal material, but rather as aspects of a larger cultural sign system that functions to "personaliz[e] social meanings and ideologies" (Gledhill 1991, xiv). Under Dyer's analytical microscope, stars became complex social constructs produced by their film performances as well as by extrafilmic factors, such as publicity, promotion, and reviews. Because he believed star images "reconcile, mask, or expose social contradictions," Dyer saw the ideological significance of stars as profound and open to divergent, even oppositional fan readings (Gledhill 1991, xiv).

In Dyer's view, star performances combined with the star's extrafilmic image to become part of a larger star text that could be investigated by the use of semiotic analysis. Dyer's introduction of semiotics to star studies was nothing short of monumental. Stars were now examined in terms of the fit between image and role; the ideological function of performance, especially as a model of acceptable social behavior; and the interconnection among star performance, publicity, promotion, and audience reception. For instance, Dyer suggested that the study of stars should examine not only the recurring features of their performances, but also what they signify ideologically to their fans. As a semiotician, he broke star performance down into signifiers (component elements) of meaning, such as physical appearance, speech, gesture, posture, hairstyle, and actions. He deconstructed star images, separating the various aspects of their "structured polysemy" and uncovering the ideas, values, and attitudes the star represents. In this way, Dyer believed star studies could expose the ideological underpinnings of stardom by showing how stars make coherent and natural what is actually contradictory, arbitrary, and socially constructed.

Thus, Dyer's approach to the study of stardom brilliantly combined semiotic with intertextual and ideological analysis. His conception of star images as amalgams of performance, promotion, publicity, and criticism revealed stars in all their complexity as unstable, always partial and constantly changing accumulations of a shifting series of elements. In order to recreate the range of meanings of a star in a given historical period, it became the difficult task of the star studies scholar to unravel the underlying pattern of constructions hidden within the star image. Thus, stars became not just images composed of a complex web of intertexual material, but rather signs with significant social value as sites of ideological contradiction and resistance. As Jeremy Butler points out, according to Dyer's ideological conception of stardom, "the (many) meanings associated with a star are seen to form a part of the meaning system of that star's society, the ideology of that particular time and place."[18]

In his second major work, *Heavenly Bodies*, Dyer's ideological approach led him to contextualize the star images of Marilyn Monroe, Paul Robeson, and Judy Garland within the discourses circulating at the time of their popularity. In this way, he was able to examine how their images negotiated current issues of gender, sexuality, and race. Dyer's ideological intertextual semiotics of the star image was extremely influential on the work of subsequent star studies scholars. For instance, building on Dyer's work, James Damico in his study of Ingrid Bergman developed the idea of the star's "image lexicon," comprising all the various intertextual elements of the star's image fused together into an "assimilatable phenomenon" labeled with the star's name. According to Damico, based on this lexicon, the star becomes a "totem figure" for fans, signifying their spiritual longings and aspirations. The star who violates the fan conception of this lexicon will be rejected by fans, sometimes very harshly.

Damico believes this was the case with Ingrid Bergman, whose star image was built by the studio to symbolize wholesomeness, purity, and devotion to work and family (246). When it was revealed that she had an extramarital affair with Italian director Roberto Rosselini, she was harshly condemned by the press as immoral and her fans quickly turned against her. Damico proposes that it was because of the false and misleading nature of Bergman's image lexicon that her fans rejected her with such anger, disappointment, and resentment. Bergman had become a "totem figure" who served as a reflection of her "audience's indefinite spiritual longings and aspirations," but when she showed herself to be a sexual rather than an entirely spiritual being, she was torn down as a false idol (251–252).

Alan Lovell believes Dyer's influence on star studies may not have been entirely positive. For Lovell, Dyer associated star studies too closely with ideological analysis, capitalist ideology, and the construction of human subjectivity. Lovell even questions whether the formation of the individual subject is as central to capitalist ideology or to stardom as Dyer suggests. As Lovell points out, stars are questionable candidates for carrying out ideological functions because they appear to be rather frivolous people who lack, rather than promote, stable, consistent identities. Lovell asks whether "the main interest of stars [for their fans] could really be, as Dyer suggests, the [social] meanings they make" (2003, 260–261).

At approximately the same time that Dyer developed his ideological semiotics of star studies, other critics were looking at stars through a psychoanalytic lens. Psychoanalysis seemed particularly appropriate to the study of stars, who function as objects of spectatorial identification, pleasure, and desire. Under the influence of Laura Mulvey, feminist film criticism in particular began to use Lacanian psychoanalytic theory to investigate female stars as objects of the male spectator's voyeuristic and fetishistic gaze, representatives of "to-be-looked-at-ness," and signifiers of "otherness" in contrast to male normality. The psychoanalytic approach connected stars to human psychological development, especially to Lacan's conception of incomplete human subjectivity and the dominance within the human psyche of a sense of unfulfilled desire and lack. Within the psychoanalytic framework, the star image as part of an endless cycle of promotion and publicity offers the viewer's incomplete subjectivity the promise of completion through identification with the image of the star. This promise, however, is only temporarily fulfilled through the star's film performances, compelling the spectator to return again and again to the cinema for another temporary sense of fulfillment and wholeness (Lovell, 263).

According to psychoanalytic theory, the spectator's cinematic experiences are intimately related to the psychic processes of narcissism, voyeurism, and fetishism. By narcissistically identifying with the star as an ego ideal, the viewer is said to form a sense of self. Through the voyeuristic component of the cinematic experience, the spectator purportedly derives a feeling of sadistically controlling the star as an exhibitionist object of screen spectacle and off-screen gossip. Finally, it is proposed that fetishism allows the spectator to assuage the fear of lack (in psychoanalytic terms, castration anxiety) by positing the star as a fetishistic figure with magical attributes. Through what John Ellis has called the "photo effect," the cinematic image of the star enacts within the spectator Freud's *fort-da* game. In watching a film, the spectator experiences the star's cinematic presence on the screen and the absence of the star's physical presence in the theater at the time of the film screening. The star is in a sense there and not there, activating the audience's desire for wholeness and completion, but ultimately only reinforcing their sense of lack.[19] The female star's glamorization, the cult-like devotion of her fans, and her function as an object of spectacle are all said to partake of this fetishistic aspect of stardom.

If Dyer's ideological semiotics of stardom places too much emphasis on stars as representations of human individuality, psychoanalysis has its problems, some of which we will consider more fully when we deal with psychoanalytic approaches to the female star. In general, however, psychoanalytic star studies are hampered by a gendered division of spectatorship that posits female stars as inevitably the objects of the male gaze, ignores the "to-be-looked-at-ness" of male stars, and makes female spectatorship difficult to theorize.

Also neglected are the complexities of cinematic and star identification, which would seem to involve not just gendered, but also shifting cross-gendered and multiple-gendered processes of identification. Psychoanalysis is also flawed by its limited conception of fandom as homogenous and monolithic, of film-going as a function merely of individual viewer psychology divorced from sociohistorical contexts, and of stars' significance as rooted in the universal childhood experiences of fans. Thus, the meanings of stars are regarded reductively as all encompassing, applicable to all audience members, and final (McDonald 2000, 92).

Another prominent approach to the study of stardom is sociohistorical. This perspective has been dominated by studies of the history of the Hollywood star system. Most influential in initiating work in this area were Janet Staiger and Richard de Cordova who, in the late 1980s, began to challenge the traditional account of how the star system began. Film textbooks attributed the development of the star system to the conflict between Edison's monopolistic MPPC (Motion Pictures Patents Company) and the competing independents. Independent producers were said to have used stars to differentiate their product from the films of the MPPC, which reputedly was reluctant to identify its players from fear that they would then demand higher wages. Cook's account identifies as the crucial event in the development of the star system Carl Laemle's promotion in 1909 of Florence Lawrence, whom he had just lured from MPPC's Biograph Studios (Butler 1998, 344). Other historians, however, identified Mary Pickford or Ben Turpin as the first real movie star.[20]

Staiger took exception to this scenario, indicating that the first evidence of players being publicized did come in 1909, but it actually came from an MPPC studio. By 1910, according to Staiger, identification of actors became so widespread that every studio was putting actor credits on its films. Fan magazines even began to be published in 1910, and the star system was in full swing by 1912. Staiger says the crucial event was not competition within the film industry, but the recognition that it was more effective to sell films by promoting their stars rather than their stories. She also makes clear that the star system was not at all new when it was adopted by Hollywood, but was inherited from the popular theater, which had already begun to promote its stars in the nineteenth century (Staiger, 9–15). In fact, the exodus of theatrical stars from stage to screen can actually be seen as crucial to the development of the star system. This arrival of theater talent legitimized film acting and shifted film discourse from the wonders of film technology to the stories film could tell and the actors who brought those stories to life (Butler 1998, 345).

Like Staiger, de Cordova also argued that the star system was developed by the MPPC and the independents, but he added an analysis of how that development took place. He pointed to a three-layered developmental schema. First, "a discourse on acting" had to develop. The focus needed to shift from documentary filmmaking and its emphasis on the magical qualities of the film medium to narrative film and the importance of acting for effective storytelling.[21] The second requirement was the development of the "picture personality," who not only was credited in the film's list of players, but could also be identified as a distinct presence from film to film. The stage and screen careers of picture personalities would be known, but they would only be famous in terms of their acting roles. For de Cordova, true stardom had not yet arrived. It was only in 1914, when information about the private lives of stars began to circulate as part of the industry's attempts to combat Progressive Era attacks on Hollywood immorality, that stardom really began (de Cordova, 24–26). Similarly, Paul McDonald sees six factors as needed for the development of the star system (2000, 24–29):

the move from the single cameraman to the director system of production with an accompanying specialized division of labor

the growth of narrative film

active circulation of information about players

the development of the close-up to allow audiences intimate identification of performers

continuity editing

naturalistic acting

More recently, critics have begun to examine not just when the star system began, but how it functioned in the studio era. For instance, Paul McDonald discusses the close ties between the power of the studios and the creation, marketing, and control of stars (2000, 40). Similarly, Martin Barker points out that the studio era star system, well in place by the 1920s and lasting to the 1950s, tied stars to long-term contracts typically extending for seven years and giving the studios extensive control not only of the stars' career decisions but also of their personal lives (4).

McDonald discusses in detail the nature of the studio contract. Individually negotiated and nonstandardized, studio contracts gave job security to apprentice actors in early career, but contained many features that were highly unfavorable to actors once they became stars. The studio determined the stars' salaries, the roles they would play, how many films they would make per year, and which ones. It could terminate the contract at will, but the star could not break it. Stars could also be loaned to other studios and typecast without their consent to create a consistent image. If stars refused to acquiesce to any of the studio's demands, they could be suspended without pay with their contract extended to make up for the time of their suspension. Contracts also customarily contained morality clauses that gave the studio extensive control of the star's personal life (2000, 62–63).

The studios used long-term contracts to control what they called their "stable" of stars and also created an elaborate system of star development. In the discovery phase, studios would send hired talent scouts to comb other entertainment venues, such as theaters, nightclubs, and vaudeville houses, for actors with star potential. These would-be stars would then be given screen tests by studio drama coaches and casting directors to determine whether they should be offered contracts. Once they became contract players, they entered a period of apprenticeship, during which they would take lessons with drama, speech, dancing, and singing coaches and work to cultivate subsidiary skills that might be required for film work, such as etiquette, movement, fencing, and horseback riding. At this time, their names and physical appearance might be changed, and they would be cast in small supporting roles in major films or in less significant "B" pictures (McDonald 2000, 43–48). All of this would eventually lead to the final goal of acting stardom.

As many critics have pointed out, stardom in contemporary Hollywood is very different from what it was in the studio era. Since the 1970s, the New Hollywood has been dominated by the package-unit system of production, which involves independent production companies and talent agencies packaging together a script, director, stars, and financing into film projects that are then sold to the major studios, which have become largely management and distribution companies (McDonald 2000, 75). The selling of these film packages relies heavily on the star power attached; with the star's agent negotiating deals per project, star's salaries and industry clout have increased greatly, as has the importance and power of talent agencies. Stars now can even opt for profit participation arrangements, also known as "back-end deals," in which they waive part or all of their salary to get a share in the net or gross profits of a film. They can also negotiate vanity deals that allow them to start production companies (McDonald 2000, 79). New Hollywood's dependence on blockbuster, high-concept, and event films and synergy to tie films to other media industries also have increased the star's importance as a marketing tool (McDonald 2000, 96).

As a result, contemporary stars are no longer studio-controlled contract players, but have become entrepreneurs selling their star status as their product. Barry King asserts that as "self-contained auteurs pursuing their personal vision" stars have moved out of what he calls the "real subsumption" characteristic of the studio era, when stars were indentured to powerful studios that formed and controlled every aspect of their public lives. In the New Hollywood, stars now exist in what King calls a state of "formal subsumption" with the freedom and the responsibility to shape their careers and images (Barker, 4). As Barker points out, however, this period of star power may be coming to an end as independent production companies become increasingly aligned with certain studios, star's vanity deals are withdrawn, star-based production companies fold, and films are sold less on star power than on special effects and the notoriety of superstar directors. According to Barker, all of this may signal the beginning of a new studio era with the concomitant decline of star power (8–9). Currently, however, the star–actor is still able to shape his or her career in significant ways.

If the sociohistorical approach has led to analyses of the star system as it existed during various eras of Hollywood production, audience studies have investigated star images in relation to the perceptions of their fans. This approach has also had a sociohistorical dimension because stars are studied in terms of how they have influenced the actual movie-going public in a given historical period. The most important work in this area is Jackie Stacey's *Star Gazing*, an ethnographic study of the relationship between British female fans and Hollywood stars in the post-World War II era. Although she focuses on a particular time and place, her conclusions, are widely applicable to star–fan relationships in different historical periods.

Stacey proposes eight different ways in which female fans can use star images to fashion their identities. She delineates four cinematic identificatory fantasies: adoration; desire to become the star; pleasure in the star's female power; and using the star to escape one's life, and four extracinematic identifications: pretending or fantasizing about being the star; accentuating one's resemblance to the star; changing oneself to imitate the star; and copying one physical aspect of the star.[22] Similarly, Richard Dyer has constructed four categories of fan–star relationships: emotional affinity (the fan feels involved with the star because of the characters he or she plays); self-identification (the fan puts himself or herself in the same place as the star); imitation (the fan takes the star as a role model); and projection (the fan lives a life bound up with that of the star) (1979, 20).

The use of audience studies has been problematic in star studies because of the difficulties involved in conducting and interpreting interviews, surveys, and other potential means of ascertaining viewers' actual reactions to stars during the cinematic experience and outside of the cinema. This is especially true in regard to audiences of the past, whose memories are now, after many years, notoriously vague and unreliable; however, even contemporary viewers are difficult to investigate because they are often inarticulate about the reasoning behind their star preferences. Box office statistics, fan magazine polls and letters, fan club news, fan mail, Internet fan sites, and reviewers' opinions have all been used to provide insight into the popularity of certain stars, but they do not always reliably reveal exactly why viewers feel a connection to certain stars. As Alan Lovell suggests, we are not even sure how aware audiences are of the contributions stars make to films, how fans' star preferences guide their choices of film viewing, or what fans' criteria are for judging star performances (2003, 269).

Richard Dyer suggests that the audience studies approach is also limited by the fact that fans can only choose from the array of performers offered to them by the film industry and studying audiences does not tell us why certain stars are offered to filmgoers in the first place (1979, 20). Still, audience studies have made some important contributions to the study of film stardom. First of all, they have pointed to the active and diverse nature of fan culture. Fans are not passive dupes subject to the wholesale manipulation of the Hollywood industry; instead, audience studies have shown that, rather than simply accepting the star images offered to them, fans use stars in unique and varied ways to serve their social and psychic purposes.

One other approach that is prominent in star studies is typological. Just as scholars have documented types of actors, they have also developed theories of star types. Christine Geraghty's work is most notable in this regard. She has divided stars into three types: the star as celebrity, the star as professional, and the star as performer. The fame of stars as celebrities is based on the public dissemination of intimate revelations about their private lives in publicity, interviews, star biographies, and other sources of celebrity gossip. This gossip is not matched by excellence in performance; stars as celebrities are famous for being themselves and not for the success of their films or their reputations as actors. Geraghty proposes that female more often than male stars fit into this category (2000, 187–189); among the actresses that we will study, Gwyneth Paltrow is a perfect example of a female star who rose to stardom based on gossip about her personal life, rather than because of her acting accomplishments. She clearly began her career as a star as celebrity.

The fame of stars as professionals rests on the "seamless public persona" they present through their work as acting professionals, rather than on their private lives (Geraghty 2000, 187). Another way to put this is to say that these stars are typecast into certain roles that they make their own and exploit throughout their careers. Stars known for their performances in certain genres and television actors who play recurring roles in series fit into this category. Geraghty proposes that in film it is dominated by male action and comedy stars (2000, 187–189), such as Sylvester Stalone and Eddie Murphy. Stars as professionals are associated with the acting style of personification, playing the same type of character in each role. Among contemporary actresses, Julia Roberts' and Meg Ryan's romantic comedy personas fit into this category. They have established stable star identities that are crucial to their audience acceptance, and any changes they have made in their images have seriously threatened their established fan base. Among the actresses that we will study, Jodie Foster comes closest to this category of actress. She has established her career playing heroic survivor roles and has really not deviated from this persona.

The final and most prestigious category is the star as performer, where the skill, craft, and talent of actors are placed in the forefront of their image lexicons and put on display in their performances (Geraghty 2000, 187). This star type is associated with the acting style of impersonation; the actor shows his or her talent by becoming a different character in each role. Actors within this category of stardom have prestigious acting reputations and their performances garner high critical accolades. The paradigm of this acting type among the actresses that we will study is Meryl Streep, whose career has largely been created around her renown as a great actress and her talent for impersonation.

Another attempt to delineate acting types is John Ellis's distinction between film stars and television personalities. Ellis proposes that television does not create stars. Only film has the rarity value, the glamour, the "photo effect," the fetishism, and the combination of the ordinary and the extraordinary needed for the "ultimate confirmation of stardom" (Gledhill 1991, xiii). Television for Ellis has too much immediacy, familiarity, and frequency for TV personalities ever to rise to the level of real stardom. He believes rock stars, rather than television actors, are closer to the star status that comes with film stardom (313–315). Recently, scholars have also begun to consider the category of the virtual star, created by computer-generated imagery (CGI). They raise questions concerning the unique qualities of this category of stardom and how its new prominence will affect the star system and the acting techniques of real stars.[23]

Clearly, star studies have contributed enormously to the study of film stardom. These attempts to define the concept of stardom in all its permutations and complications have been extremely valuable, as has been the examination of intertextual and ideological components of the star image. Sociohistorical accounts of the history of the star system have also been of crucial importance. What has not been so carefully examined, however, is how these theories of acting and stardom relate to the study of the Hollywood star–actress. It is to this matter that we turn in our next chapter.

References

1. Lovell, Alan. 2003. "I Went in Search of Deborah Kerr, Jodie Foster, and Julianne Moore but Got Waylaid..." p. 259 in *Contemporary Hollywood Stardom*, eds. T. Austin and M. Barker. London: Arnold; hereafter cited in text.
2. McDonald, Paul. 2000. *The Star System: Hollywood's Production of Popular Identities*. London: Wallflower Press, p. 1; hereafter cited in text.
3. Amossy, Ruth. 1986. "Autobiographies of Movie Stars: Presentation of Self and its Strategies." *Poetics Today* 7(4): 677; hereafter cited in text.
4. Dyer, Richard. 1986. *Heavenly Bodies: Film Stars and Society*. New York: St. Martin's, p. 8; hereafter cited in text.
5. Damico, James. 1991. "Ingrid from Lorraine to Stromboli: Analyzing the Public's Perception of a Film Star." p. 252 in *Star Texts: Image and Performance in Film and Television*. ed. J. Butler. Detroit: Wayne State University Press; hereafter cited in text.
6. Geraghty, Christine. 2000. "Re-examining Stardom: Questions of Texts, Bodies, and Performance." p. 185 in *Reinventing Film Studies*, eds. C. Gledhill and L. Williams. London: Arnold; hereafter cited in text.
7. Gledhill, Christine. 1991. "Signs of Melodrama." pp. 208, 216–217 in *Stardom: Industry of Desire*, ed. C. Gledhill. London: Routledge.
8. Dyer, Richard. 1991. "Charisma." p. 59 in *Stardom: Industry of Desire*, ed. C. Gledhill. London: Routledge; hereafter cited in text.
9. King, Barry. 2003. "Embodying an Elastic Self: the Parametrics of Contemporary Stardom." p. 52 in *Contemporary Hollywood Stardom*, eds. T. Austin and M. Barker. London: Arnold; hereafter cited in text.
10. Barker, Martin. 2003. "Introduction." pp. 22–23 in *Contemporary Hollywood Stardom*, eds. T. Austin and M. Barker. London: Arnold; hereafter cited in text.
11. Dyer, Richard. 1991. "Four Films by Lana Turner." p. 216 in *Star Texts: Image and Performance in Film and Television*. ed. J. Butler. Detroit: Wayne State University Press; hereafter cited in text.
12. Eckert, Charles. 1991. "Shirley Temple and the House of Rockefeller." p. 185 in *Star Texts: Image and Performance in Film and Television*. ed. J. Butler. Detroit: Wayne State University Press.
13. Wells, Paul. 2003. "To Affinity and Beyond: Woody, Buzz, and the New Authenticity." p. 92 in *Contemporary Hollywood Stardom*, eds. T. Austin and M. Barker. London: Arnold.
14. See, for instance, Geraghty, Christine. 2000. "Re-examining Stardom." p. 188 in *Reinventing Film Studies*, eds. C. Gledhill and L. Williams. Oxford: Oxford University Press.

15. Clark, Danae. 1995. *Negotiating Hollywood: The Cultural Politics of Actors' Labor.* Minneapolis: University of Minnesota Press, p. xii; hereafter cited in text.
16. Butler, Jeremy. 1991. "Introduction to Charles Affron's 'Generous Stars.'" p. 91 in *Star Texts: Image and Performance in Film and Television*, ed. J. Butler. Detroit: Wayne State University Press.
17. Gledhill, Christine. 1991. "Introduction." p. xiv in *Stardom: Industry of Desire*, ed. C. Gledhill. London: Routledge; hereafter cited in text.
18. Butler, Jeremy. 1998. "The Star System and Hollywood." p. 345 in *The Oxford Guide to Film Studies*, eds. J. Hill and P. C. Gibson. Oxford: Oxford University Press; hereafter cited in text.
19. John Ellis' formulation of this theory in *Visible Fictions: Cinema: Television: Video* (London: Routledge, 1982) is the most noted.
20. Staiger, Janet. 1991. "Seeing Stars." pp. 5–6 in *Stardom: Industry of Desire*, ed. C. Gledhill. London: Routledge.
21. de Cordova, Richard. 1991. "The Emergence of the Star System in America." p. 21 in *Stardom: Industry of Desire*, ed. C. Gledhill. London: Routledge; hereafter cited in text.
22. Stacey, Jackie. 1991. "Feminine Fascinations: Forms of Identification in Star–Audience Relations." pp. 150–156 in *Stardom: Industry of Desire*, ed. C. Gledhill. London: Routledge.
23. Austin, Thomas. 2003. "Star Systems." pp. 27–28 in *Contemporary Hollywood Stardom*, eds. T. Austin and M. Barker. London: Arnold.

CHAPTER 3

Star Acting and the Hollywood
Star–Actress

Star Acting

Because of the division within film scholarship between studies of stars and of film acting, the acting techniques of Hollywood stars have received far too little scholarly attention. This chapter will attempt to fill that gap. Even within the field of star studies, the focus has been placed so much on ideological criticism of star images and the historical examination of the star system that the study of stars as actors has been pushed to the side. Also, the common conception that stars actually cannot act but merely play themselves on screen has interfered with the examination of their acting methods. The idea that stars are not really actors stems from the common association of star acting with the mode of acting labeled as personification.

The belief that star acting is merely playing oneself in each role has interfered more than anything else with the study of the star–actor. The essence of this association is that the "star is always himself or herself, only thinly disguised as a character." Thus, star–actors are seen as not acting, but just "being" on the screen, and their characters are considered merely "fictional extension[s] of the actors' true personalities" (Maltby, 384). Barry King has called this type of acting "concerted cynosure," which involves the fusion of the roles actors play with their personalities (King 2003, 46). Because of this fusion, star acting has become identified with nonacting or, even worse, with bad acting. It is contrasted unfavorably with the acting mode termed impersonation, which is said to involve the actor's personality disappearing into the role or the actor becoming or transforming himself or herself into the character.

Impersonation is associated in somewhat different theoretical forms with Method and Broadway repertory acting and has gained considerable prestige from this association. In Method acting, as we have seen, the actor is said to become the character, whereas in Broadway repertory acting the actor instead pretends to be or imitates the character's actions and emotions. However, in both acting styles, actors give up their personalities to become someone else. Thus, their methodology is said to be impersonation. Personification, on the other hand, never involves this sacrifice of the actor's personality. The star is always seen behind the role and, for this reason, someone employing the acting mode of personification is often condemned as a poor actor. Because star acting has been strongly associated with this mode, the film apparatus has even been accused of making acting unnecessary and requiring stage actors to undertake a "deskilling process" (Geraghty 2000, 192).

More recently, however, scholars have begun to question the validity of the distinction between personification and impersonation. For instance, Paul McDonald suggests that the two are not exclusive acting types at all, but rather are always combined in acting performances (1998, 32). Barry King even proposes that impersonation has actually been cultivated in film acting because of the prestige to be gained from its strong association with craft and technique (King 1991, 147). Recently, Alan Lovell has gone so far as to say that criticisms of star acting as personification reflect only the anti-Hollywood sentiment of film scholars, rather than representing legitimate critiques of modes of film acting. He questions the notion that playing oneself is necessarily bad acting, pointing out that accomplished people in all occupations concentrate their talents on a limited area of expertise that provides them with an avenue to success. He sees star–actors who use personification and typecasting as a means of establishing a stable "picture personality" as simply placing themselves in a venue where they feel their talents will most benefit them, and he characterizes Hollywood stars as "the best actors by and large"(2003, 263).

Even before Lovell, James Naremore examined the work of Cary Grant as an example of the acting effectiveness of personification. Naremore characterized Grant as the epitome of the star–actor, "a famous personality who is performing a role but is [also] the essence of stardom—that is, as a remote, glamorous object who emits a glorious light simply by being 'himself.'" Naremore proposed that stars of Grant's magnitude have an "aura" that interferes with the audience's ability to see them as acting (221). The audience tends to lose sight of star–actors' craft because their image overshadows their acting technique; therefore, their acting is regarded as just "being natural" or playing themselves. Naremore points out that there is nothing really natural about looking natural on the screen and at the same time projecting an image that viewers find interesting. He proposes that the screen portrayal of "a vivid star personality is itself a theatrical construction" and one that necessitates considerable acting ability (234).

Actually, it seems to be the combination of personification and impersonation in star acting that provides the star with a considerable amount of market value. Impersonation brings with it the cultural capital of acting as a craft or art, allowing stars to present themselves as artists and the industry to market their films as having artistic merit. Personification, on the other hand, serves Hollywood's capitalistic structure by making stars famous not for their technical skills and acting talent, but rather for their personal features, which makes them easier to market as commodities (King 1991, 142, 148). As Virginia Wright Wexman points out, personification can actually add to the verisimilitude of star performance by connecting it with the intimate details of stars' lives as revealed in promotion and publicity. Thus, it affords yet another way of making characters on the screen come alive and seem real (1993, 24).

The combination of impersonation and personification in star performances is just one aspect of the hybrid nature of star acting, which, as Naremore points out, always involves a mixture of role, actor, and image (158–159). Similarly, Richard Maltby has suggested that all acting really entails the dual presence of the actor and character, but Hollywood's commercial aesthetic in particular encourages performance styles that accentuate this duality and allow the two halves of a performance to play against each other with the actor's persona and the character alternating throughout (380). It is not just actor and character that are combined, however. The star's image is also part of the alchemy of star acting, raising the issue of what is the appropriate proportion of actor, image, and character in the concoction that makes up an effective star performance.

Clearly, it is necessary for actors to show a certain amount of craft in order to impress the audience with their acting ability, but they are also expected to inhabit the role they play by making themselves one with the character. At the same time, some of the star's image is expected to shine through in every performance because this image, after all, is one of the major reasons the star's fans come to see the film. In many star performances, the star's off-screen persona actually is used to give added resonance to the role played, and stars are said to create their ideolect, "a set of performing traits that is systematically highlighted in films" (Naremore, 4). The balancing act needed to create a proper combination of star presence, demonstrated acting ability, and absorption in a character to make that ideolect work in a given performance is no easy acting task.

The hybridity of the star–actor is also a result of the mixture of the commercial with the aesthetic, box office clout with personal charisma, and industry creation with artistic expression that characterizes successful star acting. Scholars have speculated about the proper combination of these elements needed for an effective star performance. For instance, James Naremore argues that successful star–actors play characters who are "fictional extensions" of their image, thus allowing the part and the actor to be seen as one. As a result, the star–actor is not perceived as *acting* so much as *being* the character. However, Naremore also sees star performances as structured to give the audience a chance to appreciate the star's acting accomplishments and posits that one of the pleasures of film spectatorship is feeling that the star–actor is doing something remarkable on the screen (26).

John Ellis proposes three ways in which a star's image can relate to a character played. First of all, star–actors can perform their images so that image and role perfectly mesh. Ellis sees this as a rare occurrence, however, and one that is easier for male than for female stars because male characters are defined more by action than feelings. More commonly, the image exceeds the role and then the performance "goes to one side" of the image, using only certain components and refusing others. At other times, the role will contradict the image, going completely against the star's perceived personality as established on- and off-screen. Although Ellis proposes that star performances can thus resemble, contradict, or utilize only one side of the star image, he says they always reveal "something of the essence of the star's personality," a situation that he believes results in "cultism, of an inquisitive voyeuristic kind or a fascinated fetishistic type" on the part of fans (312).

Ellis has also suggested that star acting commonly involves one of two modes: stars underperform or overperform. According to Ellis, one reason why stars are not seen as acting is because their performance style tends to be more naturalistic than that of the supporting cast. Ellis attributes this to stars not having to work so hard to attract the audience's attention because they are already so well known. At times, however, stars, especially those interested in demonstrating their acting ability, will overperform in order to demonstrate their craftsmanship (311–312).

More persuasively, Richard Maltby has argued that star acting always involves interaction between different acting modes. It combines integrated acting, in which the actor becomes bound up with the character and plot of the film, with autonomous acting, when the star's performance stands out from the plot and the star's personality emerges from behind the characterization. Maltby associates these two acting modes with representational or invisible acting, which involves the actors seemingly having no conception that they are performing for an audience, and presentational acting, in which the actor acknowledges the audience's presence (381). The presentational mode is used most frequently in musicals and comedies, whereas the representational mode is associated strongly with drama.

Star acting can also be contrasted with character acting. Some critics have even argued for a hierarchical Hollywood structure with stars at the top assuming the major roles in films and acting through personification and character actors below them making supporting roles come alive through impersonation (King 1991, 148). Others have proposed to the contrary that the acting of supporting players is actually more likely to involve overperforming in order to draw attention to themselves and away from the film's stars (Naremore, 249). In the contemporary period, a middle rung in the acting hierarchy is said to exist composed of industry famous working actors, who lack the fan base of stars, but have performed in supporting roles in so many films that they are well known in the industry.[1] Barry King has suggested that, even among stars, a distinction can be made between those with high and low autonomy. Highly autonomous actors have considerable control over the shaping of their performances, usually because their stardom has brought them considerable clout within the industry; actors with low autonomy are merely the tools of their directors with little control over the characters they create and minimal input into the artistic dimensions of the films they make (1991, 145).

Recently, Allan Lovell has called into question all of these distinctions between stars and other actors. He believes stars are really no different from character actors in their acting techniques. The only reason their personalities seem to be more evident behind their characters is because the audience knows them better. Character actors only seem to disappear into their roles because the audience is unfamiliar with their personalities. Lovell believes that, if one followed the career and knew the private life of a character actor, that actor would no longer seem to disappear into a role, but would be seen to develop a recognizable screen personality (2003, 264).

A major venue for star acting is the star vehicle, a film specifically made to promote a given star. The star vehicle is often thought of simply as a film written to showcase a star's talent, but several types of star vehicles exist.

A film can be written to suit the character type, setting, genre, or theme favored by a star; a literary work can be adapted to the screen with a star in mind to play the lead role; or a script can be rewritten or a part changed or expanded to accommodate a star's image or abilities (Dyer 1979, 70). Because the star vehicle showcases its star's particular talents and plays upon the star's image, it encourages the acting mode of personification, with the star just doing what she or he has become famous for doing or just being the way fans expect the star to be. In many ways, as Barbara Klinger has suggested, the star vehicle is a form of "dramatic striptease," with the film's character gradually losing its fictional characteristics and developing the skills or personality traits the star is reputed to possess. Thus, "the 'real' image of the star behind the disguise of the character in question" is gradually revealed, and the star's authentic star quality is validated (quoted in Maltby, 386).

Paradoxically, star vehicles are showcases for star talent, but because they identify stardom with the acting mode of personification, they in turn render that talent suspect. The typecasting of stars in roles that accord with their established star personas and the hypersemiotization of stars' screen images also call their acting abilities into question. As we have seen, hypersemiotization converts the star into a bigger-than-life supersign invested with meaning beyond the context of the film. Because hypersemiotized stars are always visible behind the characters they play, they can never fully embody their characters. All of this results in a vicious cycle in which hypersemiotization, personification, and typecasting become inevitable and stars' acting talent is recognized less and less (King 1991, 143).

However, an argument can be made, and certainly will be made in this book, that stars are actually very talented actors and that the demands of film acting call for highly developed acting skills. Despite the claim that star acting primarily involves personification, Hollywood actors rarely admit to playing themselves on the screen. They focus instead on their work in creating believable characters and mastering the technical demands of film acting. As Sarah Knobloch proposes, screen actors must learn to "organize a wide variety of bodily postures and vocal textures into the classical narrative pattern with a clear beginning, middle and end, always cognizant of how much of the body (and voice) the framing makes available for the audience to perceive" (Knobloch, 122). Given the fragmented, discontinuous nature of Hollywood filmmaking, effective screen acting is no easy task. The association of screen acting with personification has obscured the acting talents of star–actors, and the substantial demands placed upon them to create believable characters within a medium that is not always conducive to effective characterization have not always been recognized.

According to Barry King, contemporary star acting has developed in very different directions from star acting under the studio system and requires somewhat different skills. For instance, because of the transformation from the studio to the package-unit system of production, stars are now required to take more control of the shaping of their careers through role choice and image construction. King argues that they must cultivate a star image characterized by "plasticity," rather than the consistent "commercial identity" associated with stardom in the studio era (2003, 45). According to King, contemporary star actors must be prepared to take on the identity appropriate to their current film performance. Thus, they are not expected to have a uniform star identity, but to create a vast "wardrobe of identities" from which they can pick and choose for different occasions (3003, 49).

They are also expected to "play down" to the acting requirements of "high-energy, low-intellectual demand blockbusters," where all the star–actor needs to do is to be a "simple presence" with "the ability to *seem* deeply meaningful" (Barker, 19). Blockbusters also require that male stars become objects of spectacle, as female stars have always been, but this masculine spectacle involves a different type of "to-be-looked-at-ness" that is connected not so much with facial beauty and romance, but rather with special effects and sensational action sequences. According to King, the physical screen presence of contemporary male stars has thus taken on so much importance that they have become "corporeal signifiers" on screen, rather than actors (King 2003, 51).

King argues further that film acting no longer involves what he terms the "metanymic servitude" of the studio era, when star acting rested on the analogical relationship between the stars' images and their screen roles, making them "narrative 'guests.'" For King, contemporary star acting is characterized by "metaphoric servitude," whereby stars are expected to subordinate their personalities completely to the purposes of the film and become essentially "narrative functions" without personalities beyond the roles played (2003, 48). Yet King also insists that because of the increased circulation of media gossip and publicity, stars are required more than they were in the past to be performers in their personal lives. They are now expected to create and recreate themselves as "characters in the drama of their own biographies."

Because of the "global market for celebrity gossip" and the increased competition within the acting profession, stars must constantly reaffirm their star status by heightening the sensationalism of their image and the hyperbole of their performances. King proposes that stars must prove over and over again that they are sensational on screen and in their personal lives in order to create the illusion of perpetual success. The ubiquity of contemporary star images, however, also creates what King calls a "dissipation of star persona" as stars become almost perpetually on display (2003, 51). As a result, it is increasingly difficult for stars to distinguish themselves from other stars and to establish an authentic star quality.

In spite of these insightful forays into the investigation of star acting, it remains an area that calls out for further analysis. As Allan Lovell suggests, the scholarly neglect of stars as actors ignores the fact that the most important aspect of stardom and the thing that really makes actors stars is their success as performers. Not to look at the career planning, technical skills, physical attributes, knowledge, and intelligence needed to attain film success is really to fail to discuss the essence of stardom. Lovell proposes that, to undertake this study, we need to return to an aesthetics of star acting, to look at the "beauty, pleasures, and delight" produced by the star–actor (2003, 270).

I would agree that the aesthetics of star acting merit further study, but I would also suggest that to limit our investigation to the aesthetic approach alone is yet again to ignore the complex, intertextual, multifaceted nature of stardom and star acting. What seems to be needed instead is a combination of approaches that illuminate the essential aspects of the contemporary star—actor's career, image, and acting. It is just such a combination of approaches that I utilize in the second part of this volume to construct case studies of five contemporary star–actresses.

The Star–Actress

If star acting has been neglected as a subject for scholarly analysis, the work of the star–actress—especially the contemporary star–actress—has been particularly ignored. This is not to say that Hollywood actresses have not been studied at all. Feminist film critics in particular have made some interesting observations about female stars, but these stars have not been studied as actresses per se, but more as ingredients within patriarchy's ideological conception of an objectified femininity. As we have seen in Chapter 1, feminist approaches to the star–actress have been limited by the conception that she represents a social stereotype of women or a fetishized object of the voyeuristic male gaze. In both instances, the star–actress is not regarded as a skilled acting professional in her own right, but as "a construction, a product of culture, industrially manufactured, and prefabricated by men."[2]

Another reason for the neglect of the star–actress is a long-standing tendency to denigrate the acting abilities of female stars in comparison to those of male stars. The classic expression of these sentiments is Josef von Sternberg' comment that

> To study acting is one thing, but to study the actor and the female of the acting species is something else again. There would be no need to study them at all were it not that [films are] dominated by them, and it is necessary to become familiar with the material one is compelled to use (quoted in Naremore, 131).

Overwhelmingly, female stars' work as actresses has been compared unfavorably to the accomplishments of their male counterparts. For instance, the acting abilities of female stars have traditionally been more naturalized than those of male stars, who are much more likely to be described as highly skilled and well-trained professionals whose success is the result of hard work and mastery of the craft of acting, rather than of their physical attractiveness and natural talent. Physical beauty has always been more important as a criterion for female stardom, but, as Virginia Wright Wexman points out, the work that an actress puts into her appearance has never been recognized as part of her acting skill (1993, 136). Instead, actresses are viewed merely as passive beauty icons who have risen to stardom due to their physical attractiveness or because they are willing to use their sexuality "on the casting couch" to get roles.

Star biographies are notorious for "emphasizing the training and work habits of men while focusing on the romantic adventures and pampered irresponsibility of the women" (Wexman, 1993, 134). This emphasis on work, training, and professionalism for male stars helps them to maintain their stardom even as they grow older, whereas female stars notoriously have great difficulty sustaining their careers once they reach the age of forty.[3] One way ageing male stars extend their careers is by advancing from acting to directing and producing, but female stars rarely make this move; when they do, they are seen as exceptional, like Jodie Foster, or difficult, like Barbara Streisand. Female stars have also often been portrayed as "Galatea figures," whose careers are launched and managed by powerful male directors or producers, but male stars are almost never portrayed in this way (Wexman, 1993, 135).

In addition, female stars' box office clout is traditionally lower than that of male stars. A few female stars, and Jodie Foster is said to be one of them, can "open" a film on their star status alone without a major male star opposite them. Actresses over forty lose almost all of their box office appeal and are no longer seen as candidates for high-profile roles. As Peter

Krämer points out, stars cannot get the choice parts that would allow them to ascend into the pantheon of major stardom until they have built a reputation in the industry. Thus, an actress would not be able to become a top box office draw until she hit her thirties, and given that an actress's career begins to decline when she turns forty, this leaves her with only a ten-year window when she can enter the highest box office ranks, which are overwhelmingly dominated by male stars whose careers often thrive well into their old age.[4]

If female stars have been neglected as actresses, one reason may be that they are more closely identified with celebrity than with acting. In discussing star types, Christine Geraghty argues that female stars are much more likely to be perceived as celebrities than as professionals or performers because their private lives are more often the subject of celebrity gossip and their stardom is more commonly based on this gossip than is the case for male stars. In fact, some type of celebrity status distinct from acting, such as rock stardom or fame as a model, is often a female star's means of entrée into Hollywood. It is especially common for popular singers to make the transition to star acting. One benefit of this situation is that a female star can maintain her star status through her "consistent extratextual interest as a celebrity," even when her films are only intermittently successful. Her celebrity accords her the star power that allows her to maintain her career even in the face of a string of bad performances (Geraghty 2000, 196–197). This celebrity status is especially important given that female stars have lower box office clout than male stars and often do not benefit as much from their reputation for acting ability. At least, they have their celebrity to fall back on.

Most studies of female stars do not look at them as actresses, but as figures of commercialism and conspicuous consumption, especially in regard to fashion and beauty products. Much more than male stars, actresses are seen as "simplified frozen schema for commercial purposes" (Amossy, 681). Partly, this comes from the strong cultural association of femininity with physical beauty, yet the intricacies of this association in terms of the female star have yet to be fully investigated. The need for physical perfection on screen has commonly been seen as a result of film technology, especially the importance of the close-up and the larger-than-life quality of film projection, both of which tend to enlarge and accentuate an actor's smallest imperfection.

Why the burden of this requirement has fallen so heavily on female stars, however, is not entirely clear. Part of the problem is that the standards of physical attractiveness required of male stars are only beginning to be investigated, so it is difficult to compare the importance of beauty for male and female stars. As noted earlier, the emphasis on female stars' physical attractiveness has traditionally been used to denigrate their talent and craft by attributing their fame to good looks, fashion, make-up, and, more recently, to plastic surgery, diet, and intensive exercise routines. Yet, as Virginia Wright Wexman points out, major questions about the relation of female stardom to beauty have yet to be resolved. For instance, how important is physical appearance to an actress's success when some of the most beautiful actresses never make it to the top level of stardom and others who are attractive but not sensationally beautiful do? What is the effect of physical beauty on the film audience? How much of stars' beauty is natural and how much is constructed, and how much do contemporary female stars rely on cosmetic surgery and other extreme beauty-enhancing procedures and products to improve their physical appearance? Should beautification be considered a major aspect of the craft of the film actress (Wexman, 1993, 133)?

Several studies have shown that studio publicity departments early determined that using female stars as walking advertisements for fashion and cosmetics was not only a good way to establish tie-ins with these industries, but was also effective in creating a special bond between actresses and their female fans. Charles Eckert was the first to recognize what he termed the "symbiotic relationship" between the studios and consumer culture, a bond that he sees as especially taking hold in the 1930s. Eckert proposes that, in the studio period, films were used as "living display windows" for consumer products. The major models within these windows have been and continue to be female stars, whom Wexman has called "passive images of beauty and romantic desirability" within the film industry's "mystification of glamour" (1993, 145, 142).

Jane Gaines and Charlotte Herzog have carefully traced throughout the studio period the progression of Hollywood's long relationship with the fashion and beauty industries. They point to the development of "clotheshorse" stars, who are promoted by the fashions they wear on- and off-screen. Behind them, one finds prominent male costume designers, such as Travis Benton for Marlene Dietrich, Orry for Grace Kelly and Bette Davis, and Gilbert Adrian for Joan Crawford and Greta Garbo.[5] Like directors and producers, these Svengali-like figures are often given credit for making an actress into a star by dressing her in their celebrated fashions. Lucy Fischer, for instance, argues that Greta Garbo's star image in the 1920s was built on her status as an Art Deco icon through costuming and set design. According to Fischer, Garbo came to represent the "coveted 'look' of the era," the look of "the 'New' or modern woman."[6]

Gaines and Herzog also point to the development of particular types of film sequences, known as the "social whirl" montage and the fashion-show-within-the-film, which became staples of woman's films of the 1930s and 1940s and were constructed just to display fashions on screen.[7] Thus, within the studio period, a female star's fashion wardrobe became an essential tool for solidifying her claims to stardom. It helped to give her an easily identifiable star image based on her sense of fashion and also linked her off-screen star image with her screen personality.

This association of female stars with the fashion and beauty industry has certainly not diminished, although it has not been studied in regard to contemporary stardom to the extent that it has been for the studio era. As we shall see, Gwyneth Paltrow is a contemporary example of a "clothes-horse" star, and each of the stars in our case studies has been lauded for her beauty, fashion sense, and glamour. Although the association of the female star with beauty can lead to her worship as a screen goddess, this association has a dark side. Many female stars have been the victims of sexual and commercial exploitation inspired by Hollywood's obsession with female sexual allure. The tragic lives of Marilyn Monroe and Judy Garland have been the subject of numerous star biographies, but serious scholarly analysis has yet to investigate fully the effects of commercial exploitation on female stars. This exploitation is exacerbated by the fact that contemporary stars now suffer from a new form of commercial commodification not found in the studio era: exploitation by the Internet porn industry.

Internet porn sites place stars, and most often female stars, in a new context of commercial exploitation for the sexual titillation of fans. Paul McDonald discusses two types of sites: celebrity nudes and fake celebrity nudes. The former shows stars in intimate scenes from their films, in porn films or nude photos they made before they became famous, or in paparazzi photographs that catch them in various states of undress at private moments when they had no idea they were being photographed. Fake celebrity nudes, on the other hand, provide fans with "more intense voyeuristic fantasy" by using computer technology to alter star photos to place them in erotic fantasy contexts. McDonald proposes that these new forms of commercial exploitation, like older forms of star publicity, sell revelations of the intimate caught-off-guard private moments of stars' lives as a way for the fan to get at the "hidden truth" behind the star's image. He proposes, however, that fake celebrity nudes have a more sinister underlying purpose. They seek to mock and humiliate stars by placing them in erotic contexts that never really existed and that might cause them embarrassment. This is done to reduce the star's power and to give fans a sense of control over the star's image.[8]

Much has been written about the relationship of Hollywood actresses to consumerism, but female stars have only rarely been examined for their acting talents. The closest that scholars have come to this type of analysis is to delineate certain typologies of female stars. These typologies, however, tend to divide female stars into categories based on their screen image, role choice, or the social stereotypes prevalent at the time of their popularity. For instance, Richard Dyer divides the screen images of female stars into the categories of the pin-up, independent woman, exceptional woman, girl next door, and figure of sexual ambiguity. Similarly, Molly Haskell breaks down the film portrayals of studio era female stars into the categories of the superfemale and the superwoman. Because the former is too intelligent and ambitious for traditional women's roles, she is led to demonic behavior (e.g., Bette Davis), whereas the latter adopts male characteristics in order to survive in a male-dominated society (e.g., Katherine Hepburn) (Dyer 1979, 61).

Dyer and Haskell query the exact social significance of these roles. Do they challenge the status quo by showing women's dissatisfaction with their allotted position in society or do they teach women that those who seek to move away from their "proper femininity" will be punished? Haskell sees the influence of these images on female fans as largely positive; Dyer seems more uncertain of their overall effect. As Dyer points out, the superwoman, who becomes in a sense a pseudomale, is more a product of the male rejection of femininity, than of women's discomfort with their limited social status. He also indicates that the endings of films containing these socially critical star types usually contain what he calls a "climb-down" for the female character as she is shown to be finally humiliated or punished in some way and thus returned to her subservient position in regard to the male (1979, 64). Haskell proposes, however, that female fans tend to remember the personality of the star behind the role and ignore the character's "climb-down" ending (Dyer 1979, 56).

The difference between Haskell and Dyer suggests one of the main problems with the typological approach. It tends to confuse the star with the character she plays. Dyer looks at the status of the character played by the star at the film's conclusion and sees this status as significant in terms of what fans make of the star's image, whereas Haskell discusses the star's image as based upon, yet also transcending, a given role. This conflation of star image and role makes it difficult to know exactly what to make of star typologies based on characters played by stars. Do they relate to the star's overall image extracted from extratextual sources like promotion and publicity as well as to the roles the star plays or are they simply a reflection of the star's screen personality extrapolated from her roles?

Other critics have also examined common roles played by women and concluded that actresses often play some type of performer, such as an actress, dancer, or singer. Many possible reasons have been proposed for this casting choice. As Lucy Fisher points out, the role of performer places the actress's character in a glamorous, self-supporting occupation that puts emphasis on her beauty, sex appeal, and romantic involvements rather than connecting her with the mundane world of work where she might be shown in competition with men. It also provides ample opportunity for close-ups to emphasize her physical attractiveness and for highly emotional scenes to showcase the intensity of her acting.

As Fischer and Wexman suggest, the association of the actress with theatricality, artifice, and deception also connects her with roles that diminish her recognition as an artist and a respected professional. She is portrayed as a role-player who is always hiding behind a theatrical mask, whose goal is to perform for and please men, and whose success is based on natural talent rather than hard work.[9] Wexman argues further that casting female stars in roles as performers diminishes their association with power by identifying them with characters who are always guided by men, who suffer from self-destructive personalities, or who have lost their chance at love because of their career goals. As Wexman points out, however, when these same roles are enacted by aging female stars, they take on a subversive potential, threatening to demystify star glamour and expose its constructedness (1993, 145–146).

Wexman and Richard Dyer emphasize the relation between female stars' images and prevalent social types or mores. For instance, Wexman argues that female star images are strongly connected to social ideals of heterosexual romance and romantic love. Actresses are typecast in romantic roles, and these roles are complemented by close-up cinematography, an obsession with physical appearance, and an emphasis on the screen kiss—all of which works to create an "intimate rapport between actress and audience" that positions the female star as "an ideal of desirable emotional intimacy" (1993, 239, note 10). Actresses' publicity also presents them as living in a world without material problems, where the work of acting is de-emphasized and the female star is left to agonize over an endless stream of romantic relationships. According to Dyer, this presentation of female stars as ideals of romance positions stars' lives and the roles they play as models for viewer emulation. Female stars offer lessons in the need for endurance and suffering in romantic attachments, the proper roles for men and women in love relationships, and the best way to maintain a healthy marriage (Dyer 1979, 53).

Wexman believes that, in the final analysis, female stars promote an ideal of heterosexual romance that advocates long-term monogamous romantic relationships. Even though female stars usually engage in many romantic attachments throughout their careers, they always practice serial monogamy, moving from one great love affair to another and always suffering from a failure to find, or from the tragedy of just having lost, their one true love (1993, 24). As Wexman points out, this emphasis on romance in the biographies of female stars works to reduce their status as successful professional women and to place them in a subordinate position to men (1993, 134). In spite of all their acting accomplishments, their ultimate goal is repeatedly shown to be the acquisition of male affection, rather than the fulfillment of their independent career ambitions.

As noted in Chapter 2, acting success in film has traditionally been considered the "ultimate confirmation of stardom" (Gledhill 1991, xiii), and television actors have been regarded as rising only to the level of TV personalities. Because they lack the "rarity value" of film stars, television actors are said never to reach the pinnacle of true stardom (Ellis, 314). The prevalence of female stars in made-for-television dramas, however, has called this division into question, and Joanne Lacey has argued for a distinct category of female television stars, including, for instance, Valerie Bertinelli, Lindsay Wagner, Linda Carter, Melissa Gilbert, Meredith Baxter, Donna Mills, and Tori Spelling. Lacey proposes that these actresses transcend the level of television personalities because their star status is used specifically to promote their made-for-television films; they can guarantee high ratings, they bring their star persona to bear on the characters they play, and they possess large communities of fans who follow their careers and celebrity gossip about their personal lives.

Made-for-television stardom has also been a traditional way for fallen or aging stars to resuscitate their careers. Yet, made-for-TV stars clearly differ from film stars in that their careers become almost exclusively confined to television, their fans do not want them to move to the big screen, and they do not cultivate the image of great beauty and glamour associated with Hollywood female stardom. In fact, Lacey argues that the made-for-television star must possess a certain amount of "plainness" to establish a connection with her fans and fit into made-for-TV dramas that are largely devoted to enacting "the trials of everyday life."[10]

Female stars not only can be typed by the medium in which they perform, but also by their style of performance. For instance, Christine Geraghty has made an interesting distinction between the acting styles employed by British and American female stars. She argues for two distinct female acting modes: heritage and glamour acting. The heritage style is associated with what is known in England as "the heritage genre," which includes period dramas and literary adaptations. It is employed by prominent British actresses such as Emma Thompson, Judi Dench, Kate Winslet, and Helena Bonham Carter and is characterized by "restraint," rendering emotions through intellect rather than feelings, and a sense of "irony, which demonstrates the heroine's superior understanding."[11] Geraghty compares the level of prestige and aesthetic worth that accrues to actresses who employ this style to what Method acting has done for many male stars, giving them a reputation for acting greatness. As Geraghty suggests, the reason for this attribution of greatness is actually very different for male and female stars. Male Method actors are seen as great artists for demonstrating emotional expressiveness, whereas heritage style actresses are granted prestige for showing emotional restraint (116).

Geraghty points to only one Hollywood actress who has cultivated the heritage style: Gwyneth Paltrow, whose penchant for British films and British accents has led her in this direction. Yet, Paltrow has not totally abandoned the dominant acting style common among Hollywood actresses, which Geraghty characterizes as glamour acting. According to Geraghty, this acting technique emphasizes sensual appeal and physical presence, rather than intellect, aesthetic achievement, or restraint, and relies heavily on acting in close-up to show the star's perfect looks and model-like body (112). Glamour acting is the style of "to-be-looked-at-ness" that contributes greatly to the female Hollywood star's status as an object of desire and concomitantly detracts from her recognition as a skilled actress.

Although most typologies of female stars characterize them as serving to support dominant social values and roles through their images, the characters they play, or both, occasionally a female star is said to break with the ideological status quo and offer herself as a figure of resistance. Richard Dyer, for instance, characterizes some stars as "alternative or subversive types," who embody positions in opposition to dominant ideological beliefs (Dyer 1993, 59). Similarly, Pam Cook has proposed that certain female stars throughout film history have resisted the conventional roles assigned to them and come to represent models of an alternative identity for their female fans. Cook even claims that this subversive quality accounts for an actress's "true star quality" (quoted in Geraghty 2003, 185).

Feminist critics have debated extensively whether the roles played and images projected by Hollywood actresses actually challenge dominant patriarchal ideological concepts in any major way or whether any challenge they offer is inevitably recuperated by patriarchy's overarching ideological power. Even if female stars may not be able to challenge the status quo, some feminist critics have argued that female viewers can read them as such. For instance, Andrea Weiss argues that in order to reinforce their sense of lesbian identity, lesbian viewers commonly read female Hollywood stars against the grain in ways that interpret their images as sexually ambiguous. She believes lesbian viewers of the 1930s did exactly this with the images of Greta Garbo and Marlene Dietrich. Using gossip about the star's lesbianism, they read these stars' androgynous, exotic, and ambiguously sexualized screen presences in ways that empowered them, resisted patriarchy, and affirmed their lesbian identity.[12] In the contemporary period, the ongoing rumors concerning Jodie Foster's reputed lesbianism can be regarded as serving a similar purpose for her lesbian fans.

Studies of Individual Female Stars

One tendency in the study of female stars is to investigate particular stars as unique individual figures, rather than seeing them as part of an overall category, and this inclination has been a pervasive one throughout the history of star studies. It is my intention in offering the five case studies of contemporary actresses that make up the second part of this book to continue with this tradition, yet to break away from it in important ways. Individual studies of prominent female stars have tended to look at them in isolation as unique instances rather than seeing them as representative figures. They have also tended to ignore the contemporary female star in favor of stars in the studio period and to laud these stars with a fan-like devotion as screen goddesses rather than seeing them as working professionals.

It is my goal to study individual stars not only for what they tell us about a particular star as a unique entity but also for what they reveal about contemporary Hollywood female acting and stardom. I am not interested in lauding the talents of these stars, although I do believe their talents are considerable, but rather in examining their careers as highly successful actresses and the role their star images play in shaping ideological conceptions of women in contemporary society.

This is not to say that studies of individual female stars have not shed considerable light on female stardom throughout film history. Studies of certain prominent stars in the silent-film and studio period are particularly illuminating. In the silent-film period, focus has largely been placed on Lillian Gish and has involved the question of her status as a great actress. Scholars have argued against the notion that she was merely a "Galatea figure" created by director D.W. Griffith.[13] They propose that she shaped her acting performances and even created her acting style by mixing naturalistic and ostensive acting techniques. Virginia Wright Wexman argues beyond this that Gish was not only a great actress in her own right, but also a subversive figure who embodied the "victimized femininity" and "aura of feminine helplessness" that Griffith cultivated in her performances and also challenged this characterization through her career success and reputation as the premier actress of her generation (1993, 63, 134).

Paul McDonald's work on Mary Pickford makes a similar argument. Like Gish, Pickford played "diminutive child-women," yet at the same time she was a shrewd businesswoman who quickly and effectively took control of her career, negotiated lucrative contracts, exploited her child-like image, and shifted from one studio to another when it was to her advantage. Finally, she even cofounded her studio, United Artists, with Douglas Fairbanks, Charlie Chaplin, and D.W. Griffith. As McDonald suggests, although Pickford's career collapsed because she was unable to move into more mature roles, she remains a female star of the silent-film period who had clout, business savvy, and the ability to move from acting to producing (2000, 38).

Studies of actresses in the studio period also often address the issue of whether they can be said to have had any real control of their careers. In regard to the early sound period, studies of Marlene Dietrich exemplify this approach. Laura Mulvey saw Dietrich as essentially reduced in her films to the position of a wax dummy manipulated by director Josef von Sternberg as an object of fetishistic scopophilia, totally subjected to the male gaze, and supportive of patriarchal dominance (22–23). Also utilizing a psychoanalytic perspective, Gaylyn Studlar envisioned Dietrich's screen image as "the cold feminine ideal of masochistic fantasy" embodied in a "powerfully sexual, androgynous … punishing woman [who] is not sadistic, but exhibits the pseudosadism (punishing function) required within the purely masochistic narrative."[14]

Other critics, however, have argued that Dietrich was far from totally controlled by von Sternberg and male desire, but instead actually had considerable control of her screen image. For instance, Richard Dyer portrayed the von Sternberg–Dietrich films as symbolic enactments of the personal relationship between director and star, with the films' male characters serving as surrogates for von Sternberg and with Dietrich representing the object of his voyeuristic scopophilia. Dyer also argued, however, that Dietrich did not passively accept this placement, but resisted it in subtle ways (1979, 180). Following Dyer's lead, other critics began to portray Dietrich as a subversive figure more sophisticated than the material she was required to perform, gently satirizing her characters and the plots of her films, and seditiously critiquing patriarchy through her "masquerade of femininity," rather than as a simple pawn of patriarchy (Naremore, 143). For others, she became a coauthor of her performances with von Sternberg, indissolubly united with him in a relationship of collaboration rather than domination.[15]

More recently, she has been proclaimed an ambiguously lesbian figure, clandestinely affirming lesbian identity (Weiss, 286–287). The progression of Dietrich criticism from her portrayal as the mindless creation of an omnipotent male director and a passive object of male voyeurism to a female star who covertly shaped her career and image in antipatriarchal directions is indicative of the movement in feminist film criticism to portray female stars not simply as passive Galatea figures controlled by a male-dominated industry, but rather as women with considerable influence and power within that industry.

In looking at actresses within the studio era, however, there is also a countertendency for scholars to see female stars as almost entirely products of the studio system or of dominant ideological conceptions of women's roles. For instance, Cathy Klaprat and Martin Shingler portray Bette Davis, a star known for her heated disputes with studio executives, as completely shaped as a screen personality by studio publicity and role assignment. They argue that the studio calculatedly shifted Davis's image first from a glamorous romantic leading lady to an independent, hard-boiled seductress and then to a highly accomplished and respected great actress.[16] Similarly, James Narmore argues that Katherine Hepburn's early image was seen as too patrician and feminist for film audiences, so the studio systematically assigned her to roles that demonstrated her "retreat from assertiveness" and served to "dramatiz[e] her complete submission to patriarchal authority" (175–176).

Whereas the studio construction of Davis' and Hepburn's images succeeded in making them huge stars, James Damico argues that studio fashioning led to Ingrid Bergman's bitter rejection by fans. As discussed in Chapter 2, her studio-promoted image of wholesome, pure, asexual saintliness and total devotion to her husband and family was completely shattered when her illegitimate pregnancy as a result of a scandalous extramarital love affair with Italian film director Roberto Rosallini was revealed, and her fans viciously turned against her.

Critics have characterized other studio era actresses as products of ideological conceptions of proper womanhood rather than of studio control. Proposing that star images resolve the unresolvable split between cultural definitions of the ordinary and the extraordinary, Richard Dyer's work has been crucial in initiating this type of analysis. For instance, he portrayed Marilyn Monroe as resolving the split that characterized the

1950s conception of womanhood dividing women into virgins and whores. Similarly, he saw Lana Turner as enacting the ordinary/extraordinary dichotomy inherent in stardom through her glamorous image, which in many ways revealed its contructedness, and the combination of her girl-next-door background and troubled private life.[17]

Jane Fonda, a poststudio Hollywood actress, is really Dyer's poster girl for the ideologically constructed star.[18] He sees her star image as an unstable and shifting combination of conflicting elements related to her relationship to her father, Henry Fonda; her sexuality; her reputation for political radicalism; and her acting talent. According to Dyer, her image moved with the times from progressive to reactionary implications. Tessa Perkins argues further that Fonda's image not only changed in response to current issues, but also became a matter of so much contention that it meant entirely different things to different political groups. According to Perkins, Fonda's image became a site of ideological struggle, especially in the 1970s when the mainstream press attacked her as an extreme radical feminist; whereas feminists' responses to her actually ranged from seeing her as a role model of feminist rebellion to regarding her as a bandwagon feminist whose life and roles did not support her feminist designation.[19] Similarly, Barbara Seidman discusses the "complex accommodation Fonda has made to reconcile her determined continuation as a Hollywood film-maker with her vocal allegiance to feminism."[20]

Although little work has been done on contemporary star–actresses, the issues raised by these studies of earlier female stars are still pertinent. It is important to consider how star–actresses fit into the male-dominated Hollywood industry and how they are shaped by and challenge American patriarchal ideology. We will keep these issues in mind as we undertake in the second part of this book an examination of the progress of the careers, composition of the images, nature of the acting, and social significance for female fans of Meryl Streep, Susan Sarandon, Jodie Foster, Angela Bassett, and Gwyneth Paltrow. It is to this examination that we will now turn.

References

1. Knobloch, Susan. 1999. "Helen Shaver: Resistance through Artistry." p. 106 in *Screen Acting*, eds. A. Lovell and P. Kramer. New York: Routledge; hereafter cited in text.
2. Gaines, Jane. 1990. "Introduction." p. 1 in *Fabrications: Costume and the Female Body*, eds. J. Gaines and C. Herzog. London and New York: Routledge.
3. Although little has been written on this issue, Lucy Fischer has made some initial forays into the examination of actresses' declining careers after they reach the age of forty in two essays: "Marlene: Modernity, Mortality, and the Biopic." pp. 29–42 in *Stars: The Film Reader* (New York: Routledge, 2004)

and "Sunset Boulevard: Fading Stars." pp. 97–113, in *Women & Film*, ed. J. Todd. New York: Holmes & Meier, 1988.

4. Krämer, Peter. 2003. "'A Woman in a Male-Dominated World': Jodie Foster, Stardom, and 90s Hollywood." p. 202 in *Contemporary Hollywood Stardom*, eds. T. Austin and M. Barker. London: Arnold; hereafter cited in text.

5. Gaines, Jane. 1990. "Costume and Narrative: How Dress Tells the Woman's Story." pp. 198–199 in *Fabrications: Costume and the Female Body*, eds. J. Gaines and C. Herzog. London and New York: Routledge.

6. Fischer, Lucy. 2003. *Designing Women. Cinema, Art Deco, & the Female Form*. New York: Columbia University Press, pp. 95, 112.

7. Herzog, Charlotte Cornelia and Jane Marie Gaines. 1991. "'Puffed Sleeves before Tea-Time': Joan Crawford, Adrian and Women Audiences." p. 78 in *Stardom: Industry of Desire*, ed. C. Gledhill. London: Routledge.

8. McDonald, Paul. 2003. "Stars in the Online Universe: Promotion, Nudity, Reverence." pp. 35–37 in *Contemporary Hollywood Stardom*, eds. T. Austin and M. Barker. London: Arnold.

9. Fischer, Lucy. 1989. *Shot/Countershot: Film Tradition and Women's Cinema*. Princeton, N.J.: Princeton University Press, pp. 145–147. See also Fischer's analysis of Douglas Sirk's representation of the actress in his 1953 melodrama *All I Desire* in "Sirk and the Figure of the Actress: *All I Desire*," *Film Criticism* 23(2–3) (Winter/Spring 1999): 136–149.

10. Lacey, Joanne. 2003. "'A Galaxy of Stars to Guarantee Ratings': Made-for-Television Movies and the Female Star System." pp. 196–197 in *Contemporary Hollywood Stardom*, eds. T. Austin and M. Barker. London: Arnold.

11. Geraghty, Christine. 2003. "Performing as a Lady and a Dame: Reflections on Acting and Genre." p. 108 in *Contemporary Hollywood Stardom*, eds. T. Austin and M. Barker. London: Arnold.

12. Weiss, Andrea. 1991. "A Queer Feeling When I Look at You: Hollywood Stars and Lesbian Identity in the 1930s." p. 297 in *Stardom: Industry of Desire*, ed. C. Gledhill. London: Routledge; hereafter cited in text.

13. See in particular Naremore, James. 1988. *Acting in the Cinema*, chap. 6, Berkeley: University of California Press.

14. Studlar, Gaylin. 1990. "Masochism, Masquerade, and the Erotic Metamorphosis of Marlene Dietrich." pp. 235, 238–239 in *Fabrications: Costume and the Female Body*, eds. J. Gaines and C. Herzog. London and New York: Routledge. Studlar develops her views on Dietrich's star image and its connection to a masochistic aesthetic more fully in *In the Realm of Pleasure: Von Sternberg, Dietrich, and the Masochistic Aesthetic* (Urbana: University of Illinois Press, 1988).

15. Zucker, Carole. 1990. "'I Am Dietrich and Dietrich Is Me': An Investigation of Performance Style in *Morocco* and *Shanghai Express*." pp. 293–294 in *Making Visible the Invisible*, ed. C. Zucker. Metuchen, N.J.: Scarecrow Press.

16. Klaprat, Cathy. 1985. "The Star as Market Strategy: Bette Davis in Another Light." pp. 351–376 in *The American Film Industry*, ed. T. Balio. Madison: University of Wisconsin Press, and Shingler, Martin. 1999. "Bette Davis:

Malevolence in Motion." pp. 46–58 in *Screen Acting*, eds. A. Lovell and P. Kramer. New York: Routledge.

17. Dyer's analysis of Monroe is found in Dyer, Richard. 1986. *Heavenly Bodies: Film Stars and Society*, chap. 1, New York: St. Martin's Press, and his examination of Turner in Dyer, Richard. 1991. "Four Films by Lana Turner." p. 216 in *Star Texts: Image and Performance in Film and Television*. ed. J. Butler. Detroit: Wayne State University Press. In her introduction to *Imitation of Life* (New Brunswick, N.J.: Rutgers University Press, 1991), a volume on Douglas Sirk's film that she edited for the Rutgers Films in Print series, Lucy Fischer also presents an interesting analysis of the way Turner's star image and publicity about her troubled personal life were used to promote her role in this film.

18. Dyer's analysis of Fonda is found in Dyer, Richard. 1979. *Stars*. London: British Film Institute, pp. 72–98.

19. Perkins, Tessa. 1991. "The Politics of Jane Fonda." pp. 237–250 in *Stardom: Industry of Desire*, ed. C. Gledhill. London: Routledge.

20. Seidman, Barbara. 1988. "The Lady Doth Protest Too Much, Methinks: Jane Fonda, Feminism, and Hollywood." p. 188 in *Women & Film*, ed. J. Todd. New York: Holmes & Meier.

PART II

Case Studies of Contemporary Star–Actresses

CHAPTER 4

"Magic Meryl"[1]: Meryl Streep

Career Trajectory: From Natural Talent to Melodramatic Mother

One might think that someone whom critics have repeatedly singled out as the "best actress of her generation" would have considerable control over the development of her career and the construction of her image; however, Meryl Streep claims neither such control, nor such construction. In fact, she describes her career as a series of random acts without design: "The progression of roles you take strings together a portrait of an actor, but … it's a completely random process."[2] She also claims to have no knowledge of the exact nature of her image. When asked to comment on what she sees as her star persona, she replied,

> I don't know what my image is. I went to France to publicize *Marvin's Room*, and one really smart young woman journalist said to me, "You know, when I told people I was going to interview Meryl Streep, they were so excited … all ze women in my office, they love you so much. But ze men—they are afraid of you."[3]

The fact that she relates this particular story suggests that, although she may not feel she has fashioned her image, she is certainly aware of its constructed nature and gender-specific effects.

Her career has, indeed, been remarkably successful. Generally recognized as the most highly trained contemporary Hollywood actress, she first began seriously to pursue an acting career when she was in college at Vassar, where biographical accounts claim she was immediately recognized as a natural talent. Her Vassar drama professor, Clinton Atkinson, is quoted as having described as nothing short of "brilliant" her theater debut as the eponymous heroine in the August Strindberg classic *Miss Julie*: "She played Miss Julie with a voluptuousness that was almost shocking in someone her age."[4] According to Atkinson, throughout her college career, Streep's performances were consistently "hair-raising, absolutely mind-boggling. I don't think anyone ever taught Meryl acting; she really taught herself."[5]

Although Atkinson describes Streep's talent as instinctive, she has never characterized herself that way. In fact, Streep has never described herself as a natural talent. She claims to have gone into acting "with this great ambivalence," stemming not so much from her uncertainty about her abilities as from questioning whether acting was "a worthwhile way to spend your whole life."[6] After graduating from Vassar, Streep studied for three years at the Yale School of Drama, arguably the most prestigious American school of acting. Reputedly nicknamed "Yale's Leading Lady," she is said to have acted in as many as forty productions while there.[7] Albert Innaurato, who cowrote the Dostoevsky spoof *The Idiots Karamazov* with Christopher Durang, proposes that in the play's Yale production Streep literally "invented the part" of the eighty-year-old crippled translator, Constance Garnett (Gussow, 24).

Beneath this fairy tale of the spectacular discovery of a brilliant natural talent are indications that Streep's stay at Yale was not entirely happy and that it actually involved a considerable amount of anguish and hard work. During her first year, she was even placed on academic probation, according to Streep, because the program director felt she was "holding back my talent out of fear of competing with my fellow students."[8] She also admits, however, to being so nervous and pressured by her studies that she developed an ulcer and had to visit a psychiatrist. Being exposed at Yale to too wide a range of acting theories seems to account for at least part of her nervousness. She describes her experience there as follows: "Every year, there'd be a *coup d'etat*. The new guy would come in and say, 'Whatever you learned last year, don't worry about it. This is going to be a completely new approach.'" Her reaction to this type of training was mixed:

> That kind of grab-bag, eclectic education is invaluable, but only out of adversity. Half the time you're thinking, I wouldn't do it that way, this guy is full of crap, but in a way, that's how you build

up what you do believe in. Still, those years made me tired, crazy, nervous. I was constantly throwing up from the pressure.[9]

After leaving Yale in 1975, Streep refused to take the conventional route through regional theater and headed directly for the New York stage, where publicity accounts describe her rise to theater stardom as nothing short of meteoric. Primarily an actress in stage comedies, she won praise for roles ranging from Tennessee Williams's *27 Wagons Full of Cotton*, for which she won a Tony Award, to Shakespeare's *Measure for Measure* and *Taming of the Shrew*. After two successful years in New York theatre, Streep moved into television and film. She quickly achieved television success; in only her third television role, she won an Emmy for her performance in the miniseries *Holocaust* (Chomsky 1978). Her move into films was somewhat more gradual, but still marked by relatively rapid progress. She began by accepting small supporting roles in major big budget films, fleshing out minor characters, and making them memorable. She won an Academy Award nomination for only her second film role in *The Deer Hunter* (Cimino 1978) and an Oscar as best supporting actress for her fourth film, *Kramer vs. Kramer* (Benton 1979).

Although Streep may see her work as a random series of roles, one can discern definite career patterns, the most notable of which is her accumulation of thirteen Academy Award nominations, the largest number of nominations that any actor has ever received. Her success in receiving Oscar nominations is perhaps the single most important factor in the development of her career, stimulating it in its initial stages and buttressing it during a midcareer decline. If not for her critical reputation, Streep's career might easily have fallen apart, especially because, since her marriage to Don Gummer in 1978 and the birth of the first of their four children in the following year, she has repeatedly turned down major roles and chosen others solely on the basis of family interests. Indeed, Streep's highly publicized determination to place her family over her work represents another major pattern in the development of her stardom.

In the early stages of her career before her family became her primary concern, Streep claims to have had only one major goal: the desire to establish her acting range by embodying a uniquely different type of character in each role. As she describes her acting in these early years, "What the people saw fed into what I wanted for myself—which was not to be typed" (Maychick, 36). Yet her film choices have always been guided by her attraction to certain kinds of roles. "A Meryl Streep film" is typically very character driven, often containing a complex, enigmatic heroine whose internal crisis provides the central enigma of the drama. Streep has said that the "great worth [of acting] is giving voice to characters that have no voice" (Lipton), that she chooses roles that involve "a certain challenge and a character with problems,"[10] and that she is "drawn to disagreeable women ... [as her] favorite characters" (Smith).

She also describes choosing films that "put a positive energy out" and that she would not be ashamed to show to her children.[11] This last consideration has led her to avoid, in particular, parts that are sexually explicit. In fact, she seems to be sensitive about roles that involve even the smallest amount of female nudity. For instance, she says she felt very uncomfortable when she was required briefly to flash her breast in *Silkwood*, and only agreed to do it because she felt the gesture was crucial to the development of her character Karen Silkwood's personality (Maychick, 154).

She is also repeatedly drawn to emotional portrayals, especially those that contain a big heart-wrenching climactic scene. Almost every Meryl Streep film has such a moment, and in most of them, Streep breaks into floods of tears. In *Kramer vs. Kramer* (1979) and *Still of the Night* (1982), her director, Robert Benton, even allowed her to write her climactic emotional monologues (Pfaff and Emerson, 45; Maychick, 125). In *The Bridges of Madison County* (Eastwood 1995), she says she was required to cry on cue for two days straight while shooting her final farewell scene with Clint Eastwood.[12] In his commentary on the DVD version of *Music of the Heart* (2000), director Wes Craven discusses his decision to cut a scene of Streep crying and to remove the musical score from behind several of her other highly emotional scenes because he felt the film was becoming too sentimental and that a character who cries as much as Streep's does would lose audience sympathy.[13]

Critic Pauline Kael, who over the years became Streep's critical nemesis, proposed sarcastically that she had "come to dread [Streep's] reflective manner and flooding tears—she could give pensive a bad name. If only she would giggle more and suffer less—she keeps turning herself into the red-eye special" (Pfaff and Emerson, 83).

Although many of Streep's films have been labeled tearjerkers, they have also been characterized as "quality projects." She is particularly attracted to literary adaptations and docudramas, which lend themselves to the "quality" label, and especially to those that in the tradition of the women's melodrama recount the lives of real-life women who may initially appear ordinary, but become extraordinary as their story develops. Streep has stated rather bluntly, "I don't do junk" (Pfaff and Emerson, 8), and in her 1983 Vassar commencement address, she attributed her "consciousness of quality" to a "taste for excellence" gained during her Vassar experience:

> Sometimes, I've wished it [her taste for excellence] would go away, because some so-called important scripts are *so* illiterate, and the

money is *so* good, that I've been tempted to toss all my acquired good taste, and hustle.

But there's always the knowledge, and this *is* from experience, that the work itself is the reward, and if I choose challenging work, it'll pay me back with interest. At least, I'll be interested, even if nobody else is (Maychick, 155–156).

Her attraction to literary adaptations and docudramas seems related not only to her tendency to regard them as quality projects, but also to her technique of character construction (discussed more fully later), which largely involves the imitation of real-life or literary models. Many of Streep's major films (*Kramer vs. Kramer, The French Lieutenant's Woman,* and *Sophie's Choice* early in her career and more recently *The Bridges of Madison County, Marvin's Room, Dancing at Lughnasa, One True Thing,* and *The Hours*) have been based on novels or plays. Others (notably *Silkwood, Cry in the Dark, Out of Africa, Postcards from the Edge,* and *Music of the Heart*) are stories of real-life heroines.

As her career has progressed, Streep's age—she is currently in her midfifties—has heavily influenced the roles she is offered. As noted in Chapter 2, once a Hollywood actress turns forty, her career choices begin to narrow. Streep has been pointedly critical of this bias:

Well, certainly in a season where most of the female leads are prostitutes, there's not going to be a lot of work for women over forty. Like hookers, actresses seem to lose their market appeal around that age. At the age of forty, however, most male actors are just approaching their peak earning potential.[14]

Indeed, Streep's career has moved through five distinct stages:

- early training and stage success (1975 to 1977)
- initial film roles as a supporting player (1977 to 1979)
- major stardom as a dramatic film heroine (1981 to 1988)
- a decline as she entered her forties and took on comedic roles (1989 to 1992)
- a resurgence as a mature actress primarily cast in women's melodramas (1993 to present)

Streep's biographers most often present the initial stage of her career, her early theater success, somewhat inconsistently as an indication of her meteoric rise to stardom as a natural talent and her extensive on-the-job training as an actress. She is said to have honed her acting skills at Yale and in New York theatre before she made her decisive move into film. As noted earlier, when she began her film career, she did so by accepting small, underwritten parts that she worked to develop and expand. These parts were, however, always in major big-budget, heavily promoted films. Also, although she was able to create memorable characters in small supporting roles in *The Deer Hunter* and *Kramer vs. Kramer*, in her other early film roles—namely, *Julia* (Zimmerman 1977) and *Manhattan* (Allen 1979)— she was decidedly less successful. In *Julia*, most of her performance was eventually cut from the final film; in *Manhattan*, director Woody Allen insisted that she stick so closely to the script that she was unable to reshape her poorly developed and highly unsympathetic character.[15]

The crucial film in this initial period was without question the enormous box office success *Kramer vs. Kramer*, which still remains her highest grossing film. It was a breakthrough film for Streep because of its popularity and because she won her first Academy Award for her performance, as well as because director Robert Benton allowed her considerable creative license in expanding and reshaping her character. As the story is told and retold by Streep's biographers, Benton and his star, Dustin Hoffman, were unsure how to approach the role of Joanna, the film's distraught wife and mother who abandons her husband and young son only later to return and sue for child custody. In the novel upon which the film was based, Joanna was a completely unsympathetic character, but Benton and Hoffman feared this type of portrayal would alienate their female audience, so they reputedly turned to Streep to give Joanna a more sympathetic dimension.

Streep is said to have entered into the project with enthusiasm, beginning by conducting research into Upper East Side New York women who juggled career and family, even consulting her mother about her life as a full-time housewife with a part-time career (Maychick, 84–85). In interviews at the time of the film's release, Streep described how, as she prepared for the role, she came to feel great sympathy for Joanna's plight. She said she went to Benton and told him that the character as written in the script was "too evil" and her conflicts "too narrowly described." Streep considered the part an acting challenge:

> There's a very interesting filmic device that's used. A lot of what other characters do and say has to do with me, but I'm really there only at the beginning and at the end. It's like a person who walks out of the room, and everybody tries to explain why she did what she did, and finally, after they've agreed on some version of things, she comes back and explains it herself. I'm set up as a villain, so I like the idea of reappearing and trying to turn that around (Maychick, 83).

Streep developed a conception of Joanna that deviated considerably from the novel's one-dimensional abandoning wife and mother. In describing the character she tried to portray, Streep emphasized her desire to make Joanna more realistic, more like women she knew and could understand, and to tie Joanna's situation to rarely discussed problems faced by contemporary women:

> In 1979, nobody was talking about depression, but this woman probably thought about killing herself once or twice every day. I could understand the compulsion to leave and not want to take your little boy wherever you were going in order to get better. I didn't think she was horrible—I read it and I was on her side.[16]

In order to engineer Joanna's transformation, Benton apparently made the unusual decision of allowing his actress to rewrite most of her character's dialogue. Streep also claims that, against Hoffman's opposition, she insisted that certain of the film's scenes be reconstructed to give Joanna more credibility. An especially heated battle between the two actors seems to have taken place over the film's crucial restaurant scene, in which Joanna tells Ted, Hoffman's character, that she intends to fight him for custody of their child. Over Hoffman's objections, Streep insisted that Joanna be allowed gradually and hesitantly to work toward the revelation of her intentions, rather than cruelly blurt out her decision as soon as Ted sits down (Smurthwaite, 49). Benton also asked Streep to rewrite her lines in two key scenes: the dramatic courtroom scene, when she explains why she felt forced to leave her son, and her final meeting with Hoffman's character, when she tells him of her decision not to take the child away from him (Pfaff and Emerson, 45–46). According to Streep, her empathy for Joanna extended even beyond the film's ending:

> The ending never felt like an ending to me. Everyone said, "There! She gave the boy back!" And I thought, "Yeah … that week." You don't know where the process of her getting herself back together would lead. And you just know when the boy became preadolescent, he'd say, "F--- you, Dad! I'm gonna go live with Mom, a--hole!" (Harris).

After winning the Oscar for *Kramer vs. Kramer*, Streep moved from supporting roles to major stardom. This second and most successful stage of her career extended throughout the decade of the 1980s, beginning with her Academy Award-nominated performance in *The French Lieutenant's Woman* (Riesz 1981) and including a string of other Oscar-nominated roles in *Silkwood* (Nichols 1983), *Plenty* (Schepisi 1985), *Out of Africa* (Pollack 1985), *Ironweed* (Babenco 1987), and *Cry in the Dark* (Schepisi 1988).

Undoubtedly, Streep's most critically admired performance in this period was her portrayal of the Polish Holocaust survivor in *Sophie's Choice* (Pakula 1982), for which she won her second Oscar—her first nomination and only win as a lead actress. *Sophie's Choice* contains all of the hallmarks that have come to characterize a Meryl Streep film. It was a quality project based on a critically acclaimed novel, placed Streep in a highly emotional role as a tragic unconventional heroine, and offered her the opportunity to demonstrate her skills at impersonational acting by creating a unique character very unlike herself. The film won Streep sweeping critical acclaim and established her unquestionably as a major star.

After an extended period of major stardom throughout the 1980s, Streep's career began to take a definite downturn as she reached the age of forty in 1989. Some critics attributed this decline to her movement into comedies, which they saw as a deliberate attempt to lighten her image and demonstrate her acting range. It seems more likely, however, that it resulted from her increasingly limited role choice as an older actress, combined with her refusal to sacrifice her family's convenience for the benefit of her career.

Another factor was that, in the late 1980s, Streep had begun to star in social problem films, such as *Silkwood*, *Cry in the Dark*, and *Ironweed*, films that tended to push her image in a new socially conscious direction. It may have been Streep's belief that her movement into social commentary had precipitated her career decline that led her to look to comedic parts. She insists, however, that she made no conscious attempt to move out of serious drama when she chose to star in a series of comedies in the early 1990s: *She-Devil* (Seidelman 1989), *Postcards from the Edge* (Nichols 1990), *Defending Your Life* (Brooks 1991), and *Death Becomes Her* (Zemekis 1992). She says she was just trying to find roles that would allow her to stay in Los Angeles, where she and her family had then decided to reside (Fuller).

Despite the favorable critical reception of *Postcards from the Edge*—an adaptation of Carrie Fisher's tell-all Hollywood dramedy, for which Streep gained her ninth Academy Award nomination—the disastrous critical response to *Death Becomes Her* brought Streep to a career nadir from which she managed to recover only by abandoning comedy to reestablish herself as a serious dramatic actress. This movement back to drama launched the fourth stage in Streep's career, in which she played not tragic unconventional heroines, as she had earlier, but melodramatic, and much more conventional, maternal figures. Certain consistencies do remain between Streep's early and late dramatic roles, namely, the high quality of the projects, the attraction to literary adaptations and docudramas, and the intense emotionalism of her performances.

The River Wild (Hanson 1994) and *The Bridges of Madison County* served as transitional films between the comedic and late dramatic phases of Streep's career. Because the two films provided her with successive box office hits, critics saw them as essentially revitalizing her fading stardom. In the former film, Streep made a foray into action–adventure, playing a courageous mother who saves her family on a white water rafting expedition. In the latter, she portrayed Clint Eastwood's love interest, again a devoted mother who, out of loyalty to her husband and children, decides to give up a passionate midlife romance and remain an Iowa farm wife.

Streep's assumption of maternal roles has dominated this most recent period of her career, and she has become typed as the queen of the contemporary woman's melodrama, a film category often pejoratively labeled the tearjerker or woman's weepie. Films like *Marvin's Room* (Zaks 1996), *Dancing at Lughnasa* (O'Connor 1998), *One True Thing* (Franklin 1998) and *The Hours* (Daldry 2002) have led critics to characterize her recent films as one "Meryl Streep weepfest" after another.[17] It is somewhat disillusioning to trace the evolution of Streep's role choice. Her career began progressively with her reshaping underwritten female roles to transform negative female portrayals into more positive ones and moved in her middle years into a succession of socially conscious portrayals. It seems to be concluding rather disappointingly, however, with her typecast in a succession of melodramatic maternal roles of the sort conventionally allotted to older female stars.

Her recent decisions to take supporting roles in *Adaptation* (Jonze 2002), *Prime* (Younger, 2005) and *The Manchurian Candidate* (Demme 2004) represent notable exceptions. The former may indicate that she is again turning to comedy as a way to take her career in a new direction, and the latter suggests she is at least expanding somewhat beyond her representations of melodramatic mother figures, if only into the realm of the monstrous mother. Still, it is disheartening to see a career that started so progressively seem to be ending much less so.

The Meryl Streep Image

Meryl Streep's image is composed of two distinct image clusters centered on her renown as a great actress and her reputation as a devoted wife and mother. A more muted aspect of her star persona— one that is often masked as merely an offshoot of her maternal devotion—is her social activism.

The Greatest Actress of Her Time

The most prominent component of Meryl Streep's star image is her critical recognition as the finest actress of her generation. As is characteristic of Hollywood actresses, she has often been praised for her looks. Especially in her younger years, she was described as possessing classical beauty with a patrician manner, regal bearing, high cheek bones, long blonde hair, and a porcelain complexion. Publicity accounts, however, have always referenced her remarkable acting talent, professionalism, and perfectionist commitment to excellence, rather than her looks, as accounting for her success. She was even dubbed by one critic "the female Lawrence Olivier" (Pffaf and Emerson, 8).

Her reputation for acting prowess is said to be so impressive that her costars have claimed they took roles just to act opposite her or that they were so intimidated by her talent that they were afraid to perform with her (Maychick, 145). Always a paragon of feminine modesty, Streep has consistently played down her great actress status, insisting that she finds the designation distracting: "I'm so daunted by [reputation] that I never think about it," she says. "It's a thing bigger than I'm capable of perceiving. Other people are more aware and concerned with it than I could ever allow myself to be."[18]

Her reputation for acting prowess is largely based on her characterization as a star who acts through impersonation rather than personification. Her ability to transform herself into a different character in each role has gained her renown for chameleon-like acting abilities and remarkable talent. It has also led to criticism that she has never established a consistently recognizable screen personality. As a result, some critics have argued that she lacks a star image, but Streep does not really lack an image. Rather, her image is founded upon her recognition for superior acting talent, and the prestige from this recognition has provided her career with the kind of longevity that actresses whose personas are largely based upon their looks and personality have not been able to achieve.

Family: A Soccer Mom Deeply Involved in PTA Meetings

The longevity of Streep's career is especially remarkable given her reputed commitment to placing her marriage and family life over professional concerns. Almost as consistently promoted within Streep's publicity as her eminence as a singularly gifted actress is her reputation for devotion to her family. Perhaps the threat to ideals of conventional femininity posed by an actress such as Streep, who is renowned for her superior acting skills, rather than for her great beauty, mandates this emphasis on her much more conventional devotion to her family.

Whatever the reason, much has been made in her publicity of Meryl Streep, the great actress, also being Meryl Streep, the great wife and mother. From the very beginning of her career, accounts of Streep's personal life involve tales of her devotion to a loved one and her ready acceptance of the role of female caregiver. Early press accounts of Streep's romantic involvements were extremely melodramatic, worthy of some of her most emotion-laden roles. They involved a May–December romance ending in tragedy, a love triangle, and what appeared to be marriage on the rebound.

While performing as a young New York actress in a production of Shakespeare's *Measure for Measure* at the Public Theater, she fell in love with her costar, actor John Cazale, best known for his role as the Corleone brother Fredo in *The Godfather* (Coppola 1972). Streep was in her twenties and Cazale in his forties when they began their romance. They shared a Soho flat and even acquired supporting roles in *The Deer Hunter* together. During the shooting of the film, Cazale, earlier diagnosed with bone cancer, became gravely ill. With a prior commitment to shoot *Holocaust* in Europe after finishing *The Deer Hunter*, Streep had to leave Cazale in the throes of his illness. When she returned, he was near death. She is said to have put her career on hold to nurse him devotedly in his last months.

Accounts of Streep's early career, such as the following quote from stage director Joseph Papp, exalt her devotion to the dying Cazale, reconceptualizing it as a stimulus to her art:

> She took care of him as if there were nobody else on Earth. She was always at his side. It was such a statement of loyalty and commitment .... She spent weeks at the hospital while John wasted away. There's no way she can forget a thing like that. It's part of her life now, part of her art (Smurthwaite, 29).

Despite her pain, only six months after Cazale's death in 1978, Streep married Don Gummer, her brother's college friend, who terminated his relationship with another woman in order to initiate a whirlwind courtship of Streep. Their marriage, based, according to Gummer, "on a very deep-rooted feeling of trust" (Pfaff and Emerson, 41) has lasted for over twenty years and produced four children. Streep's publicity material repeatedly emphasizes her devotion to her family and her praise for motherhood.

Diana Maychick, in her unauthorized star biography, even proposes that Streep's determination to make her marriage work has led her to approach it as an "iron-clad commitment" and to cover over marital problems stemming from Gummer's disdain for the celebrity spotlight (99).

Since her marriage and reputedly under her husband's influence, Streep has repeatedly expressed distaste for stardom. For instance, in comparing herself to Cher, her costar in *Silkwood*, she dramatically asserted, "Cher doesn't mind being the center of attention. It isn't agony for her. It doesn't take away part of her soul" (Pfaff and Emerson, 90). Although Streep temporarily moved her family to Hollywood in the early 1990s, they have since returned to the East Coast and settled down in a secluded suburban hilltop estate in upstate New York, not far from Streep's Connecticut childhood home.

Streep's rejection of the trappings of stardom is also expressed in her nervousness and hesitancy in interviews and public appearances. For instance, in the middle of delivering the commencement address at Vassar, she dropped her speech and is said to have been so nervous after winning her Academy Award for *Kramer vs. Kramer* that she left her Oscar on the back of a toilet (Maychick, 154; Pfaff and Emerson, 58). The component of her image that stresses her extraordinariness, her renown as a great actress, is complemented (one might even say controlled), as it is in the image constellations of so many actresses, by the ordinariness of her rejecting stardom to live the personal life of a down-to-earth suburban housewife. When asked to describe herself, for instance, Streep very self-deprecatingly asserts: "Somebody always trying to give her best shot, and sometimes not making it. A sense of humor about herself. A short attention span. A lot of great ideas. Very lazy" (Smurthwaite, 123).

As she has grown older, Streep has presented herself increasingly as just a suburban housewife with only a side-interest in acting. Even early in her career, when she won her Oscar for *Sophie's Choice*, she told interviewers that she celebrated by buying a washer, dryer, and cuisinart (Pfaff and Emerson, 81). Describing her relationship with her husband, she has said, "He's a hermit and so am I. We like to be alone—with each other and our kids. We don't like the razzmatazz, the photographers and the glitz" (Pfaff and Emerson, 99). In 1996, she characterized herself as merely a soccer mom who is deeply involved in PTA meetings.[19]

Although Streep has been intent in interviews on characterizing herself as a happy homemaker, she has also been very adamant that the press not intrude on the privacy of her home life. She has been quite militant about her family's need for privacy:

> I don't mind publicizing a film. But there's a difference between that and selling my life. My life is all I have. It's not for sale. The one thing I haven't done is publicize my family to enhance me. I haven't taken a picture with the kids saying what a fabulous mother I am" (Smith, 94–98).

In fact, in a highly publicized incident in 1988, Streep accosted a photographer who took pictures of her and her children as they left a theater in Chatham, New York. She allegedly ran after him, tried to pull his camera off of his neck, and in so doing, hit him on the side of the face.[20] When later asked about the incident, she told an interviewer, "I'm sorry I didn't break his face [Streep here broke into uproarious laughter]. I get like a tigress when it's about my kids."[21]

Streep's comments about her home life have repeatedly pitted family against career. For instance, she is quoted as telling an interviewer that, if asked to choose between acting and family, she would choose the latter "because no enterprise is bigger than your life's needs or your humanity" (Smurthwaite, 118). Consistently, she has defined herself as first and foremost a mother: "I was never the kind of person who said, 'I'm going to be an actress. And if I meet somebody and have a family, great.' I always, always, since I was a little girl, wanted to have kids and a family."[22] Although she admits that she loves acting, she describes it as "that other outlet" she needs to prevent herself from becoming "short" with her family and proposes that "all the life experience in raising children [makes] my work have more depth and resonance" (Behar, Calhoun).

As noted earlier, Streep's determination always to put her family first has without question significantly affected her career design. She has said, "… my husband and children mean more to me than my career. I choose movie projects which will not inconvenience my family" (Hobson 1996), and she claims to have turned down major roles because they would necessitate her being away from home for extended periods of time. Certain films that precipitated the decline of her career in the 1980s, such as *Falling in Love* (Grosbard 1984) and *Heartburn* (Nichols 1986), she admits were selected primarily because they were shot in New York, which allowed her to go home to her family in the evenings (Maychick, 160). While shooting *Marvin's Room* and *One True Thing*, she is said to have flown home each night by helicopter to be with her children, who at the time ranged in age from seven to eighteen years old. As she describes her maternal devotion, "My children don't care what I've been doing all day. They have no interest in what particular character I'm working on. All that matters is that I'm there for them at night and know where their clean underwear is."[23]

Streep's melodramatic accounts of her extreme aversion to being away from her family make her seem not just devoted to, but neurotically obsessive about and overly dependent on, them. When shooting on location in Yugoslavia for *Sophie's Choice*, for instance, director Alan Pakula allowed her to fly to New York for a weekend so that she could attend the opening of her sculptor–husband's art gallery showing, even though, if she had returned late to the set on the following Monday, the whole production would have been jeopardized. Pakula is quoted as saying that he "knew that not being there [at her husband's opening] would eat her up" (Pfaff and Emerson, 77).

Streep has also taken her family with her when shooting in foreign locations. For example, she and Robert Redford had their families accompany them to Kenya to shoot *Out of Africa,* and Streep took her family with her to Ireland for the shooting of *Dancing in Lughnasa.* When the shooting schedule for the latter film went over the initially allotted six weeks and her children were forced to return home for the beginning of the school year, Streep is quoted as saying, "It almost killed me" (Smith).

In interviews, Streep has always described the experience of motherhood in absolutely glowing terms: "Having a baby is the greatest thing ever! I hate this myth that your life is taken over, destroyed by a kid." She proposed, "I wasn't really prepared for the enormous emotion—the love. It's really overwhelming. Motherhood is a great thing, easier and more fun than anyone told me. I definitely believe in it" (Pfaff and Emerson, 56, 70). This maternal component has become increasingly prominent in Streep's image as the ageing actress has become identified with maternal film roles.

A remarkable number of Streep's recent films—notably *The River Wild, Bridges of Madison County, Before and After, ... First Do No Harm, One*

Figure 4.1 Meryl Streep and Renée Zellweger in a scene from *One True Thing* (Franklin 1998), one of the many films of the 1990s in which Streep plays the perfect screen mother. (Reproduced with permission of Corbis.)

True Thing, and *Music of the Heart*—have fashioned her as the perfect screen mother. She even said that she chose to play a non-nurturing mother in *Marvin's Room* because she had played so many good mothers in succession that she wanted to break out of that mold (Behar). Shortly after that film, however, she accepted the role of a stereotypical nurturing maternal figure yet again in *One True Thing*, a film that she describes as a tribute to the traditional stay-at-home mother, whom she believes modern career-oriented women fail to appreciate.[24]

Social Activism: "... We Are all Political Actors, Aren't We?"

Streep's support for numerous social causes is a muted aspect of her image that her publicity often cloaks under the cover of her maternal instincts. As cofounder of Mothers and Others, an organization dedicated to the protection of children from environmental hazards, she has worked for a wide range of causes, such as nuclear disarmament, environmental protection and conservation, alleviating world hunger, women's rights, assistance to the disadvantaged, education reform, and artistic freedom. She has participated in rallies, helped organize benefits, and narrated videos for many of these causes.

This wide-ranging social activism is a part of Streep's image that her publicity rarely emphasizes. In interviews, Streep has even denied that she is "political," defining the term very narrowly and insisting that she would never think of running for political office. She has consistently presented her activism as merely based on motherly concern and centered only on issues that she sees as affecting her children:

> I figure that nuclear disarmament is the only thing worth giving up a bit of my privacy for. When I wake up in the dead of night to get Henry [her son] a glass of water, I realize that issues such as disarmament, equal rights, looking out for the disadvantaged, all are about him. I don't want to get too busy to care.[25]

In her 1983 commencement address at Vassar, she exhorted the graduates to become politically involved: "... we are all political actors, aren't we, to be judged by our sins of omission as well as commission, by our silences as much as our expressed opinions, by what we let slide as much as by the things we stand for?" But she also felt compelled to apologize for taking a political stand:

> I think we feel in this country that it's "inappropriate" for even the most vaguely expressed political views to intrude on what should be short, sparkling, and entertaining. Anyhow, I'm not

going to try to make you share my political views today, but I do exhort you to investigate your own and follow through on them (Maychick, 157).

Approach to Acting: "I Don't Know about my Approach Because I Don't Have One"

As one of the most prestigiously trained contemporary Hollywood actresses, Meryl Streep might be expected to be very articulate in discussing her acting techniques and, in many ways, she is; however, she also tends to mystify her technique and to disqualify herself as a technical actress. For instance, she has said, "I don't know about my approach because I don't have one. I just respond in a holistic way to the material."[26] She claims to have "no codified way" to begin a project and proposes that each time she starts a picture she does not know how she is going to approach it. As noted in Chapter 1, she also describes her acting process in mystical terms, claiming that she is not at all a technical actress and comparing her process to entering "a zone" and to "being in love" (Lipton).

From her training in a wide range of acting styles and theories at Yale, Streep claims to have made up, as she puts it, her "grab-bag" of techniques.[27] Clearly, however, the centerpiece of Streep's acting style and the aspect about which she is most articulate is characterization. She has said that, while doing a film, she often forgets the plot because it is "not important" to her. What is important is creating a character: "So much of acting is vanity …. But the real thing that makes me feel so good is when I know I've presented a soul" (Lipton). She has even described acting as "like painting a portrait" ("Spotlight: Close-Up," 64).

Although she has said that she does not understand the Method and has never followed it in preparation for a role, Streep's descriptions of her methods of characterization suggest a combination of Method and theatrical acting styles. First of all, in the Method tradition, she describes her need to make a connection with the character, to approach each role from a very personal place before working on a character's mannerisms: "Always work from the inside," she says. "You always connect with a piece of material from the inside, or you shouldn't do it. You always work from the inside out and then you take care of the outside business." Without this inner connection, she claims, one's acting will be nothing but "a dry husk" (Lipton). She also works in the theatrical acting tradition from the outside in, by putting together the look of the character—or, as she describes it, "You need to walk the walk"—but then she says an actor needs to "forget it" and concentrate on an inner connection that must be made with the character.[28]

Yet much of this inner connection comes from Streep's imitation of the observed behavior of others. One of her professors at Yale called her technique "clinical ... like looking into someone's life" (Maychick, 39). Streep has said, "I like peeling away the surface and presenting two sides of a person. Acting is my way of investigating human nature and having fun at the same time" (Gussow, 28).

Indeed, many of her characters are based on actual people. For instance, she says she modeled Linda in *The Deer Hunter* on girls she knew in high school who were always waiting for the right man to come along and sweep them off their feet (Pfaff and Emerson, 28); Francesca in *The Bridges of Madison County* on an Italian war bride who lived down the street from her family when she was a child (Harris); and Roberta Guaspari in *Music of the Heart* on the real-life music teacher who was the inspiration for the film. Streep even visited Guaspari's classroom in Harlem to study her teaching style: "I noticed immediately how tough she was, and I used a lot of her sharpness in my portrayal."[29] For *Postcards from the Edge*, Streep copied many of the mannerisms of Carrie Fisher, who wrote the screenplay based on her semiautobiographical novel. Fisher, who was on the set every day, says she could see Streep watching her and imitating her gestures and mannerisms in the film.[30]

Streep bases her characterizations not only on real people, but also on fictional and film characters. In *Still of the Night*, a rather obvious reworking of Alfred Hitchcock's *Vertigo* (1958), she seems to be impersonating Kim Novak, the star of the earlier thriller. Even her final speech in the film, which, as noted previously, she apparently wrote herself, reworks *Vertigo's* ending from the female perspective. Instead of a man watching the woman he loves fall from a tower, in Streep's version, her character watches her father fall to his death. Similarly, in *The French Lieutenant's Woman* and *Sophie's Choice*, Streep is said to have spent much of her time on the set between takes rereading the novel upon which the film was based to get a sense of her character (Pfaff and Emerson, 61, 75).

Although Streep's acting style may combine acting traditions, it is about as far as possible from personification, the acting style most commonly associated with star acting. In fact, Meryl Streep *never* seems to be playing herself on the screen. As she describes her process,

> I attach myself to the soul of the character when I read it. Something in the script or the story makes my heart beat faster and that's what I'm attached to in a sort of way that I cannot really analyze. But it isn't limited to people from my own culture, my own background, and my own time (Kirkland).

She even is reputed to stay in character outside of her performance. For instance, director Mike Nichols says of her,

> Weeks before we begin shooting, the company starts to get together. Whoever is playing her love is in love with her. Whoever is playing the villain is a little afraid of her. And whoever is playing her best friend is her best friend. She shifts her soul slightly and changes the chemistry of all the relationships (Lipton). ✳

During the shooting of *The Bridges of Madison County*, rumors actually began to circulate that she and Clint Eastwood were having a real-life affair after Christopher Kroon, the actor who plays her son in the film, told a reporter that on the set, even when they were not shooting, Streep and Eastwood would "dance together, hold and kiss each other's hands, have fun." Streep and Eastwood were forced to deny the resulting rumors that they were having an off-screen romance (Levitt and Armstrong).

Streep's physical and emotional mutability, which allow her to demonstrate a relatively wide acting range and to take greater risks with her characterizations than is common among star actresses, does not mean that she advocates entirely separating one's personality from the characters one plays, although some critics have described her acting style as too detached and aloof. She has been accused, for instance, of working too much from the outside in and getting hung up on the technical aspects of the part to the detriment of the character's inner life (Proudfit).

Streep maintains to the contrary that, although she must forget herself when playing a character, she also needs in the tradition of Method acting to call upon her feelings and experiences to relate to that character's inner self. For instance, she says about her part as the elder sister, Kate Mundy, in *Dancing at Lughnasa* that she particularly related to the character's need always to dominate her family: "I can get a little relentless, and I could bring that to the part." She says that, as a mother of four and an elder sister, she could connect with Kate's determination to be "always right" because "there is an element of that in my personality" (Lipton).

She has even described acting as a means of cathartic psychological release. She describes it as "a place to tap into all sorts of feelings that I had never admitted to myself I felt or felt like parading in front of a group of people" (Lipton). She has said she uses acting as "what they call in therapy acting out. I get to do it and get paid. And that's very healthy for me because it's something that does need expression" (Fuller). In particularly emotional scenes, however, she recognizes a need to distance herself from her characters:

These characters that are in precarious life and death circumstances are dangerous characters to visit with your body and soul. It's dangerous to go there. We spend our whole lives as real human beings trying to get beyond the fears and the terrors that are there everywhere for us and to be an actor is to want to visit those places—those dark places and scary parts. I use it as my therapy and as a place to exorcize those things that in my real life I would never want ever to have to deal with (Lipton).

In order to develop a close connection to a character, Streep finds rehearsals useful:

The first encounter with a script is always the same … sitting around a table trying to make connections. A lot of actors will tell you that the most valuable work and the most interesting and spontaneous discoveries are made at those moments—those first times you look into the eyes of the other person. Shooting in snippets makes it difficult to keep your interest up. You can easily flag and get bored (Smurthwaite, 22).

She also demands a realistic setting to provide an authentic backdrop for her process of characterization. For instance, Alan J. Pakula, who directed her Academy Award-winning performance in *Sophie's Choice*, claims that she needed very little direction. All that she required was "the reality there for her to react to" (Pfaff and Emerson, 76). In order to provide her with that reality, he had a concentration camp survivor serve as an advisor on the set and promised to take the whole cast and crew to Europe to shoot the film's concentration camp sequences. When Pakula began to reconsider this trip because of its expense, even though it required leaving her husband behind in New York, Streep persuaded Pakula that the authentic European setting was absolutely crucial to her performance (Pfaff and Emerson, 76–77).

Streep seems to need to identify a foundation on which to build her characters. If not a realistic setting, a real-life model, or literary figure, then a line of dialogue or a secret only she knows about the character will serve this purpose. For example, she says that every film has a problem scene that must be put aside because it is hard to figure out, or a line that every actor does not want to say, but "when you solve that, it's the 'Rosetta Stone.' It's the one that turns the understanding of the whole piece" (Lipton).

She found that line in *Out of Africa* in a single sentence her character, Isak Denisen, speaks to her lover, Denys Finch Hatten (Robert Redford). Streep did not want to say the line until she realized that the key to Denisen's character could be found in her saying, "I won't allow it, Denys"

Figure 4.2 Meryl Streep being directed by Alan J. Pakula on the set of *Sophie's Choice* (1982), the film that made her undisputedly a star. Pakula claims that Streep needed very little direction. All that she required was "the reality there for her to react to" (Pfaff and Emerson, 76). (Reproduced with permission of Corbis.)

when he tells her of his plans to have another woman accompany him on one of his expeditions. According to Streep, this line showed Denison's imperviousness and her determination to claim Denys' life (Lipton). She also says that she likes to keep a little secret from all the other actors in a film, something that only she knows about her character. In *Kramer vs. Kramer*, for instance, she remembers thinking that her character, Joanna, never loved Dustin Hoffman's character, and this secret provided the key to Joanna's inner life and helped her shape her portrayal.[31]

Another foundation upon which Streep builds her performances is her facility with accents and dialects, and it has come to represent a hallmark of her style. She has done Polish, English, Irish, Danish, New Zealand, Southern, and New York accents. Often she has been praised for this linguistic facility, but at other times she has been mocked and ridiculed as "Hollywood's queen of the foreign accent" (Kirkland). Streep has been known to "bristle" when her fluency with accents is brought up in an interview.[32] She is said to feel that critics have used it to reduce her acting talents to "automechanics." As she puts it, her facility with accents is "just something that's sort of—you know—it's not the most interesting part of the work. It's not emotional; it's just like something you put on."[33] She works to make the accent she uses "organic to the character."[34] As she describes her method,

> You don't start with an accent. You try and find the person first. The accent isn't a problem. It comes with the rhythm of the writing. Of course, I have to work at it, but you hope it comes from the heart of the story—not as some trick like jumping through a hoop (Vincent).

In fact, she says that while doing an accent she cannot think about it and tells a story about having a speech coach on the set of *Dancing at Lughnasa* to help her with her Irish accent. When he was there, she was completely unable to remember her lines, so he had to be "banished" from the set (Lipton).

Streep is known not only for accents, but also for certain mannerisms that some critics see as enriching her performances. Others, however, feel her acting is needlessly cluttered with fluttery hand movements, facial expressions, head twitches, and the running of her fingers nervously through her hair. Many of these gestures may actually stem from the fact that Streep is genuinely nervous about her performances. She is even said to suffer from stage fright (Maychick, 95). Some of her anxiousness can perhaps be attributed to her reputed perfectionism. Jeremy Irons, her leading man in *The French Lieutenant's Woman*, describes her as "never satisfied … strong, opinionated, and nearly always right" (Smurthwaite, 61–62). Paradoxically, she is also said to like to work very quickly. She prefers to do just two or three takes because, as Carl Franklin, her director in *One True Thing*, says (attaching rather strange sexual connotations to her process), "She gets there fast. She isn't at all precious about it" (Seiler).

Although Streep's methods of building a character may seem very personal and internal, she nevertheless acknowledges a strong connection with her audience. She attributes her realization of the need for this connection again to observing someone else's behavior. In watching Liza Minnelli perform on stage, she says, "Her desire to give you something was so fantastic. That's an element you can't forget in the private integrity of your work that makes everything real right in here. It's nice to open it, you know, and give it" (Lipton). This desire for a close relationship with her audience may at least partially account for her stated preference for stage over film acting and her reputed desire someday to return to the theater. When she first moved from theater to film, she proposed,

> Working on movies is very economical, clean, pared down. You can afford to do so little. You don't have to be a good actor, or even an actor, to be effective in the movies …. My fear is that in doing so little I will not be able to do what I do on stage, which is to be brave, to take the larger leap (Smurthwaite, 26).

Falling in line with other film actors who give privilege to theater over film acting, Streep has proposed that on stage, "[Y]ou give more of yourself," and she has designated the theater as her real home (Maychick, 75).

Streep has been prevented from returning to the theater, where she also believes roles for older actresses are more plentiful, only by its grueling schedule, which she fears would interfere with her commitment to her family. In fact, one reason she agreed to take the part in *Dancing at Lughnasa*, the film version of Brian Friel's play, was to "begin circling the theater, to see if I could fit my large, overly important self into an ensemble again in the way that everybody does seamlessly in the theater" (Harris). Over the years, there have been many rumors that Streep was about to be coaxed back to the New York stage. She was said to have considered lead roles in Tom Stoppard's *The Real Thing* in 1983 and in Wendy Wasserstein's *An American Daughter* in 1996. In the summer of 2001, she finally made what was heralded as her triumphal return to New York theatre, fittingly playing the great actress Madame Arkadin in a Public Theater production of Chekhov's *The Seagull* performed outdoors in Central Park.

Although Streep may see film acting as less creative than acting on the stage, her work in both media is very auteurist. Throughout her career, Streep has always had a great deal of creative input into her films, not only because of her meticulous characterization, but also through her initiation of script changes. Director Robert Benton, who, as noted previously, seems essentially to have allowed her to construct her roles in *Kramer vs. Kramer* and *Still of the Night*, has proposed that working with Streep is "like working with another writer. She's a wonderful collaborator. She's a combination of intelligence, imagination, and instinct" (Maychick, 125).

Spontaneity and improvisation are also crucial aspects of Streep's auteurist acting. She has said that she does not like to read a script too much for fear that her acting will become "like writing, not like talking." What inspires her performance is the "idea of the dream that was created in my head the first time I read it [the script], and then I often don't like to read it again" (Lipton). Having early demonstrated a talent for improvisation at Yale, Streep has expressed a strong belief in the need for spontaneity in acting. In discussing improvisation, she says, "That's the only thing that's worth looking at—what nobody expected to happen in a scene .... The unexplained, the tangent energy, the spontaneous is what you dream of and wish for and hope happens. So you get all ready before the first reading and then... forget it" (Lipton). She has also described her acting skill as involving the ability to listen carefully: "I don't feel I exist until I'm with someone else in a scene" (Proudfit).

Many of her screen performances were, in fact, heavily improvised. For instance, Kevin Kline says he found working with her in *Sophie's Choice* very different from his previous experiences in the theater:

> Absorbing the lines the night before then changing them all day is alien to a stage actor. Meryl loves to act dangerously, to surprise. Alan [Pakula, the director] went along with her because he gets worried if a scene comes out as it's written on the page. In the end, we were all trying to surprise each other (Smurthwaite, 82).

Streep also experimented liberally with improvisation in her films with Robert De Niro: *The Deer Hunter, Falling in Love,* and *Marvin's Room.* Streep and De Niro improvised almost all of the dialogue in *Falling in Love* in two months of marathon sessions before shooting (Pfaff and Emerson, 103). Streep also speaks glowingly of her experience working with Clint Eastwood in *The Bridges of Madison County* because of the freedom he gave her to improvise. She says shooting the film was like doing a two-character theater piece with both actors "free to explore how it evolves, almost as if we were making it up as we went along."[35] In fact, Streep seems to require very little direction. Carl Franklin proposes that he directed her and costar William Hurt in *One True Thing* "almost not at all."[36] In characterizing her favorite type of director, Streep describes someone who "doesn't say anything to me ... leaves me alone ... someone who inspires your confidence, who sets up a safe world for you to make your mistakes and go as wild and as far out as you want" (Schickel).

Although critics have widely praised what have been called Streep's meticulously constructed invisible acting techniques and the verisimilitude of her portrayals, she does have her detractors. As noted previously, the most vehement of these has been the influential film critic Pauline Kael, who before her death wrote for *The New Yorker*. The essence of Kael's criticism, as Streep has pointed out, is that Streep's performances, as Kael sees them, are too mannered, and not naturalistic enough, and that they do not follow the tenets of traditional star acting, in which the actor through personification seems to be playing himself or herself in every role. When asked to respond to Kael's criticism, Streep said that Kael "wants to believe that the person that she sees [on the screen] *is* that person" (Gell). In describing Streep's most highly acclaimed performance in *Sophie's Choice*, for instance, Kael was, as always, harshly critical:

> Streep is very beautiful at times, and she does amusing, nervous bits of business, like fidgeting with a furry boa, her fingers twiddling with our heartstrings. She has, as usual, put thought and effort into her work. But something about her puzzles me; after I've

seen her in a movie, I can't visualize her from the neck down. Is it possible that as an actress she makes herself into a blank and then focuses all her attention on one thing—the toss of her head, for example, in *Manhattan*, her accent in *Sophie's Choice*? Maybe by bringing an unwarranted intensity to one facet of a performance she in effect decorporealizes herself. This could explain why her movie heroines don't seem to be full characters, and why there are no incidental joys to be had from watching her. It could be that in her zeal to be an honest actress she allows nothing to escape her conception of a performance. Instead of trying to achieve freedom in front of the camera, she's predetermining what it records (quoted in Smurthwaite, 85–92).

Fortunately for Streep, the majority of reviewers have not agreed with Kael; instead, they have praised Streep for creating a unique acting style characterized by emotional intensity, surety of detail, and realism of presentation. The critical acclaim Streep has accumulated throughout her career, not to mention her extensive collection of Academy Award nominations, testifies to the fact that, in Hollywood today, traditional schools of acting are of minimal consequence. The star–actress effectively creates her acting style, employing whatever techniques suit her immediate purposes, and Meryl Streep has done just this. As a result, she has been able to put together a remarkable succession of critically acclaimed film performances and has gained a reputation as an actress who can create a completely different and uniquely individual character in each film. During the height of her career, she even became known as "the only woman in Hollywood who [could] do any script" (Proudfit).

Meryl Streep: Actress and Image

Meryl Streep's image is a mixture in almost equal parts of the progressive and the reactionary.[37] Because she has been recognized primarily for her acting ability, rather than for her beauty, and singled out as one of the greatest Hollywood acting talents of her generation, even of the contemporary period as a whole, she is in many ways a very progressive figure in the history of the Hollywood female star. She is also an actress who has made substantial artistic contributions to her films. The auteurist nature of her acting has paved the way for other actresses to seek more involvement in the shaping of their characters. In addition, Streep's role choices have frequently been progressive. She has extended female roles beyond stereotype, even taking underwritten parts and playing unattractive female characters so that she can flesh them out and make them sympathetic or at least understandable. Furthermore, the idea of being a sex object has always been repellent to her. In fact, for a major Hollywood star, she has played remarkably few sex scenes and none that are particularly graphic.

Throughout her career, Streep's films have been consistently female centered, most often with her character's emotional life serving as the focal point and central enigma of the drama. Many of her films are even overtly feminist, presenting the lives of exceptional women and giving voice to those whose stories would not otherwise be heard. Streep has played a strongly independent Victorian heroine in *The French Lieutenant's Woman*, an antinuclear activist in *Silkwood*, a strong-minded plantation owner in *Out of Africa*, an adventure heroine in *The River Wild*, and a dedicated inner city music teacher in *Music from the Heart*.

Yet some of her roles that might on the surface seem progressive are less so upon close analysis. For instance, her fleshing out of the character of Joanna, the wife who abandons her husband and child in *Kramer vs. Kramer*, does not prevent the film from developing a theme strongly critical of the independent woman. Although Streep does her best to make the situation less black and white, as she has said herself, her character is still the film's "heavy," who is only seen at the beginning and end, but is talked about in the most unfavorable terms for most of the film (Maychick, 83). By far the most regressive aspect of Streep's role choice has been her turn as a mature actress to playing stereotypical maternal figures in women's melodramas.[38] Although in making these films Streep has been instrumental in bringing a number of novels that focus on female characters to the screen, many of these works, such as *The Bridges of Madison County*, *Marvin's Room*, *Dancing at Lughnasa*, and *One True Thing*, are unabashedly women's tearjerkers that associate femininity stereotypically with uncontrolled emotional expression and maudlin sentimentality.

In addition, a number of extremely traditional aspects of Streep's star persona render her a very safe female role model for contemporary women and recuperate her progressivity for the patriarchal status quo. Her strong identification with motherhood and family devotion, complemented by her recent maternal roles, connects her image strongly with conventional femininity. When Streep, often portrayed as the greatest living Hollywood film actress, presents herself as a soccer mom who uses her career merely as a way to keep from becoming "short" with her family, she demonstrates that she has so internalized established notions of traditional femininity that she herself initiates the cultural recuperation for patriarchy of her image as a strong, successful career woman. Divided between her reputation as an extremely accomplished star–actress with enormous talent and power and her self-construction as a stereotypical homemaker who willingly has sacrificed her career for her family's happiness, Streep's image perfectly embodies the contemporary social conception of the postfeminist woman in crisis, torn between her career aspirations and her desire to be a traditional housewife.

Richard Dyer's conception that star images magically reconcile the oppositional terms of historical dilemmas seems particularly relevant here (1979, 30), yet Streep's image enacts this conflict between career and family without reconciling its binary oppositions, as Dyer suggests it should. Rather than offering women accommodation to their traditional domestic role or a radical subversion of that role, Streep's image provides only an uneasy compromise, resulting in the confusion, rather than the clarification, of gender issues. Streep repeatedly has asserted that if she had to choose between family and career, she would without question choose her family; however, she has never really had to do this in any significant way. She has always had both, and although she has at times perhaps limited her career because of family concerns, this has not prevented her from establishing herself as a major star.

Additionally, Streep has been an outspoken critic of the film industry's failure to consider actresses the equals of male stars or to provide a wide enough range of women's film roles. When asked in 1990 to present the keynote address at the Screen Actor's Guild's First National Women's Conference, she delivered some very pointed criticism of the current employment situation for Hollywood actresses. Lamenting the lack of good roles for women, she proposed:

> If we don't have these images of women we feel for, admire, recognize, and esteem, then we stifle the dreams of our daughters; we put our hands over the mouth of their inspiration. If we erase our dreams, we disappear.

> If most of the women we've seen in film this year are slapped, kicked, raped, murdered, bruised, begging for help or duplicitous and just asking for it, this is not an indication that *actresses* are confused about their roles. It is rather an indication of the kind[s] of images the industry has confidence in, green lights and feels will sell (Streep, 15–17).

Yet, when asked if she feels any pressure to work to change this situation that she so deplores, she says that she does not feel she has the power. To bring about significant change, she believes she would need to start her own production company, and she does not have time for this effort because of her desire to be with her family (Behar). It is exactly this split between career and family at the heart of Meryl Streep's image that makes her a symbol for her time.

References

1. The sobriquet "Magic Meryl" was first given to Streep by John Skow in "What Makes Meryl Magic," *Time* 118 (Sept. 7, 1981): 38.
2. Fuller, Graham. 1998. "Streep's Ahead: An Adult Conversation with Meryl Streep." *Interview* Dec. <http://www.articles.com/m1295/12_28/53368755/pl1/article.jhtm>; hereafter cited in text.
3. Smith, Liz. 1998. "The Meryl Streep Nobody Knows."*Good Housekeeping* 227(3) (Sept): 94–98. EBSCOhost Academic Search Premier. GALILEO. <http://galileo.peachnet.edu>; hereafter cited in text.
4. Gray, Paul. 1979. "A Mother Finds Herself." *Time* Dec. 3: 81.
5. Gussow, Mel. 1979. "The Rising Star of Meryl Streep." *New York Times Magazine*, Feb. 14: 24; hereafter cited in text.
6. Schaefer, Stephen. "Mr. Showbiz Interview: America's Drama Queen Fiddles with the School System in Music of the Heart." Mr. Showbiz.com, <http://www.mrshowbiz.go.com/celebrities/interviews/510_1.html>; hereafter cited in text.
7. Pfaff, Eugene E., Jr. and Mark Emerson. 1987. *Meryl Streep: A Critical Biography.* Jefferson, N.C.: McFarland & Co., p. 16; hereafter cited in text.
8. "Spotlight: Close-Up." 1977. *Seventeen,* Feb: 64; hereafter cited in text.
9. Maychick, Diane. 1984. *Meryl Streep: The Reluctant Superstar.* New York: St. Martin's Press, 36; hereafter cited in text.
10. Wiener, Thomas. 1983. "In Search of Silkwood." *American Film* (Dec.): 52.
11. Behar, Henri. 1996. "Film Scouts Interview: Meryl Streep on Marvin's Room." Film Scouts.com, Dec. 23, <http:/www.filmscouts.com/scripts/interview.cfm?file=mar-stree>; hereafter cited in text.
12. Levitt, Shelley and Lois Armstrong. 1995. "Heartland." *People* 43(25) (June 26): 70–75. EBSCOhost. GALILEO. <http://www.galileo.peachnet.edu>; hereafter cited in text.
13. "Scoring Session: Behind the Scenes" (Making of Featurette), *Music of the Heart* DVD, directed by Wes Craven (1999; Burbank, CA: Miramax/Walt Disney Home Video, 2003).
14. Streep, Meryl. 1990. "When Women Were in the Movies." *Screen Actor* (Fall): 15–17; hereafter cited in text.
15. Smurthwaite, Nick. 1984. *The Meryl Streep Story.* New York: Beaufort Books, p. 47; hereafter cited in text.
16. Mark Harris, Mark. 2001. "Depth Becomes Her." *Entertainment Weekly* (June 12). <http://www.ew.com/ew/archive/0.1798.1[28020]meryl%streep.00.html>; hereafter cited in text.
17. Waszczyna, Susan. 1998. "Dueling Stars Step Maternal Tale Up in Class." *USA Today* (Dec. 21): 40.

18. Hobson, Louis. 1996. "It's So Nice to Be Nasty." *Calgary Sun* (Dec. 8), <http:// www.cgi_canoe.ca/jammoviesarticlesS/streep_meryl.html>; hereafter cited in text.

19. Kirkland, Bruce. 1997. "Streep Is Just Another Soccer Mom." *Calgary Sun* (Jan. 18), <http://www.cgi_canoe.ca/jammoviesarticlesS/streep_meryl.html>; hereafter cited in text.

20. Landon, Ruth. 1988. "Meryl Streep Picks a Fight." *New York Daily News* (July 25): np. Meryl Streep Clippings File, Billy Rose Theater Collection, New York City Public Library.

21. Plaskin, Glen. 1990. "Feeling the Life." *New York Daily News Magazine* (Sept. 16): 18.

22. Calhoun, John. 1996. "Mother's Nature." *Toronto Sun* (Dec. 15), <http:// www.cgi_canoe.ca/jammoviesarticlesS/streep_meryl.html>.

23. Hobson, Louis B. 1998. "Dying for Attention." *Calgary Sun* (Sept. 15), <http://www.cgi_canoe.ca/jammoviesarticlesS/streep_meryl.html>.

24. Seiler, Andy. 1999. "Meryl Streep's One True Role." *USA Today* (Dec. 17): np. Meryl Streep Clippings File. Margaret Herrick Library, Beverly Hills, CA; hereafter cited in text.

25. Dutka, Elaine. 1982. "Talking with Meryl Streep," *Redbook* (Sept.): 14.

26. Gell, Aaron. "Let's Get Small." *Time Out New York.com*, http://www.time-outny.com/hotseat/164/164hotseat.htm.

27. Dworkin, Susan. 1979. "Meryl Streep to the Rescue!" *Ms. Magazine* (Feb.): 88.

28. Proudfit, Scott. 1999. "Behind the Magic." *Backstage West Drama–Logue* (Feb. 18): np. Meryl Streep Clippings File. Margaret Herrick Library, Beverly Hills, CA.

29. Erman, Lynn. 1999. "From Harlem to Hollywood." *Good Housekeeping* 229(5) (Nov.): 28.

30. Commentary by Carrie Fisher, *Postcards from the Edge*, DVD, directed by Mike Nichols (1990; Culver City, CA: Columbia Tristar Home Video, 2004).

31. Transcript, *The Oprah Winfrey Show*, Dec. 9, 1996. http://www.geocities. com/Hollywood/Hills./2844/mss_oprah.html.

32. Mal Vincent, Mal. 1999. "Meryl Streep Talks about Her Latest Role." *The Virginian–Pilot* (Feb.5). http://www.thehollandsentinel.net/stories/020599/ ent_meryl.streep.html.

33. Transcript, *The Rosie O'Donnell Show*, March 6, 1997, http://www.geocities. com/Hollywood/Hills/2844/msr.html.

34. Dowling, Claudie Glen and Ken Regan. 1995. "Madison County Confidential." *Life* 18(8) (June): 46–52. EBSCOhost, GALILEO. http://www.galileo. peachnet.edu.

35. Schickel, Richard. 1995. "The Cowboy and the Lady." *Time* 145(93) (June 5): 62–64.

36. "Spotlight on Location" (making of featurette), *One True Thing*, DVD, directed by Carl Franklin (1998; Hollywood, CA: Universal Studios Home Video, 2003).

37. I am aware that the use of the terms "progressive" and "reactionary/regressive" in terms of judging films, star images, and film performances is

problematic. Certainly, I do not want to suggest a return to the "positive image" approach to criticism and require all film representations to have a progressive dimension, and I do not want to pigeonhole a performance or star image reductively in one category or another. At the same time, however, I do think that in assessing the ideological significance of a star's image one can, and really must if the assessment is to have any meaning, delineate certain aspects of that image that seem to relate to a progressive social mind-set and others that represent conservative views.

38. I am not defining a "women's melodrama" as a work necessarily written by a woman, but rather as one directed to a female audience.

CHAPTER 5

Susan the Siren: Susan Sarandon

**Career Trajectory: "You can't build a career …
you know how irrational this business is"**

Attributing her success almost entirely to chance, Susan Sarandon, even more than Meryl Streep, seems to subscribe to the Hollywood myth that stardom is based on magical circumstance. Streep only believes her acting comes from a magical place, whereas Sarandon claims her whole career magically materialized. According to Sarandon, she began acting only because she thought, "This is easy and fun and I'll pay off my school debts."[1] She failed to take her career seriously, not because she lacked ambition, but rather because she says she always approached acting as

> A means to an end but not an end in itself … It's not something I dreamt about becoming and then dedicated myself to and struggled for. It happened very quickly, and I thought it was a lark for at least ten or fifteen years. I wouldn't even call myself an actress for a long time because it seemed so silly.

As her career progressed, her lack of seriousness about acting changed into a distaste for the Hollywood system: "And then I became somewhat disillusioned with it [Hollywood] because, as a woman, you're not necessarily treated very respectfully in the industry."[2] Later in her career, like Meryl Streep, Sarandon began to place family obligations above professional concerns: "It's complicated by the fact that I have a family; they come everywhere with me. My children are young. I could do three films in a row, but I don't want to leave my kids or take them out of school. It's not that important for me."[3]

Sarandon's tendency to be "not incredibly aggressive about her career"[4] also derives from her rejection of the whole idea of a career design. She proposes that actors merely "choose from what you're given" (Moynihan and Warhol). "You can't build a career ... you know how irrational this business is."[5] She says she never made her career her primary focus because "life is so much bigger than my craft that I would rather invest my genius in my life. It has many more challenges, many more surprises. It may even demand more from the imagination."[6] She sees not only filmmaking but also life as unpredictable: "Almost everything in my own life has been unplanned. I got here because all the things that were going to happen, didn't happen" (Shapiro, 220). As part of her overall conception of life as a succession of unplanned events, Sarandon maintains that acting chose her, rather than she it.

An introverted, introspective child alienated from her deeply conservative Catholic parents and her eight younger siblings, Sarandon embarked on her college career at Catholic University in Washington, D.C. in order to escape what she considered to be an oppressive home environment. She says she had little real interest in college and her "sole ambition was to get out of Jersey. Once I did that I thought my life would just unfold" (Shapiro, 40). As an English major in college, she says she "never studied" (Shapiro, 41) and "never wanted to be an actor."[7]

The crucial event in her college years was her romance with Chris Sarandon, whom she met in her freshman year and later married. She credits Chris with educating her and getting her interested in acting: "I was just a baby and he was six or seven years older, and I thought he knew everything. And he just took me to foreign movies and stuff" (Moynihan and Warhol). After graduating from college and doing some modeling, Sarandon was "discovered" when she went to an audition with Chris, who was reading for New York Agent Jane Olivier. Sarandon says that she went only to accompany Chris and "give him a warm body to play against" (Shapiro, 49). Olivier signed Chris, but liked Susan's performance so well that she asked her if she would also like to be represented.

Olivier quickly got Susan an audition for her first movie role in *Joe* (Avildsen 1970), a low-budget production that Sarandon describes as "the first straight film that a porn company was doing" (Lipton). She won a featured role in the film even though she says she was such a novice that, when asked to do an improvisation during her audition, she had to ask for an explanation:

> They asked me to do an improvisation. I asked them what that was. They told me, I did it, and they gave me the job on the spot. I thought "Gee, this seems easy; maybe I'll try acting for a while." Because for me, it just seemed like anyone could be an actor.

She remembers calling Olivier, telling her that she got the part, and ending the conversation by asking, "Now, what do I do?" (Shapiro, 49).

Although she denies having any career design, Sarandon did make career decisions after this initial discovery phase that unquestionably shaped her career, and not always in positive ways. Whereas actors, especially early in their careers, most often rely heavily on the advice of their agents, Sarandon from early on was known to fire agents who disagreed with her. She has said of her process of selecting roles,

> I have an agent who is a really smart guy, very literate, and very moral. I also have a female agent who's all of those things and who has different opinions and reasoning to mine. Finally, they give their opinion and I do listen but, in the end, if I want to do it, I do it![8]

She is said to have rejected Hollywood superagent Jay Bernstein because he wanted her to give up her political activism and to have fired Aaron Russo when he proposed that the way for her to gain superstar status was to take roles in commercial films of questionable quality.[9]

In accord with her notion of stardom as magically attained, Sarandon presents herself as an iconoclast who has broken all of the rules of conventional career wisdom and still has miraculously become a star: "I am always incredibly shocked that I still have a career. I've done everything wrong, so there must be some kind of angel watching over me."[10] However, Sarandon did not really do everything wrong, and in fact, she did many things right. One thing that she did very right was to pursue aggressively certain key, career-shaping roles and then work very hard to make them memorable (Moynihan and Warhol). Although she has been in a remarkable number of unmemorable films, she has also kept her career afloat by searching out career-defining parts in commercially and artistically successful films,[11] often against the stated advice of her agents (Bates).

In interviews, Sarandon has talked about her dogged pursuit of key roles. For instance, she struggled to get the attention of Louis Malle so that he would cast her as Brooke Shields's prostitute mother in *Pretty Baby* (1978), a film whose controversial presentation of child prostitution increased

Sarandon's visibility and gave her already sexualized image an art house respectability. She says that she was worried about her audition with Malle, "He was running around his office totally preoccupied," and she could not be sure that she had gotten his attention. So, when he followed up with a telephone call, she worked hard to impress him with her analysis of the script and conception of the character. As Malle describes the conversation, "She had a lot to say. She was critical of some aspects of the script. And I thought this conversation was terrific."[12] She got the part.

Even more indicative of her aggressive pursuit of key roles was her determination to play Annie Savoy in *Bull Durham*, a role that really made her a star. Sarandon has described Annie as her favorite role:

> She doesn't apologize. She's one of the few women I know in film who likes sex, has sex and doesn't have to die at the end of the movie. She has a great sense of humor, she's philosophical, she's vulnerable, she's literate, she wears funny clothes, she can hit a ball. You get to go to bed with Kevin [Costner] and Tim [Robbins] (Lipton).

The role would be particularly instrumental in the construction of Sarandon's star image because it combined the quality of earthy sexuality already well established within her image lexicon with the added elements of wit and intelligence. Sarandon proposes that she only got the role because of casting difficulties: "Lucky for me it was a very difficult part to cast because you had to move an amazing amount of verbiage and at the same time have a sense of humor and some legs. I guess that narrowed it down" (Newman). There are other reasons why the part may have been available, however. In addition to its highly sexualized nature and the acting challenges it posed, writer–director Ron Shelton insisted that every actress considered for the role, no matter how prominent, had to audition (Shapiro, 127).

Sarandon's account of the auditioning process for the film reveals not a magical success story, but rather an actress who was willing to pursue any avenue to secure a highly desirable acting opportunity. She says that when she read the script, she realized

> It was the first part in a long time that I hadn't been kind of over-qualified for, you know, that really on the page had so much going for it so that when you read it every time you get towards sort of a film cliché moment he would take it and completely reverse it and that was exciting (Lipton).

In order to audition, she flew back to Hollywood from Rome at her own expense only to discover that, as she puts it, "nobody wanted" her. She describes herself as having "groveled completely" (Lipton), "spent some time with Kevin Costner, [and] kissed some ass at the studio" (Lovell, 91). Ron Shelton says that, although he allowed her to audition, Sarandon was not on the studio's list of actresses from which he was supposed to cast the role. Somehow, Sarandon got wind of this fact and, to persuade studio executives of her qualifications, paraded up and down the hallways at Orion Pictures in a skin-tight red dress that, according to Shelton, "was fabulous. It looked like something Sophia Loren would have worn. Susan knows how to stop traffic" (Newman). Everything she did paid off because the studio put her on their casting list and Costner and Shelton recommended her for the part (Newman; Shapiro, 128). As Alan Lovell suggests, this was "one clear example where Sarandon was able to take control of her career and shape it decisively" (91). There would be others.

In addition to these instances of Sarandon's decisive career management, however, many times she simply refused to play the Hollywood game. As one interviewer commented, Sarandon has "broken all of the rules regarding conventional career wisdom" (Bates). In fact, Alan Lovell lists the extraordinary length of time—about twenty years—it took Sarandon to establish herself as a star as one of the most notable aspects of her career, and he points out that "her career contrasts interestingly with comparable actresses of her generation like Meryl Streep, Jessica Lange, and Sigourney Weaver, all of whom achieved star status relatively quickly" (92).

What Sarandon's early career really illustrates is how difficult it is for an actress to build a career if she refuses to play the Hollywood game. Even after two series of potentially breakthrough roles, *Pretty Baby* (Malle 1978) *and Atlantic City* (Malle 1980) in the late 1970s and early 1980s and then *The Witches of Eastwick* (Miller 1987) and *Bull Durham* (Shelton 1988) in the late 1980s, her career still continued to have what Lovell calls a "miscellaneous character" (89). Individual films "var[ied] greatly in ambition and scope," and Sarandon won "recognition as an interesting actress without that interest being strongly defined" (Lovell, 90).

Sarandon's screen career developed through three successive stages, each characterized by a particular type of role.

- It began with a lengthy early stage (1970 to 1987) of discovery, sporadic success, and strong identification with earthy eroticism in films such as *Joe, The Rocky Horror Picture Show, Pretty Baby, Atlantic City, Tempest, The Hunger,* and *The Witches of Eastwick.*
- A stage of gradual development from minor to major stardom (1988 to 1992) saw her cast in roles that were still highly sexualized but also associated with intelligence and what can perhaps best be described as "an attitude"—a brash "ballsy, don't-give-a-shit" manner

(Shapiro, 54). This period was initiated by *Bull Durham*, includes *White Palace* and *Light Sleeper*, and ends with *Thelma & Louise*, which finally, after twenty-two years, made Sarandon a major star.

- A final period of de-eroticized older women roles in which Sarandon has played a wide range of mother figures (1992 to present) begins with *Lorenzo's Oil*, extends through *Safe Passage, Little Women, The Client, Dead Man Walking, Stepmom, Anywhere But Here, Igby Goes Down*, and *The Banger Sisters*. *Twilight, Cradle Will Rock, Illuminata, Alfie*, and *Shall We Dance* also fall within this period, but represent deliberate, and not entirely successful (at least in terms of box office), attempts by the ageing actress to create a more mature version of her earlier sexualized-intelligent-heroine-with-an-attitude persona.

Throughout these periods, one major mistake Sarandon repeatedly made in terms of career planning was not to capitalize fully on major film successes by following them up with a second big movie. As Lovell points out, wiser choices after *Pretty Baby* and *Atlantic City* might have made her a major star in the early 1980s, but instead she chose a series of Hollywood disasters: *Loving Couples, Tempest, The Buddy System*, and *Compromising Positions*. Similarly, after her huge success in *Thelma & Louise* and at the height of her career, she did *Lorenzo's Oil*, a film that initiated a long series of mother roles. The film's grim portrayal of a child suffering from the ravages of adrenoleukodystrophy (ADL) makes it a harrowing viewing experience and, to judge from box office receipts, one to which many filmgoers chose not to subject themselves. Then, after finally getting her big-budget Hollywood star vehicle, *The Client*, Sarandon took two glamourless mother roles in *Sage Passage* and *Little Women*. She would also follow up her Oscar-winning performance in *Dead Man Walking* by taking three years off to spend time with her family. When she finally did return to the screen, she chose to star in *Twilight* with the much older Paul Newman, Gene Hackman, and James Garner, a film that one critic dubbed a "geezer-noir" that emphasized all of its characters' advancing age.

Throughout her early career, Sarandon routinely alternated her Hollywood roles with parts in independent films, two of which, *The Rocky Horror Picture Show* and *The Hunger*, brought her cult status. As she has suggested, they also served to detract from, rather than enhance, her position in Hollywood:

> I've been in so many independent films, which is why my price took years and years to get up. Almost every other film I've done has been for no money. Every time you do something for a small

amount of money, they quote the last price …. But a script comes along and you want to do it, so you take it for no money, and you're back to square one just about …. If there's a good project that people believe in, you can do it independently and do it fast, but then you have to subsidize yourself by doing something else (Grundmann and Lucia).

Sarandon may joke about her disastrous choice of roles, but she also seems to realize that it seriously delayed her rise to stardom: "I've been discovered at least four times. Somehow, I've managed to keep bouncing back—without having to check into the Betty Ford Clinic."[13]

Sarandon's career also suffered from the reputation she gained as an actress who is "difficult," meaning that she is not easy to work with during shooting and inclined to express her displeasure to the press about an unpleasant filmmaking experience once the film has wrapped. Very early in her career, Sarandon began to feel disenchanted with Hollywood. She has spoken openly of what she calls her "nervous breakdown" in 1975 at the age of twenty-nine and her subsequent year-long depression. After the breakup of her first marriage, Sarandon experienced what she has called an "identity crisis" (Shapiro, 64). She says she completely lost confidence in herself, in her acting career, and in the movie industry. As she somewhat cavalierly describes her mental state:

> I think everyone has to go through a kind of crash between how you've been told the world functions and then how you really have to see it, and somewhere in between there is a Blanche DuBois trying to get by without losing your magic, so that was my moment, and I went way, way out and came back and regrouped (Lipton).

She describes seeing and hearing things that were not there, losing so much weight that she was down to eighty-five pounds (Moynihan and Warhol), and even feeling that she was losing her hearing (Wadler, 39).

She credits her experience in *Bull Durham* thirteen years later with finally restoring her faith in the movie industry and her acting talent. Sarandon says *Bull Durham* "gave me faith in myself again. My disillusion had to do with working with mediocre people who had mediocre dreams, who didn't particularly feel passionately about what they were doing" (Smith). She credits the film with having "changed her life" by reconvincing her that there were "people invested with any kind of passion" in moviemaking.[14] In the 1980s, rumors of Sarandon's mental problems coupled with stories of recurrent problems on the sets of her films tarnished her reputation in the industry.

In fact, Sarandon's difficulties on the sets of her films are notorious and not confined to Hollywood productions. She was said to have had problems getting along with the other members of the mostly British cast while shooting *The Rocky Horror Picture Show* (Shapiro, 63). Afterwards, she claimed that the set was so cold that she contracted pneumonia. Although she complained to the film's director, she said he refused to do anything about it and even accused her of being self-indulgent. She was forced to perform "wet in my half slip and bra for two months on a stage that ha[d] no heat" (Lipton). She threatened to quit from several other productions, including *Loving Couples, Tempest, The Witches of Eastwick,* and *Sweet Hearts Dance,* because she was displeased with the scripts.

The Witches of Eastwick is a particularly notorious example of Sarandon's reputedly "difficult" personality on the set. As Sarandon describes her experiences, they can be seen instead as an example of a strong-minded actress refusing to submit to unfair and demeaning treatment by a male-dominated film industry. Having aggressively pursued the lead female role opposite Jack Nicholson in *Witches*, Sarandon was told she had won it. Then, only four days before rehearsals were set to begin, she was unceremoniously informed that her original part had been given to Cher and that she would be playing a subsidiary role that Sarandon describes as virtually "nonexistent" in the existing script (Shapiro, 121–122). She threatened to walk off the film, but was told that she had an ironclad contract. She says, "I was pretty much a single mom at that point, and I could have fought it in court but I didn't have any money and the studio's lawyers could have prevented me from working elsewhere if I walked away" (Shapiro, 122–123). Sarandon also accused the film's producers of blaming the film's actresses, whom they always called "girls," for all the movie's problems because they were afraid to confront its male star, Jack Nicholson.[15]

Although she remained on the film and was successful in having her part expanded (see the acting section later for further details concerning her auterism in this regard), she told the press at the time of the film's release of the "complete betrayal and a constant humiliation"[16] she experienced while making the film: "[It] broke my heart. I felt like such a fool. At each step they [the film's producers and director] asked me to trust them, and I kept doing it. And every time I was betrayed" (Newman). She recounted stories of almost being electrocuted in a scene where the three female stars were levitated over a swimming pool (Shapiro, 124), having her daughter and the girl's father thrown off the set by producer Jon Peters when they came to take her to lunch, and being given remaindered gowns from Cher's television variety show as wardrobe (Dreifus, 66). Needless to say, she became *persona non grata* in the industry after her revelations concerning *Witches*: "Not only was I not on the A list, I wasn't on any list at all" (Shapiro, 127).

She even had problems on the set of *Dead Man Walking*, a film written and directed by her domestic partner, Tim Robbins. Rumors spread during the shooting that Robbins and Sarandon were feuding so much that they decided to live in separate apartments. Sarandon said of the shoot: "We definitely had those days when tensions were high. I'm out there working unadorned without lipstick or mascara. So I definitely had moments when I wasn't particularly tactful in terms of trying to figure out what I was doing" (Shapiro, 184). Her criticism of Robbins' script apparently provoked the difficulties. According to Sarandon, Robbins was very sensitive about his role as screenwriter and saw her criticisms as "betrayals" when she meant them as constructive comments (Jeffreys). When asked about making the film, Robbins would only say: "It was a nightmare but I'm not going to talk about it" (Shapiro, 185).

During shooting, the press began to speculate that problems on the set would precipitate the breakup of the Sarandon–Robbins relationship. Since this incident, both Sarandon and Robbins have refused to discuss in public any details concerning their relationship (Shapiro, 186). When asked about Sarandon in interviews, Robbins is said to get "mopey," respond only with the stock reply, "You'd have to ask her," and even on occasions abruptly terminate the interview.[17]

If Sarandon is reluctant to talk about her relationship with Robbins, she has been all too eager to use press interviews to criticize her films. For instance, when she disapproved of the release version of *The Other Side of Midnight*, she reputedly agreed to go on press junkets, but said she would not promote the film; instead, she informed the studio that she would actually try in interviews to mention the film as little as possible. She openly complained in an interview at the time of *White Palace*'s release that the last minute addition of a happy ending had "negated every character trait I'd spent two hours building," and then added, "It's frustrating. You put your guts out there on the line; then finally somebody takes your entrails and puts them before the public" (Shapiro, 138). Her press comments on *Witches of Eastwick*, however, are probably her most devastating. In describing what she took away from the film, she said: "I learned a promise is not a promise, and a person's word is not a person's word" (Shapiro, 124). Broadening her attack on the film's producers to encompass the whole industry, she lamented: "I think they [producers and studio executives] encourage people to be difficult. I think we may be at a low point in terms of integrity, honesty, self-respect, and obviously they're very patronizing toward the movie audience" (Shapiro 125).

Although she has been nominated five times and won for best actress for *Dead Man Walking*, Sarandon has even criticized the Academy Awards, that sacred Hollywood institution. In 1980, when she was first nominated for *Atlantic City*, she said she did not expect to win because "you know how political the Academy Awards are" (Moynihan and Warhol). When she was not nominated for *Bull Durham* in 1988, she complained that all films are not equally considered, especially those that come out early in the year or are not heavily promoted by their studio (Grundmann and Lucia). Describing herself and Robbins, who make their home in New York, as "outcasts" or "inside–outsiders" from what she refers to sarcastically as that "company town" Hollywood,[18] Sarandon confided to interviewers that they keep their Oscars in their bathroom.[19]

Perhaps even more than Sarandon's outspoken criticism of the industry, her political activism has undeniably hurt her career. In the 1980s, the press even began to refer to her as "Hanoi Susan" (Shapiro, 108), suggesting that she was following in the footsteps of Jane Fonda, who in the 1960s was dubbed "Hanoi Jane" for openly opposing the Vietnam War. Like Fonda, Sarandon has challenged Hollywood's taboo on actors' using their celebrity to propagate their political views. Her most flagrant offense came at the 1993 Academy Awards ceremony when she and Robbins as presenters made a short statement criticizing the U.S. detainment of Haitian refugees with AIDS. Their behavior was condemned by Academy President Bob Rehme and the show's producer Gil Cates. Cates commented after the ceremony, "For someone who[m] I invite to present an award to use that time to postulate a personal political belief I think is not only outrageous, it's distasteful and dishonest" (Shapiro, 168). She and Robbins were reputed to have been unofficially blacklisted by the Academy for a year after their appearance (Shapiro, 23). Sarandon has even expressed fear that someday her political activism will put an end to her career. During an anti-Persian Gulf War demonstration, when a photographer commented to her, "You've got a lot of guts," she replied, "Thanks, I hope you'll cover me when I can't work" (Shapiro, 143).

For whatever reason, whether it is her criticism of the industry or her political involvement, there seems to be little doubt that Hollywood refused to treat Sarandon as a star long after she had established herself as meriting that designation. Marc Shapiro enumerates a list of indignities she has suffered, including being asked to audition for roles that a star would automatically be offered, not being paid the kind of money top-echelon actresses receive, being cast in roles only after they had been turned down by two or three other stars, being asked to commit to a film even though she had only been shown an early draft of a script that producers promised would be rewritten to expand her role, and being offered supporting roles in films dominated by male stars (24–25, 138). Sarandon has said, "I was always called in to make something more of a part that was lacking in at least two dimensions. I'd been in a lot of situations that weren't particularly respectful and where I wasn't treated very well" (Shapiro, 126).

Sarandon's commitment to her family also has hurt the development of her later career. She took off an average of eighteen months after the birth of each of her three children, turned down roles so that she would not have to leave her family (Shapiro, 25, 176), and tried to alternate with Robbins working on film projects so that at least one of them would be at home with their children (Grundmann and Lucia). According to Sarandon, "My kids are so much more interesting than most of the scripts that I read that it's certainly not even tempting to spend more time chasing more work" (Shapiro, 177).

The slow progression and troubled nature of Sarandon's career, however, obscures its other most important aspect: its longevity. The fact that, despite the many obstacles enumerated here, Sarandon has been working within the movie industry for over thirty years suggests some career design on her part, her belief in fortuitous circumstance aside. As Joel Schomacher says, "She is a big star. Many actors who have had much hotter launches than Susan didn't last as long as she has. Which tells you something about how smart she is" (Shapiro, 26). Even though Sarandon has always presented herself as a natural talent rather than a hard worker, Alan Lovell singles out her slow career development as an indication that Hollywood stardom results not so much from innate talent or good fortune as from hard work and determination (92). I would argue, however, that Sarandon's career perhaps says more about how difficult it is for an actress who is not entirely accepted by the Hollywood industry to reach star status. As a female star who has bucked the Hollywood system, still reached the status of a major star, and maintained this status into her fifties when almost all Hollywood actresses suffer a crippling, if not fatal, career decline, Sarandon is an inspirational figure.

The Susan Sarandon Image

Susan Sarandon's image is composed of only two major image clusters: one centered on her sexuality and the other on her rebelliousness; the two clusters are linked under the umbrella of unconventionality. Although the combination of these two qualities is not necessarily unique in terms of female star images, what is particularly interesting is the transformation of Sarandon's image from the sexual rebellion of her early years to the political and social activism of her later life. Also significant is the combination of sexuality with intelligence that has dominated her persona.

Sexuality: "A Thinking Man's Object of Desire" (Smith)

As Alan Lovell points out, the combination of sexuality and intelligence in Sarandon's image lexicon is based on a very selective reading of her films (93), but then a selective reading of a star's films, complemented by extratextual material, is often exactly the foundation upon which an image is based. Sarandon's early films strongly associate her with earthy sexuality and youthful incredulity and not really with intelligence at all. One would be hard put to claim keen intelligence for the characters she plays in *Joe*, *The Rocky Horror Picture Show*, *Pretty Baby*, and *Atlantic City*, although in moving from one film to the next, each character seems to be more intelligent than the last. In these early films, however, Sarandon's large eyes, accompanied by a rather blank, open-mouthed stare, give her characters a spacey, sex kittenish appearance that does not mesh well with her later reputation for intelligence. It was her role in *Bull Durham* that transformed her from spacey sex kitten to the "hot but smart" woman with an "attitude" who would become Susan Sarandon, the star.

Sarandon is notorious for the amount of nudity she has done in her films. Lovell even proposes that she "has probably appeared nude more than any other actress of her age and generation" and adds, "This might appear odd for an actress who is keenly aware of the position of women in the movies and society" (105). Odd it might be, but Sarandon's penchant for screen nudity certainly fits well with—and, in fact, did much to establish—the highly sexualized component of her image. In 1981, her infamous topless scenes even led *Playboy Magazine* to grant her the dubious distinction of having the "celebrity breasts of the summer" (Dreifus, 64). In fact, the first scene she did in her first film, *Joe*, required that she remove her clothes and jump into a bathtub with her coactor. In *Pretty Baby*, her character poses topless for a photographer (Keith Caradine) as she seductively lies on a divan and strokes the nipples of her breasts with her moistened finger to make them more photogenic. *Atlantic City* opens with what is commonly referred to as her infamous "lemon scene" in which Burt Lancaster's elderly character watches voyeuristically through an open window as Sarandon rubs her shoulders and breasts with a lemon, ostensibly to remove the fish smell on her skin from her job as a waitress in a casino restaurant.

Similarly, *White Palace* contains an explicit sex scene that includes the vivid portrayal of Sarandon's character performing oral sex, and *Bull Durham* includes a steamy sex scene between Sarandon and Kevin Costner.

In *The Hunger*, Sarandon engages in what has come to be regarded as a classic lesbian nude sex scene with Catherine Deneuve (although it is really only Sarandon's nude body that is shown). This scene's steamy passion gave Sarandon and Deneuve almost immediate cult status as lesbian icons.

In interviews, Sarandon has downplayed her reputation as a diva of cinematic nudity and, in accord with her reputation for intelligence, has waxed philosophically about the deeper significance of her sexually charged performances. About winning the award for the best celebrity breasts, she quipped, "My breasts are highly overrated …. The nicest thing I've ever heard about my breasts was said to me by a fan: 'You have the kind of breasts I could take home to my mother'" (Dreifus, 64). She has said, "I've never been incredibly comfortable just walking around naked, and I think that nipples upstage you anyway so no one's listening to anything you're saying for the first fifteen seconds, so why would you do it, right?" (Lipton). She has also criticized sex scenes that are "not scripted … [and] have no purpose" (Dreifus, 64), and she has proposed, "I've never done nude scenes that are just generalized groping and heavy breathing while trying to hide behind the other person's body" (Goldman).

According to Sarandon, the best sex scenes that she has done do not really focus on eroticism, but on the romantic relationships involved. For instance, about *The Hunger* she has said,

> Doing a love scene, whether it's with a man or a woman, in front of a room full of people, for three or four days is probably the most unnatural thing you could do. Forget about the gender of the person you're with …. When you're doing a scene that's sexual, what's interesting is what leads up to it and what happens afterward. Everybody kinda knows what's going on in between, and there's not that many variations on that that you can believe.[20]

She singles out her sex scene with Kevin Costner in *Bull Durham* as particularly effective because it "is like a real friendship kind of sexuality. I'm not naked. It's hot because [Costner's character] and I really like each other. And we're friends as well as lovers."[21] On the other hand, she has ridiculed her infamous "lemon scene" in *Atlantic City*, saying, "God knows how that fish smell ever got to my breasts, but okay …. It's a European thing" (Lipton) and "Anyone who would rub lemons on her chest is completely insane" (Dreifus, 64). She also complained that, as a result of the scene's notoriety, for a long time afterwards she kept getting lemons sent to her in the mail by fans (Dreifus, 64).

Although Sarandon has at times downplayed the glamorous sexual component of her image, she expressed genuine dismay when she had to play Sister Helen Prejean in *Dead Man Walking* with an unflattering hairstyle and no make-up. She said of the role, "I've gone all the way to the other end of the sexual spectrum. I hope I can come back" (Shapiro, 184). The real Sister Helen, on whose memoir the film is based, told a reporter that she heard Sarandon cried when she first saw how she looked in the part.[22] Sarandon later would admit that after *Dead Man Walking* she jumped at the opportunity to play an ageing movie star in *Twilight* because she "was looking for a role where I would wear make-up and fuck-me pumps, and have breasts again" (Johnston).

In spite of the strong sexual component to her image, Sarandon has never been regarded as having attained a stardom that is primarily based on her sexuality because, within her image lexicon, a duality developed between sexuality and intelligence that became central to her persona. In interviews and in personal appearances, Sarandon consistently presents herself as a mix of tough-minded independence, keen perception, and earthy sexiness. When asked by *Rolling Stone Magazine*'s interviewer how she wanted to be photographed, she said she would like a cardboard cutout of herself in "something slinky, something very sexy" with the real Sarandon holding the cutout and looking out from behind. She then elaborated on her reasoning: "I have no objection to being sexual—I hope you make me look great—but I'd also like to have people feel that I don't take myself incredibly seriously and that I have some sense of irony and am intelligent—however you can figure that out" (Wadler, 39).

Sarandon is perhaps best characterized as a sex symbol with "an attitude." Kevin Costner has called her the "Lauren Bacall of her generation. She's a throwback to the old actresses—feminine but tough" (Dreifus, 64). Promoting her reputation for sexual candor, what has been called her "ballsy, don't-give-a-shit attitude" (Shapiro, 54), Sarandon is, for instance, very apt to spice her interview comments with sexual innuendoes. She offered this description of working in European films: "It's like a woman making love to another woman. If you do a movie in Europe and it doesn't work, nobody holds it against you."[23] Explaining the distinction between film and theater, she likened it to the difference between making love and masturbation and compared making a film to having an orgasm: "And you know it's like any profession. There's good ones [film-making experiences] and there's bad ones and if the shoot goes smoothly doesn't mean the movie's going to be any good ... It's like the orgasm" (Lipton).

Sarandon has also established herself as the poster girl for middle-aged female sexuality, claiming that she does not mind getting older (Shapiro, 197) and that her ambition is to be "the world's oldest actress" (Smith). She has repeatedly been on lists of Hollywood's sexiest women over forty and has said that she would prefer to let herself age naturally without resorting to cosmetic surgery. She claims to be afraid a face lift would "terrify" her children and says she actually prefers her more mature looks: "Nowadays, I think I look lived-in. When I was younger, I looked blank. Just blank, interchangeable with other people. Now I don't think there's anybody who looks like me" (Shapiro, 147). She also pointed out, however, that even in middle age, she could still fit into the skin-tight red dress that she wore to audition for *Bull Durham*.

As a mature actress, Sarandon seems to have chosen roles in films like *The Banger Sisters, Cradle Will Rock, Illuminata,* and *Twilight* to solidify her image as the epitome of the sexy older woman. She has said, "And I've recently been hearing from other actresses—some maybe seven to ten years younger than me—who say, 'I'm looking to you as the person who's going to say my career can continue into my fifties with interesting parts.'"[24] Her long-standing relationship with Robbins, who is twelve years her junior, coupled with her roles in older woman–younger man romances, such as *Bull Durham, White Palace,* and *Earthly Possessions,* has contributed greatly to her image as a mature female sex symbol. Sarandon has said, "They keep paying me to jump into the sack with these guys. There is no reason why a middle-aged woman shouldn't have the same needs as a middle-aged man. It's brave of some movie-makers to head in that direction. I'm game" (Shapiro, 231).

Rebelliousness: "I just naturally have a
problem with institutionalized anything."

Throughout her career, Sarandon has had a reputation for unconventionality. When asked if she could relate to the rebel image the media has created for her, she proposed, "I think it's true … for better or worse, I don't have a good sense of what's 'normal.'"[25] After the breakup of her first marriage and before her relationship with Robbins, she was reputed to lead what she herself called a "pretty adventurous lifestyle."[26] She became romantically involved with a long list of actors and directors with whom she worked: French director Louis Malle; Italian director Franco Amurri, with whom she had a daughter outside of wedlock; David Bowie; the considerably younger Sean Penn; Christopher Walken; Kevin Kline; playwright Tom Noonan, while she was performing in his off-Broadway play; Don Johnson; and finally Tim Robbins. She also has expressed a cavalier attitude toward her first marriage and a disdain for the marital institution. When asked after their divorce to describe her marriage to Chris Sarandon, she said,

> We decided it would make things easier for everybody if we got married. I didn't think that much about it. The way I saw it, we would just renew every year. It was just one of those things you did for other people to make them comfortable. To my way of thinking, sex and love just went together (Shapiro, 46).

In response to many inquiries over the years about her relationship with Robbins, she has maintained: "I believe in love and commitment but not in marriage. Marriage may do something for lawyers and mothers but not for husbands and wives" (Shapiro, 27). She told another interviewer, "I just naturally have a problem with institutionalized anything."[27]

Yet Sarandon seems to have formed what she describes as a perfect companionate romantic partnership with Robbins. When rumors circulated during the shooting of *Dead Man Walking* that they were experiencing relationship problems, Sarandon countered by declaring passionately, "I've always been committed to Tim's whole being. It's a sexual, intellectual, emotional relationship. I've loved him since we met on *Bull Durham* and I love him more since *Dead Man Walking*" (Hobson). Although they live in Greenwich Village, which many would see as a bastion of unconventionality, the two stars have always maintained that they live a perfectly normal family life with their two sons and Sarandon's daughter. Sarandon, who was diagnosed with endometriosis in 1983 and thought for several years that she would be unable to have children, has repeatedly sung the praises of motherhood: "For me motherhood gives your life a bigger meaning. You can have your career and that's incredibly satisfying, but there's something to be said about watching those little lives that come through you turn out the way they turn out."[28]

Like Meryl Streep, Sarandon tries to have her career interfere as little as possible with her family responsibilities. She has even said that she is jealous of Streep, whom she characterizes as a "superwoman" with a "perfect life ... so pulled together compared with most of the rest of ours—so smooth." Yet Sarandon's attitude to her family life is very different from Streep's. What Sarandon admires about Streep is not really her dedication to her family, a dedication that Sarandon clearly shares, but rather that even with this dedication, Streep still manages to have the "pick of the best parts" (Dreifus, 80), or at least she did at the height of her career. Although Sarandon has given up roles to be in what she has called "domestic paradise" with her children during the school year (Shapiro, 172), she also emphasizes the importance for a woman of having her children later in life so that she can first establish a career. She has said, "I became a mother really late, and I had done more than enough of everything that I needed to do beforehand, and so I wasn't sacrificing anything."[29]

Figure 5.1 Susan Sarandon speaking at a prochoice rally. Sarandon's political activism has challenged Hollywood's taboo on actors' using their celebrity to propagate their political views, and she has said that her career has suffered for it. (Reproduced with permission of Corbis.)

Sarandon's image as a rebel extends beyond her personal life to her political and social activism. Although she has really done only a handful of overtly political roles, Sarandon has a reputation as "a political actress" largely because of her support for a wide range of causes and her willingness to use her celebrity to promote them. Her wide spectrum of political activities includes participating in rallies, protests, and marches; speaking at political events; donating her time to charitable activities; spearheading organizations; lobbying Congress; traveling for political causes; narrating political documentaries; and using personal appearances and celebrity interviews to express her political views.

Her activist spectrum is extensive and involves, to name only some of the most notable of her causes, support for

- gun control
- gay rights
- abortion rights
- food relief for underdeveloped countries
- protection of endangered wildlife
- first amendment rights
- funding for the National Endowment for the Arts
- food for the homeless and aged

- supplies for hurricane victims
- nontraditional political candidates
- AIDS funding.

She opposes corporate monopolies, U.S. policy in Nicaragua, and the war in Iraq.

Sarandon is a founding member of MADRE, an organization dedicated to making U.S. women aware of the situation in Nicaragua, and a member of the Creative Coalition fighting reduced NEA funding. In 2000, she was appointed a Special Representative for the United Nations Children's Fund and traveled to India and Tanzania to promote UNICEF-sponsored programs. Earlier in 1984, she had traveled with MADRE to bring milk and baby food to needy mothers in Nicaragua and contracted typhoid fever as a result of the trip (Shapiro, 105–106).

Sarandon has frequently explained why she feels justified in using her notoriety as a political forum:

> As a celebrity who has access to the media, I think you have certain responsibilities. I have enormous respect for the decency of humankind and I believe that if people had information they would behave differently, you know, so I have access to information that a lot of people don't have and what am I going to do with that? So I'm kind of a reluctant flashlight (Lipton).

Sarandon perhaps best summed up her political activism, as well as her entire image, when she was asked by an interviewer to describe herself: "That I am somebody who feels passionately about feeling passionately ... I feel that political commitment can save us all" (Dreifus, 80).

Approach to Acting: "An Organic Actress"

Over the years, Susan Sarandon has outlined her views on acting more thoroughly than most actresses. She characterizes herself first and foremost as "an organic actress," someone who lacks formal training and works from a strong sense of intuition, which she describes as "finding out what I have in common with the character in terms of emotional life, motivation, background, and going on from there."[30] She says she got her training "on the job" and especially credits as essential her work in the television soap operas *A World Apart* and *Search for Tomorrow* in the early 1970s. She found acting in soaps applicable to film and theater acting "because basically you're performing live, but you're dealing with all this equipment" (Lipton). Although she lauds this early experience, Sarandon describes her approach to creating a scene as instinctive: "I just try to be there and be open and not push too much to have something happen that's not really happening. It helps when you have another actor who's giving you what you need. And then it's just praying that something will happen ..." (Smith).

Throughout her career, Sarandon has consistently characterized acting as "not really that complicated" and as a way "to have a good time" (Chaudhuri; Johnston). She also says rather contradictorily that what really attracted her to acting is its challenge:

> It's impossible to get it right, so acting becomes addictive. Every time I see one of my performances, there's always something I think I could have done clearer, better, faster. When a film is finished, you see, in hindsight, what it was really about. When you see it you think, "Wow, I was on the right track with that, I wish I had been braver. I wish I had been committed 100% to that mistake" (Grundmann and Lucia).

In accord with her self-conception as an instinctive actress, Sarandon feels she accomplishes the most when she approaches a scene with no set preparation: "I do know that the most interesting actors are people who take chances. I do my best work when I don't have the faintest idea what I'm going to do—no plan—because I know I'll have to find a way!"[31] Sarandon also calls herself "a money actor" who can only "indicate" in rehearsal what she will do in performance. Her real performance comes only when the cameras are rolling. She sees rehearsal as a time when actors need "to sniff around and get a common language" and "to agree on what you're trying to accomplish in each scene, kind of what the director really wants" (Lipton).

Because she sees the actor as "a vessel for a project," she prefers a director who gives her plenty of guidance and has "a vision," but she also wants a director who is open to actors' creative input. Sarandon seems to be describing as her ideal what is commonly termed an "actor's director," one who concentrates on working with actors rather than on the technical aspects of filmmaking (Smith; Shapiro, 161). She says she works best in a situation in which the director has provided her with "parameters" so that she does not feel she is "in free fall" (Shapiro 76). According to Sarandon, "What a director needs to do and has to do is to create an atmosphere in which the creative process can happen and people feel safe, you know, whatever you have to do to trick yourself ...." (Lipton).

One reason Sarandon acquired her reputation for being difficult on the set is her tendency to complain about the quality of her directors. It is not often that she finds a director who meets her criteria for making actors "feel that everything that you could contribute is just so welcome and so appreciated and so smart," while at the same time providing "a very secure structure within which to explore things, so it's not like everything's all over the place and chaotic" (Smith). Sarandon tells the story about one director who tried to stimulate her performance by slapping her and giving her an onion, rather than just telling her that he wanted her to cry in a scene. Sarandon says she resented him because she felt she was being "approached on the dumbest level" (Smith). On the other hand, she complained about the lack of direction she got as a novice actress from John Avildson on the set of *Joe*. She said he was so unavailable to actors that when she asked him a question concerning her performance, he replied, "Susan, if I thought I would have to talk to you, I wouldn't have hired you" (Shapiro, 52).

Sarandon finds direction so important because she sees the filmmaking process as a personal and a communal experience. She believes an actor must take something on a personal level from a performance, especially in film, because so often one's acting ends up on the cutting room floor (Lipton). What she takes from her acting is a knowledge of human psychology (Lovell, 93). Repeatedly, she has discussed acting as a form of "self-discovery" (Jeffreys) in which the actor experiences a sense of healthy catharsis. By "living those things [through acting] you don't have to live them at home" (Lipton). She describes acting as having "forced" her "to really see and really hear ... to live life in a clearer, ultimately more compassionate way—to be present in my life" (Smith). Associated with this self-discovery is a sense that acting is also a way to understand how others think and feel, "to overcome the narrowness of your vision" (Johnston), and to gain empathy for other people.

Sarandon also describes acting as a way to escape the confines of the self: "The minute you start protecting your ego is when you're in trouble. An actor has to throw all that shit out the window and take a plunge. It may be scary, but I find anything that frightens me to be terribly appealing."[32] Yet acting is not just a means of personal discovery for her; it is very importantly a collaborative experience. She describes the filmmaking process as something that "you have to do in a cooperative group," like "a family of dysfunctional people" or

> ... pioneers going to a land. They know kind of where they want to go, they don't know exactly where they are going, and then they kind of circle their trailers and then try to keep off all the suits and everybody who is trying to ambush them on the way (Lipton).

Because she sees acting as "an exercise in letting go," she confesses to feeling very dependent on other cast and crew members. It is for this reason that she describes shooting *Dead Man Walking* as one of her most satisfying filmmaking experiences because cast and crew all felt they were friends involved in a project to which they were really committed (Lipton).

Like Meryl Streep, Sarandon does not subscribe to any established school of acting. Dan Shapiro says she early gained a reputation in the industry as a raw talent with a slightly unorthodox approach (71–72). For instance, Director Louis Malle said when he directed her in *Atlantic City*:

> One of the things I like about Susan is that she has no system. A lot of actors in this country go through schools where they learn a strictly disciplined, highly intellectual approach—such as The Method—where there's a lot of psychological interpretation. This can cause you to lose a lot of the stamina, the spontaneity, the surprise that is an essential part of acting. Susan reminds me of Jeanne Moreau, who hardly ever reads her lines, even on the night before a scene, because she wants to be completely open before the camera. Susan, too, comes to a role fresh and innocent and flexible.[33]

Because she lacks a systematic approach to her craft, Sarandon's acting has been categorized in widely divergent ways. Allen Lovell says her expressed views on acting place her squarely in the tradition of Stanislavskian naturalism. Indeed, as Lovell points out, in the Stanislavski tradition, she characterizes good acting as listening to the other actors and being open, spontaneous, and fresh, rather than coming to a performance with a set of prepared responses. She also gives her characterizations a strong sense of individuality by avoiding stock mannerisms and inventing responses that seem specific to the character (Lovell, 93). She has said, "If you're not drawing from real life, then all you're doing is rehashing images you've seen in films. Even the image of yourself."[34] Chris Columbus, who directed her in *Stepmom*, uses the terminology of Stanislavskian naturalism to describe Sarandon's creation of her character in the film. He proposes that he could envision no one else playing the role of Jackie because Sarandon was able to "disappear" into her character so completely that she simply "became Jackie."[35]

Despite these aspects of naturalistic performance, Sarandon also possesses many of the qualities of personification commonly associated with Hollywood star acting—a lack of formal training; instinctual, larger than life performances; and a tendency essentially to play herself in each role. Although she has said that she does not see herself as a star, but as a "character actress," Sarandon defines star acting very narrowly as "being glamorous for a living," which she says does not interest her.[36] Yet, as Wayne Wang suggested after directing her in *Anywhere But Here*, Sarandon unquestionably has a "larger than life quality"[37] and she does seem repeatedly to play "characters not unlike herself in many respects— straight-talking, independent women who attain the self-knowledge which enables them to ask questions and take charge of their lives and their sexuality" (Grundmann and Lucia).

Even the progression of her film roles seems to parallel events in her life. Her initial sexualized image coincides with her early reputation as a free spirit who often became involved with her male costars and directors, her older woman–younger man romantic roles parallel her relationship with Tim Robbins, and her later assumption of maternal roles corresponds with her dedication to family life. Her comments about some of the parts she has played also suggest that she feels most comfortable playing characters similar to her off-screen personality. For instance, she describes her role as Michaela Odone in *Lorenzo's Oil* as extremely difficult—not so much because of its emotional content but because the character's "whole personality, the way she speaks, the fact that she's so contained" was very far from herself (Smith).

Although Sarandon does not claim any affiliation with the Method school of acting, she has worked very effectively with actors, such as Christopher Walken and Sean Penn, who are noted for subscribing to its tenets. As Lovell points out, her acting is much too script dependent to be characterized as Method (93); nevertheless, some of the statements she has made about her technique do draw on the Method approach. For instance, she has commented upon her need to be "in the moment" when acting and advocates the use of improvisation to make "something unexpected" happen. She also says that when doing a scene, "you want to personalize it. You have to make every scene very specific, you have to know what it is in the scene that triggers what, depending on what you're going after. Something very specific is triggered and you have to isolate that, and sometimes adding a word helps." She also finds it useful to respond emotionally to another actor by imagining that that actor's character is someone from her real life who "has some emotional resonance for me" (Smith). When performing on the stage in New York in the early 1980s, she was part of a group of actors, including Richard Dreyfuss, Carol Kane, Peter Boyle, and Andre Gregory, many of whom were Method trained, who formed an improvisational acting workshop to develop their technique (Shapiro, 85).

All of this does not indicate that Sarandon belongs to one school or another, but rather that she, like Meryl Streep, draws from a number of schools to form an eclectic style that adheres to no single approach. Her eclecticism led her early in her career to theater as a means of challenging herself and perfecting her technique. In 1972, she debuted on Broadway as Tricia Nixon in Gore Vidal's *An Evening with Richard Nixon and ...*, and after her film career stalled briefly in the early 1980s, she returned to New York to do two off-Broadway plays, *A Coupla White Chicks Sitting Around Talking* in 1981 and *Extremities* in 1982. She has insightfully discussed the differences between film and theater acting, characterizing film acting as much more singular and personal with the actor

> ... working on a little moment, possibly by yourself even, to try to make something work that's not connected to hardly anything. On stage, it's much more relationship and you can tell when you're off .... It's more like life. You've got people there. You have to learn how to give focus, and when something doesn't work, you know it and you have an entire evening either to fall on your face or to build something that really pays off. But in film all you have to do is get it right maybe once, twice, have it happen and even then you're not sure anybody's gonna see it because it depends on whether or not anyone else has the same aesthetic in terms of how it's edited (Lipton).

In spite of her brief forays into theater and made-for-television movies, however, Sarandon has established her stardom almost exclusively on the basis of her work in film. Her acting style is particularly suited to the screen because it is very controlled, precise, and unostentatious. As Tim Robbins explains, "She understands how to go to the heart of a character without resorting to flashy acting" (Shapiro, 180). Like so many contemporary film actresses, Sarandon's acting is very focused on characterization. Her memorable depiction of Annie Savoy in *Bull Durham* early gained her a reputation as an actress who could add substance to characters who seemed on the surface to be stock and predictable. As Ron Shelton pointed out, "Annie could easily be played as a flake ... [but] Susan brought experience and commitment, substance and dignity to the part" (Lovell, 101). Sarandon made a woman who seemed scripted as a stock sexy airhead into "a vibrant character, funny, imaginative, and intelligent, and more than able to hold her own with the two male characters" (Lovell, 101).

Sarandon is a very script-centered actress; her characterizations are primarily based on an intelligent reading of the character as written, effective execution of dialogue, and "a deep understanding of the dramatic context" (Lovell, 104). Lovell points out, for instance, that her performance in *Atlantic City* is particularly effective because Sarandon makes her character's insecurities and anxieties so vivid that she fits perfectly with the "overall antiheroic perspective of the film" (98). Sarandon is also very adept at finding "strong and varied physical movements, gestures, and facial expressions to define the characters she plays" (104). She has even described the actor's job as "to get the little specific things and put them into the structure" (Hobson). Lovell compares two of her early performances in *Atlantic City* and *Bull Durham*. In the former, she plays Sally Matthews, a familiar character type: an ambitious, but romantically naive young woman trying desperately to escape from her small-town background. Yet Sarandon manages to make Sally interesting by using her voice, facial expressions, gestures, and body movements to convey in a "detailed and innovative way [how] she struggles to express and contain her feelings" (Lovell, 96).

In *Bull Durham*, Sarandon uses the way Annie Savoy sits, moves, stands, and gestures to create quite the opposite effect. Annie Savoy is a woman completely comfortable, easy, and confident in her sexuality. Lovell points out that Sarandon uses physical cues to set up the emotional tone of her character in the film's opening scenes and then maintains this tone throughout the film (99). In other films, Sarandon has employed physical cues—not to maintain her character's personality throughout the film, but rather to signal character transformation. For instance, in the opening scenes of *The Witches of Eastwick*, she uses physical awkwardness to show her character's discomfort with her body. Then, to convey her release from sexual repression when she meets Jack Nicholson's devil figure, Sarandon goes into what she has described as "a frenzy" (Smith), exchanging sexually charged looks with Nicholson, assuming a provocative attitude, and seductively slinking about.

Sarandon has also taken roles that proved to be quite physically demanding. She did her own stunts in early films such as *The Great Waldo Pepper,* in which she walked on an airplane wing and drove a car under a low flying prop-plane, and *The Other Side of Midnight*, in which she performed a boating stunt that left her with whiplash and bruises (Burrows, 14). Her most physically demanding role, however, was not in film, but on the stage. Her 1982 off-Broadway stint in the rape-revenge drama *Extremities* had her fighting off a brutal rapist for the whole first act. She stayed in the role for four months and one hundred performances, although she suffered as a result a fractured wrist, several jammed and one broken finger, chipped bones, frequent black eyes, bloody noses, and significant weight loss.

The physicality of Sarandon's performances allows her to impart to her characters an "expressive energy" that gives them an extraordinary dynamism (Lovell, 104). This dynamism comes not just from her physical movements and gestures, but also from her dynamic rendering of dialogue. Sarandon, who has complained that contemporary actors have lost the ability to handle dialogue effectively, seems to give each of her characterizations a distinctive "vocal energy" (Lovell, 100). As Lovell points out, she combines her natural tendency to speak quickly with a line delivery that, through variations of rhythm and volume, makes her words "shaped and pointed so that they have maximum effect."

Lovell concludes that Sarandon's dynamic technique works best when she plays characters who are active, rather than reactive (105); however, I would argue that some of her most impressive acting accomplishments involve the animation she imparts to characters that would otherwise be extremely passive and reactive. Lovell insists, for instance, that one of Sarandon's least interesting performances is the ageing film star Catherine Ames in *Twilight*. He argues that Catherine is "a passive 'iconic' figure" whom Sarandon cannot render dynamic because Catherine's film successes are all behind her (105, note 9). I would argue to the contrary that Sarandon is actually quite effective in the role because she refuses to play Catherine simply as a stereotypical *femme fatale*; instead, she humanizes her by showing how her twisted version of marital fidelity led to her involvement in several murders.

Catherine Ames in *Twilight* is not the only reactive character to whom Sarandon has brought an "expressive energy." Her memorable characterization of Louise in *Thelma & Louise* also falls into this category. In fact, Sarandon says that she learned in *Thelma & Louise* that reactive acting need not be boring:

> In that movie, mainly what I had to do was drive and listen. I had to concentrate on keeping the car in a certain relationship to the camera truck. Geena had all the lines. I was just concentrating on driving and occasionally replying. And somehow that would work. And I realized from that, you can do your best work when you're concentrating on something else (Shapiro, 155).

As Lovell points out, the roles played by Sarandon and Geena Davis in *Thelma & Louise* were extremely demanding because they involved extended dialogue exchanges taking place primarily in the confined spaces of moving cars and hotel rooms, which offered restricted acting opportunities. Sarandon managed to intensify these exchanges by acting with her eyes, using them to register strongly in close-up (Lovell, 101).

Sarandon's Academy Award-winning performance in *Dead Man Walking* is another role that is almost exclusively reactive. Sarandon's characterization is limited to her emotional reactions to other characters' intense suffering. Lovell argues that because the role is reactive, Sarandon is relatively unsuccessful and that her performance won her first Oscar only because the Academy likes to reward noble, suffering heroines, like Sarandon's character Sister Helen Prejean (104). Although I do not deny the Academy's penchant for awarding actors Oscars for the nature of the roles they play rather than for the quality of their performances, Lovell's harsh criticism of Sarandon's performance in *Dead Man Walking* seems unjustified. Sarandon has characterized her role in the film as one of her most challenging. She proposes that Sister Helen was an extremely difficult character to make interesting because she spends most of the movie "just go[ing] around saying, 'I'm so sorry, let's pray.' She's leading you through the more interesting characters, who all have much better hairdos and it's hard to make that work" (Johnston).

In the director's commentary on the DVD version of the film, Tim Robbins discusses extensively the extremely restrictive acting environment in which Sarandon and her costar, Sean Penn, had to construct their performances. Sister Helen's conversations with the imprisoned Matthew Poncelet all took place in confined spaces with very limited props, where the actors were able to use few gestures or bodily movements and were always divided from each other by a grated partition, glass door, or prison bars. Every emotion they wanted to convey had to be communicated through facial expressions. Robbins points out that in spite of these obstacles Sarandon and Penn developed such a strong "chemistry" that he tried to find innovative ways to get them both on screen at the same time. He used a split screen, shots through a grating, and reflections in a glass window to capture their interactions.

Additionally, Robbins explains that Sarandon's performance in the film showed her restraint and generosity as an actress. She was required to play most of her scenes with Penn, whose role of a condemned murderer, according to Robbins, was much more flashy and had greater depth and subtext than Sister Helen's.[38] As Sarandon describes the requirements of her role, "Yes, I had to eliminate myself—my personality, my ego—as much as possible. I tried to become a vessel for the other characters, especially Sean, to pour into."[39] Robbins proposes that Sarandon's refusal to let her ego get in the way of her performance helped to create the chemistry she developed with Penn, who by some accounts employed a "festering, angry Method approach that was making being around the actor uncomfortable both on and off the set" (Shapiro, 183).

Some of Penn's Method acting apparently rubbed off on Sarandon, who seems to have delved very far into her character. Robbins' decision to shoot their scenes chronologically also facilitated his actors' strong identification with their roles. As Sarandon described her experience,

> What helped was taking all of our scenes together and doing them in order, right in the prison. And yet, it was terrifying right then, with each scene building to the next. I just wanted to give Sean all he needed to make his journey. And then it was so strange: I've never had a costar taken off and executed before. After all that intensity, I really felt he was gone (Stoner).

In discussing the process she and Penn used to create their scenes together, Sarandon, like Robbins, emphasized her need to put aside her ego to serve Penn's performance:

> If we had gotten into some kind of ego battle it wouldn't have worked, but we just said at the very beginning, we're not gonna ... we were so right on the same wavelength and he was so generous and completely there and not messing with me in any way (Lipton).

One of the most significant aspects of Sarandon's acting is its extraordinarily auteurist nature. Throughout her career, she has had an enormous creative influence on her films in a wide variety of ways including role choice, shaping roles through performance, influencing directorial decisions, and, recently, even assuming the role of producer. Gavin Smith calls Sarandon "a great actress who lacked great roles"; certainly her haphazard process of role selection and, at times, unfortunate role choice have placed her in some terrible films. Her tendency to reject safer projects for riskier choices, however, also allowed her to play a wide range of different characters and to take roles in films that have a distinct relationship to the historical period in which they were made.

Her character in *Thelma & Louise* represents the quintessential Sarandon role. It has also had a particular significance for female viewers because it so clearly reflects debates about contemporary gender issues. Louise fits perfectly with what Sarandon has described as her ideal role; she is a "well-rounded woman who gets to change in some way, has a sense of humor, and doesn't have to deny her intelligence or her sexuality" (Grundmann and Lucia). As Lovell points out, Louise represents a combination of Sarandon's previously most successful roles: Sally Matthews in *Atlantic City*, Annie Savoy in *Bull Durham*, and Nora Baker in *White Palace* (92). A larger than life iconic figure of feminist rebellion, Louise is one of several Sarandon roles in what she has labeled

Watershed Films. Movies that are controversial. They all hit very specific political and social changes that I've gone through. I think you choose projects to come into your life. And in doing so, in being true to yourself, it reflects what's going on for yourself and a lot of people (Shapiro, 234).

Other Sarandon films, including *Joe*, *The Rocky Horror Picture Show*, *Pretty Baby*, *White Palace*, *Lorenzo's Oil*, and *Dead Man Walking*, like *Thelma & Louise*, relate strongly to cultural issues prominent at the time of their release and as a result caused a certain amount of controversy when they came out.

Although Sarandon has said that her role choice is not determined by politics,[40] she has been drawn, especially later in her career, to films with sociopolitical significance. She says the only films she admires are those that "moved me, challenged my perspective, which is what I think film should do" (Grundmann and Lucia). She also proposes,

And if there's somebody that's trying to leave an abusive relationship, and they see *Thelma & Louise*, and they get out, I'm happy about that, you know? And if any of the movies that I do make people have conversations after they leave the theater, then I think that's great (DiClementi).

In particular, Sarandon has gravitated in her later career toward films that address social issues, with distinctly feminist implications. She spent the decade of the 1990s starring primarily in maternal roles, attempting, as she sees it, to reinvent the contemporary perception of motherhood (Shapiro, 207):

I'll make a career to do every kind of mother there is. No one's tapped into this category because of the taboo. Most of the mothers we've seen on the screen have been one-dimensional, sappy, stand-by-your-man moms. Once you crossed that line, there was no turning back. You don't go to bed with someone as a mother.[41]

Sarandon has discussed this stereotypical cinematic presentation of motherhood in distinctly feminist terms, arguing that it represents yet "another way of compartmentalizing women—you have your slut, your mother, your ice princess who's smart—but you can't be a mother who has a brain and also has fun" (Grundmann and Lucia).

Sarandon has played a wide variety of mother roles, beginning well before she entered into her 1990s series of maternal melodramas. They started very early in her career with *Pretty Baby*, a film that was condemned on feminist grounds as offering a voyeuristic treatment of female prostitution and childhood sexuality. Sarandon says she was attacked in particular for doing the film and was repeatedly asked, "How could you be a hooker and a feminist?" Sarandon argues, however, that the film contained a feminist message of female empowerment: "Just because I wore frilly lingerie and was sexy doesn't mean she [her character] wasn't feminist. She turned her life around and went back for her kid."[42] Since *Pretty Baby*, which Sarandon did when she was only thirty-two years old, she has portrayed a remarkable range of mother figures, including failed or irresponsible mothers in *White Palace, The Client, Anywhere But Here,* and *Iggy Goes Down;* devoted mothers in *Lorenzo's Oil, Safe Passage,* and *Little Women;* a dying mother in *Stepmom;* an ex-rock-group-roadie mother in *The Banger Sisters;* and pseudomother figures in *The Client* and *Dead Man Walking.*

That this wide variety of mother roles actually represents an innovation in the cinematic presentation of women, as Sarandon suggests it does, is much less certain. Elaine Rapping, for instance, regards Sarandon's mother series as a reaction to the subversiveness of *Thelma & Louise,* relegating Sarandon "to the sentimental sidelines" after she had made a film like *Thelma & Louise* that actually "let a grown woman loose on the screen." Rapping attacks Sarandon for playing "martyr-like mothers" in *Lorenzo's Oil, Safe Passage,* and *Little Women* and an "over-the-hill, recovering-alcoholic mother substitute" in *The Client.* She points out that these roles are devoid of any hint of sexuality and each becomes "paler, more one-dimensional, and more maternally sacrificing and virtuous than the last." Rapping singles out Sarandon's role as Marmee in *Little Women* for particular disdain, proposing that "the smug, humorless political correctness of every smarmy line she uttered made [Rapping] cringe on behalf of progressive women everywhere."[43]

Writing in 1995, Rapping focused on Sarandon's earlier mother roles; however, those Sarandon played in the late 1990s can also be seen as regressive in terms of what they say to female viewers. In *Dead Man Walking,* Sister Helen extends unconditional love to a man who committed a brutal rape and murder. *Stepmom,* which contains Sarandon's next maternal role, is a particular disappointment because, as its executive producer, she nurtured the project for years through extensive script changes, was heavily involved in creative decisions, and seems largely responsible for finally getting the film made. She speaks of it glowingly as an innovative attempt to reconceive the melodrama of the dying mother by making it "a life-affirming film rather than one that was sad and weepy" (Shapiro, 201). Sarandon sees the film as progressive because it was headlined by two female stars (Sarandon and Julia Roberts), something that, in promoting the film, she was quick to point out is very rare in Hollywood. Sarandon also liked the film because the two female characters are not divided into a "clear heroine and bad guy. I fought very hard for that. It would have been a different movie if it had just been me falling apart" (Shapiro, 208).

In spite of these progressive features, one still wishes that *Stepmom* were a better movie. Reviewers condemned it, and I think rightly so, as a backlash women's "weepie." Although Sarandon's and Roberts' performances were praised, critics pointed out that the film mythologizes Sarandon's stay-at-home mom as a dying earth-mother and portrays Roberts' professional woman as so eager to assume this earth-mother role that she will jettison her career at a moment's notice. Sarandon's attempt to avoid the weepie aspects of the maternal melodrama also seems to have failed miserably. The film contains a maudlin reconciliation scene between Sarandon and Roberts in which Sarandon's dying character (Jackie) tearfully awards her children to her former husband's new girlfriend and two gut-wrenching farewell scenes in which Jackie says goodbye to each of her children separately, giving them hand-made Christmas parting gifts. Sarandon's proposing that a film containing such scenes avoids the trap of presenting motherhood as "sad and weepy" is really quite remarkable.

Sarandon's auteurism extends beyond her role choice and her attempts to shape characters through performance. By making extensive suggestions for script changes and character reformulations, she has had an enormous amount of creative input on her films. As Lovell points out, because Sarandon's acting is so dependent on the script, throughout her career she has always asked for script changes if she feels a scene is not working (93). She has also gone off in her own direction in shaping a character if she believes the script is inadequate or that her director is not providing sufficient guidance. She has said, "I like to contribute, to make suggestions when I work. I don't like somebody saying, 'Just trust me, rip off your sweater, walk three steps backwards, and stand on your head, and it'll be perfect.' I want to understand what I'm doing and why" (Pachero, 34).

This attitude helped gain her the reputation for being difficult, but it also allowed her to engage in remarkably auteurist acting. Examples of her creative input into her films extend all the way back to her first film. She says that, when she was asked to cry in *Joe,* she improvised a line of dialogue that was kept in the film to provide the motivation she felt her character lacked (Shapiro, 52). When Louis Malle needed a screenwriter for a quick script rewrite for *Atlantic City,* Sarandon claims it was she who proposed John Guare, and then when Guare's script converted her character into a "kind of quasihooker," she fought for changes (Wadler). In *The Hunger,* she takes credit for reconstructing her sex scene with Catherine Deneuve. She says she fought against appearing to be drunk during the scene because she felt that suggested she was a "victim" who was merely "taken" by Deneuve's character. She also objected that the scene seemed to be "apologizing for the [lesbian] sex." For the sex to be convincing, she felt it needed a prelude: "So I constructed a little scene when I spilled something on my blouse and handed it to Catherine; she handed me something to put on and that was the first time we touched" (Dreifus, 80).

Sarandon also made significant artistic contributions to *Bull Durham*. Near the end of the original script, Annie was supposed to confess to Kevin Costner's character that her Southern accent was phony. Sarandon objected that this confession of deceit would destroy the integrity she had worked so hard to give Annie's character. Honoring her objections, director Ron Shelton asked Sarandon and Costner to improvise the confession scene instead of performing it as written, and then Shelton rewrote it based on their improvisation (Smith).

Sarandon's contributions to *Thelma & Louise* are extensive. She says simply, "Ridley [Scott, the film's director] and I fought about things. We changed scenes" (Shapiro, 153). If Sarandon's account is correct, they changed many scenes. First of all, Sarandon says that she only took the part because Scott met her demand that the ending not be changed: "The first thing I demanded from the director was that I die in the last scene. I didn't want the movie to end with me in Club Med. Once he assured me I was definitely on the death list, I accepted the part" (Shapiro, 152). She also demanded other changes. She insisted that, in packing for the trip, Louise should show her meticulousness by putting her belongings in ziplock bags, that the women had to get progressively more dirty as they moved along down the road to their final doom, that at some point her character would exchange her jewelry with an old man for his dirty hat, that Louise should stop and have a pensive moment in the middle of the desert, and that it would be inappropriate for Louise to have a love scene with her boyfriend, Jimmy, after she has just shot a man:

> Originally in the script they were supposed to do a little marriage ceremony and sing songs and fuck, and I felt it was just so unrealistic. Not only would the film lose some of its tension, but also a woman who's just killed somebody because she's remembering having been raped—it's pretty hard to have sex under the circumstances and have it be great. Somehow that would cost us a lot of credibility (Lovell, 93–94).

Sarandon also says she persuaded Scott not to have Geena Davis do a topless scene in the film. As Davis tells the story,

> I thought this was a bad idea but I didn't say so. We broke for lunch and I ran over to Susan and said, "What am I going to do? Ridley wants me to take my shirt off in this scene." She said, "Oh for heaven's sake, Ridley, Geena is not going to take her shirt off in this scene." He said, "Okay, okay" (Shapiro, 154).

In addition to insisting that she and Davis die in the end, Sarandon says, "I also kissed her, which nobody expected" (Lipton). Sarandon confesses that there was some question about whether or not to reshoot the scene to eliminate the kiss, which has, in fact, served as support for lesbian readings of the film[44]: "They weren't sure about me kissing Geena at the end, because of the gay thing, but the sun was setting, we had to finish it in two takes, so I knew they'd have to go with it" (Chaudhuri).

Sarandon was even more forceful in demanding script changes in *The Client*. She said that, when she first read the script, she found "huge holes" in it and insisted on changes to make her character more active (Shapiro, 177; Jerome). Reputedly, Joel Schumacher wanted her so badly for the film that he begged her on his bended knees as they were having lunch in a New York restaurant to take the part. He then allowed her so much artistic

Figure 5.2 Susan Sarandon, Sean Penn, and Director Tim Robbins on the set of *Dead Man Walking* (1995). Sarandon had considerable influence on the making of the film in terms of auteurist acting with Penn and working closely with Robbins to develop the project. (Reproduced with permission of Corbis.)

input into the film that she told the press that she was afraid it would result in an unfocused self-indulgent performance (Shapiro, 176–177).

Sarandon also had considerable influence on Tim Robbins' screenwriting and directing efforts in *Dead Man Walking*. She was the first to read Sister Helen Prejean's memoir and to meet with her. She then persuaded Robbins to do the film (Shapiro, 178–179). When he was reluctant to drop his pet project, *The Cradle Will Rock*, Sarandon says she had a "breakdown" with him on Seventh Avenue and insisted that he begin writing the Prejean adaptation. She also says she was the one who suggested Sean Penn as her costar (Lipton). She and Penn then worked together in a way that is a perfect example of auteurist acting:

> The other great thing about Sean, of course, is that he's a writer and director himself and each time we would get a scene out of the way we would see that there would be more that we could pare down in the next one because we'd accomplished whatever it was. Besides the fact that we didn't have any props and we couldn't move, it came from trying to make it very pared down and pure (Lipton).

Sarandon has shaped roles considerably through performance in other films as well. The most notable example is *The Witches of Eastwick*. As noted earlier, Sarandon came to the set of that film believing she had the lead part only to find out that she had been relegated to what she described as a "nonexistent" role. In discussing her character, she says:

> She had the one scene in the beginning and then she disappeared; nobody knew what happened to her. When we started filming there was no part. Since there was no through-line we could agree on—there was no through-line for my character, it didn't exist in the script—my way of dealing with that was to never read the script, never read all these new pages that were coming in all the time, get there in the morning and try to make each scene work, because I knew they didn't have the faintest idea what they were doing with my character .... I just tried to come up with ideas for each scene to make things work (Smith).

Given that Sarandon seemed to have little in the script upon which to base her character and that she felt very alienated from director George Miller and the film's producers, what she accomplished in *Witches* is astounding. Compared to the film's two other female stars, Cher and Michelle Pfeiffer, Sarandon is the only one whose performance does not get swallowed up by Jack Nicholson's. Although they spent most of their time lauding Nicholson's flamboyant star turn, many reviewers did find time to praise

Sarandon for effectively constructing her character's transformation from a drab repressed cellist to a seductive devil's mistress. Although just after the film was released, Sarandon told the press that in order to keep "from sobbing and feeling humiliated" during filming she had to "sever whatever ego involvement was there," later she would say: "I'm actually very proud of what I did in that movie" (Shapiro, 124; Lipton).

Interestingly, in spite of the creative input she has put into her films, Sarandon has expressed no desire to direct:

> It's tough to direct. You need an incredible amount of diplomacy and stamina and patience with the studio and certain other attributes that I don't, at the moment, have. The directing part of it I like, but not dealing with the studio. I would produce something that I was going to do, because that's the fun of it (Moynihan and Warhol).

Perhaps, she feels that by combining her auteurist acting with her newly acquired role as executive producer she can place her artistic stamp on her films without assuming directorial control.

Susan Sarandon: Actress and Image

In spite of the fact that Susan Sarandon has done numerous films in which she has allowed herself to be objectified in scenes involving graphic sexuality and nudity, her image nevertheless has decidedly feminist implications and a progressive social significance. The combination of sexuality and intelligence that is so prominent in her image is progressive in that it reconciles feminism with femininity. *Thelma & Louise* is crucial to this reconciliation. The film has gained a well-deserved reputation as a contemporary Hollywood feminist classic and alone would place Sarandon within the pantheon of cinematic feminist icons. Other films, such as *The Hunger, Bull Durham, White Palace, Little Women,* and *Dead Man Walking,* have contributed further to Sarandon's iconic feminist status.

Sarandon's extrafilmic image also contains several progressive elements. Her long-standing companionate relationship with the considerably younger Tim Robbins, her rejection of conventional marriage, and her combination of a thriving acting career with her much publicized dedication to her family present a progressive amalgam of unconventionality, careerism, and family values. Her advocacy of the vibrancy, sexuality, and employability of women over forty also has progressive connotations. Her current project to reconstruct film images of motherhood speaks of her determination to refashion roles for mature actresses. Another progressive aspect of Sarandon's image is her willingness to use her celebrity to promote political and social causes. She sees her role as an actress from an activist perspective: "When you make a film, you have a responsibility to not keep strengthening stereotypes that are unjust and that encourage racism and sexism. You have an opportunity to give people a basis to start overcoming those destructive isms. The whole point is to question and challenge the system" (Fuller).

Sarandon's activism involves a very auteurist approach to acting. Through role choice, developing characters through performance, engineering script changes, influencing her directors' decisions, and entering the field of executive producing, Sarandon has had some of the most significant creative input on her films of any contemporary Hollywood actress. Starting as a featured actress in roles that were always secondary to the film's male star, Sarandon eventually established herself with *Thelma & Louise* and *The Client* as a female star who could carry a film, a position held by only a handful of actresses. Sarandon's career has, in fact, been very influential in moving other female stars into marquee roles. As many critics have pointed out, *Thelma & Louise* proved that a film headlined by two female stars could be a major box office success. As noted earlier, in executive producing *Stepmom*, Sarandon identified as one of her main goals the development of a star vehicle with two strong female leading roles, a great rarity in Hollywood films (Shapiro, 201). She has advocated and seems to practice a grassroots approach to bringing about change for women in the industry:

> I don't think the studio system is going to do anything unless it is going to prove to be commercial. I don't know that there are very many women executives out there who haven't gotten where they've gotten by playing the game the way the guys play it. But I think that finding your passion and writing about something you really care about is going to be the only way things are going to change. And hire me! (Lipton)

This is not to say that Sarandon is a paragon of progressivity. What is so interesting about her celebrity is that it can combine such a high degree of the progressive and regressive at the same time. The strong emphasis on sexuality in her image unquestionably promotes the exploitation of the female star as sexual spectacle. Films such as *Pretty Baby, Atlantic City,* and *White Palace* do make important statements about the connection between gender and class as sources of women's victimization, but audiences will more likely remember the working-class characters that Sarandon so effectively creates in these films for their graphic displays of female sexuality rather than for their social significance. In addition, Sarandon's activism is certainly impressive in terms of the depth and range of her conviction, but press releases too often describe her as extreme, radical, or far left. As a result, her activist work can too easily be dismissed as the ravings of a zealot rather than the thoughtful protests of a committed reformer.

Perhaps the most distressing aspect of Sarandon's image is her ambivalent relationship to feminism, which she claims to reject, although she strongly advocates many of its tenets. In numerous statements, she has taken pains to disassociate herself from feminist ideas. In one interview she characterized a discussion of her feminism as "so boooring" (Pachero, 35). She has proposed, "I don't have the faintest idea what feminism is now," suggesting that at some point in the past she may have understood it, but that feminism has moved far beyond her comprehension. When asked if she has read any feminist works, she stated unequivocally that she had not, and she has on several occasions demonstrated her very limited conception of what feminism actually is.

For instance, she has said, "I find that the label feminist is so self-defeating, because most people tend to think of feminists as strident, self-serving, and antimale, and that's not what it should be about" (Fuller). If she had read any of the feminist books that she is so quick to disavow, she would know that it not only should not be about this, but that feminism *is* not about this. She has argued that she sees herself as a humanist rather than a feminist, offering the conventional argument that feminism fails to be all inclusive:

> I consider myself a humanist—only because if you label yourself a feminist at this point in time, most people are so defensive that you can't accomplish anything. Surely if you're a humanist it encompasses everything that is feminist. People want to call me a feminist because I'm strong and I'm a woman who has some opinions. I certainly wouldn't go against it, but it's become a very divisive term—why not go for something broader? I don't disown the feminist movement, but I'm into something that encompasses the rights of men, the rights of children, the rights of gays. I think it's time for human rights (Grundmann and Lucia).

Of course, if Sarandon knew more about feminism, she would know that it does work for the protection of all human rights.

Sarandon has even refused to accept characterizations of her films as feminist. This issue came up repeatedly in regard to *Thelma & Louise*, which many critics characterized as a feminist manifesto. Sarandon adamantly fought that label, making comments that demonstrate conclusively that she indeed does not know what feminism means now, or really what it has ever meant. Sarandon suggested that *Thelma & Louise* is not a feminist film because it is "very entertaining"—not "a movie that tells people what to think," and because it deals with two women who "are still concerned about the guys in their lives" (Fuller). Thus, she seems to believe that films that express feminist sentiments are necessarily tendentious, unentertaining, and hostile to men. She even went so far as to propose that *Thelma & Louise* would not have been as good if it had been directed by a feminist and to imply that a feminist filmmaker is a "lesser filmmaker" than someone who does not advocate feminist ideas:

> Had this film been directed by a lesser filmmaker who hadn't given it such a heroic vista, had he been a feminist—which I assure you he is not—maybe the film would not have been so entertaining and therefore would not have allowed people to go on that journey (Grundmann and Lucia).

While denying feminist affiliation, Sarandon has made many comments that express feminist ideals. For instance, in the same interview in which she insists that talking about her feminism would be "so booorring," she goes on to criticize Hollywood for not creating fully developed female characters. She proposes that for women in films "[s]uffering in silence is the glorified virtue," sex appeal is related to the "ability to be penetrated," and women who make "selfish choices" are inevitably branded as evil (Pachero, 35). These comments seem to reflect feminist concerns to me, and Sarandon has made them not only to the press, but also on the sets of her films.

She has complained repeatedly about the limitations of her roles on feminist grounds. As early as 1982 when shooting *Tempest,* she bitterly attacked screenwriter–director Paul Muzursky for failing to understand his female characters. She told an interviewer that when she was shown the final version of the script, "I just got sick. This woman was so uninteresting. All she wanted to do was get laid" (Shapiro, 95). At a Women in Film luncheon in 1990, Sarandon advised women who wanted power in Hollywood to develop their own channels of influence:

> What is the point of seizing the desk, if you're going to have to keep quiet and stay within the confines of that structure, imitating their [men's] mistakes? Wouldn't it be better to have less power or our own independent power structures and be able to redefine how we work and how we accomplish things? (Grundmann and Lucia).

Sarandon has proposed that her film roles reflect the changing social position of women in contemporary society (Fuller). The same can be said in regard to her image as a whole. She represents the widespread social conception that modern women must combine their feminism with femininity, while at the same time refusing to accept the much maligned label of feminist. At the same time, however, by embodying the idea that women can be intelligent, independent, and sexy, she transcends traditional Hollywood images of the independent woman as someone who adopts male characteristics or becomes evil and manipulative. Sarandon's image represents independent feminist femininity as challenging to men as well as in their service, and perhaps this is the crucial reason for the longevity of her career. She is a Hollywood maverick who is also a Hollywood sex symbol—a combination not found that often among contemporary female stars.

References

1. Moynihan, Maura and Andy Warhol. 1983. "Susan Sarandon." *Interview* June 1983: np. Susan Sarandon Clipping File. Margaret Herrick Library, Beverly Hills, CA; hereafter cited in text.

2. Smith, Gavin. 1993. "Compromising Positions." *Film Comment* 29(2) (Mar./ Aug. 1993). EBSCOhost Academic Search Premier. GALILEO, <http://www. galileo.peachnet.edu>; hereafter cited in text.

3. Grundmann, Roy and Cynthia Lucia. 1993. "Acting, Activism and Hollywood Politics." *Cineaste* 20(1) (July 1993). EBSCOhost Academic Search Permier GALILEO. <http://www.galileo.peachnet.edu>; hereafter cited in text.

4. Newman, Bruce. 1994. "Susan Sarandon: Lover, Lawyer, Marmee." *New York Times* 17 July, 1994: 22; hereafter cited in text.

5. Lovell, Alan. 1999. "Susan Sarandon: In Praise of Older Women." p. 89 in *Screen Acting*, eds. A. Lovell and P. Kramer. New York: Routledge; hereafter cited in text.

6. Shapiro, Marc. 2001. *Susan Sarandon: Actress–Activist.* Amherst, N.Y.: Prometheus Books, pp. 195–196; hereafter cited in text.

7. Lipton, James. 1998. Interview with Susan Sarandon. *Inside the Actors' Studio,* Bravo Television, Nov. 15; hereafter cited in text.

8. Bates, Mark. 2000. "Simply the Best." *University of Wisconsin–Madison Journal* (online version) http://www.chrisbaker.co.uk/mb_interview.htm.

9. Wadler, Joyce. 1981. "Sarandon: Rough Edges and No Lingerie." *Rolling Stone,* May 28: 39; hereafter cited in text.

10. Johnston, Sheila. 2000. "It's Just a Chance to Use my Celebrity." *The Independent on Sunday* (London), April 2: np. Susan Sarandon Clippings File, Margaret Herrick Library, Beverly Hills, CA.

11. Chaudhuri, Anita. 1994. "Mother Complex." *Time Out* (London), Oct. 12–19: 18, Susan Sarandon Clippings File. Margaret Herrick Library, Beverly Hills, CA.

12. Mancini, Joseph. 1980. "The Other Side of Sarandon." *Attenzione,* July: 38, Susan Sarandon Clippings File, Margaret Herrick Library, Beverly Hills, CA.

13. Untitled Press Release. 1996. *Screen International,* April 5: np, Susan Sarandon Clipping File, Margaret Herrick Library, Beverly Hills, CA.
14. Jeffreys, Daniel. 1996. "A Very Grown-Up Kind of Glamour." *Independent on Sunday,* March 24: 20–21; hereafter cited in text.
15. Dreifus, Claudia. 1989. "Susan Sarandon: The Playboy Interview." *Playboy Magazine* May: 66; hereafter cited in text.
16. Goldman, Steve. 1992. "Careering Ahead." *The Sunday Times* (London), March 15: sec. 6, 10; hereafter cited in text.
17. Zehme, Bill. 1992. "Tim Robbins: The Running Man." *Rolling Stone* 642 (Oct. 29), EBSCOhost Academic Search Premier, GALILEO, http://www.galileo.peachnet.edu.
18. Beck, Marilyn and Stacy Jewel Smith. 1996. "Sarandon Sits Back and Waits." *Daily News* (Los Angeles), April 10, 1996: np, Susan Sarandon Clipping File, Margaret Herrick Library, Beverly Hills, CA.
19. "Cries and Whispers." 2002. *New York Reporter,* April 30: np, Susan Sarandon Clippings File, Margaret Herrick Library, Beverly Hills, CA.
20. DiClementi, Deborah. 1999. "Feminist Sex Symbol and Mom." *Lesbian News* 25(1) (Aug.). EBSCOhost Academic Search Premier. GALILEO, <http://www.galileo.peachnet.edu>; hereafter cited in text.
21. Bachrach, Judy. 1994. "The Mom Bomb." *Allure* July: 118–120.
22. "Susan Sarandon." 1996. *People,* May 6: np, Susan Sarandon Clippings File, Margaret Herrick Library, Beverly Hills, CA.
23. Queenan, Joe. 1989. "Miss Congeniality." *Rolling Stone* Jan.9, http://www.rollingstone.com.
24. Fuller, Graham. 1994. "Susan Sarandon: The Bigger Picture Revolution." *Interview* Oct.: 147; hereafter cited in text.
25. "The Anti-Star." 1995. *Buzz: The Talk of Los Angeles,* Feb.: 59–62. Susan Sarandon Clippings File. Margaret Herrick Library, Beverly Hills, CA.
26. Jerome, Jim. 1994. "Susan Sarandon." *Ladies Home Journal* 111(8) (Aug.). EBSCOhost Academic Search Premier. GALILEO, <http://www.galileo.peachnet.edu>; hereafter cited in text.
27. Hobson, Louis B. 1996. "Reconcilable Differences." *Calgary Sun* Jan. 14, <www.canoe.ca/jammoviesartistsS/sarandon.html>; hereafter cited in text.
28. Palmer, Martyn. 1999. "A Long Trip from Her to Maternity." *Globe and Mail* Nov. 25: 49, Susan Sarandon Clippings File, Margaret Herrick Library, Beverly Hills, CA.
29. Stevenson, Jane. 1998. "Sarandon Makes Her Own Role." *Calgary Sun* Dec. 30, <http://www.canoe.com/jammoviesartistsS/Sarandon.html>.
30. Burrows, Roberta. 1977. "Susan Sarandon: The Other Side of Midnight." *Interview* May: 14; hereafter cited in text.
31. Plutzick, Roberta. 1982. "Susan Sarandon." *Moviegoer* Oct.: 16.
32. Pachero, Patrick. 1970. "Susan Sarandon: Pretty Woman." *After Dark* June: 35; hereafter cited in text.
33. Flatley, Guy. 1978. "Susan Sarandon Summer Stardom."*Cosmopolitan* March: 66.

34. Seymour, Gene. 1994. "She's Her Own Best Counsel." *LA Times* July 17: np, Susan Sarandon Clippings File, Margaret Herrick Library, Beverly Hills, CA.

35. Koehler, Robert and Jerry Roberts. 1999. "Julia Roberts, Susan Sarandon." *Variety* Jan. 4: np, Susan Sarandon Clippings File, Margaret Herrick Library, Beverly Hills, CA.

36. Mcaleney, Peter. 1995. "Susan Sarandon." *Venice* Dec.: 35, Susan Sarandon Clippings File, Margaret Herrick Library, Beverly Hills, CA.

37. Phillips, Brandon. 2000. "Sweet, Sassy, Sultry Sarandon." *Variety* Sept. 28, http://www.findarticles.com.

38. Commentary by Tim Robbins, *Dead Man Walking*, DVD, directed by Tim Robbins (1996; Culver City, CA: MGM Studios, 2004).

39. Stoner, Patrick. "Excerpts from Interviews with Tim Robbins and Susan Sarandon." <http://www.whyy.org/Robbins_and_Sarandon_interview.html>; hereafter cited in text.

40. She has said, for instance, "I've played a lot of people who don't have my politics, whether or not it's the way they deal with men or the way they deal with their job or whatever. Your job as an actor is to suspend your judgment to a certain extent and to care about them and to understand what they do." (Annlee Ellingson, 2000. "Making a Sweet Margarita," *Box Office Online*. Jan. <http://www.boxoffice.com/issues/janoo/Susan_Sarandon.html>).

41. Davis, Tonya and Brian D. Johnson. 1999. "Reinventing Motherhood." *Maclean's* 112(45) (Nov. 8): 80.

42. Carroll, Jack. 1984. "Susan Sarandon: An Original." *Northeast Woman* Feb.12: np, Susan Sarandon Clippings File, Margaret Herrick Library, Beverly Hills, CA.

43. Rapping, Elaine. 1999. "Movies & Motherhood." *Maclean's*, 112(45) (Nov. 8): 80.

44. For a lesbian reading of the film, see Cathy Griegers, Cathy. 1993. "Thelma & Louise and the Cultural Generation of the New Butch–Femme." pp. 129–141 in *Film Theory Goes to the Movies*. New York: Routledge.

CHAPTER 6

"A Perfect Acting Machine": Jodie Foster

Career Trajectory: From Mother to Daughter

If any actress can be seen as a star–entrepreneur who has directed her own career, it is Jodie Foster. Foster began acting at the age of three in Coppertone suntan-lotion commercials. After she made her first commercial in 1963, her mother, Brandy, set out very deliberately to make her daughter a star. As an adult actress, Foster would later adopt the same model of career construction originally formulated by her mother. Its major tenets were to formulate carefully a specific career design and then actively to seek out roles that fit with this overall plan.

In the initial stages of Jodie's career, Brandy Foster worked hard to broaden her daughter's acting range gradually from initial work in commercials to television series and eventually to films.[1] In 1972, Foster made her film debut in the Disney children's feature, *Napoleon and Samantha*, but her mother soon realized that, if she wanted Jodie's career to flourish, she needed to transfer her from children's films into adult fare. To this end, she managed to place Jodie in a small, but significant role in Martin Scorsese's *Alice Doesn't Live Here Anymore* (1974), playing a tough little girl who befriends the heroine's son. Then, she fought against objections to Foster's young age, even reputedly agreeing to have her undergo psychological evaluation, to get Jodie the controversial and career-making role of the teenage prostitute in Scorsese's *Taxi Driver* (1976). Nominated for an Academy Award for best supporting actress for this performance, Foster entered national stardom when she was only sixteen.

After *Taxi Driver*, Foster's mother apparently felt that the way to keep her daughter in adult films was to sensationalize her image. In the same year in which *Taxi Driver* was released, Foster also starred as a gangster's moll in *Bugsy Malone*, Alan Parker's gangster film parody with an all-child cast, and in the next year she played a teenage murderess in *The Little Girl Who Lived Down the Lane* (Gessner 1977). As Foster moved into her twenties, her image became increasingly sexualized with such films as *Carny* (Kaylor 1980), *Foxes* (Lyne 1980), *The Hotel New Hampshire* (Richardson 1984), and *Siesta* (Lambert 1987), none of which was notably successful.

With her career making little progress in spite of her newly sexualized image, Foster temporarily abandoned acting to enroll as a student at Yale University in 1980. Although she took time off from her studies to make several movies during her college years, she seems to have used her college experience as a time to decide whether or not she wanted to continue to pursue an acting career. The myth of the star in the right place at the right time waiting to be discovered certainly cannot be applied to Foster. She

Figure 6.1 Jodie Foster with Robert De Niro in a scene from *Taxi Driver* (Scorsese 1976). Foster's sexually provocative role as a teenage prostitute in this controversial film won her an Academy Award nomination and national stardom at the early age of sixteen. (Reproduced with permission of Corbis.)

says her mother always insisted that she consider other career options: "I just assumed that I'd do something else [other than acting] when I grew up."[2]

After college, Foster apparently came to the conclusion that acting was her career of choice: "I always thought actors were stupid, and I thought if I went to college I wouldn't be a stupid actor. But I realized what I really wanted to do was to act and there was nothing stupid about it at all" (De Angelis 70). Yet it took her several years after her college graduation to find the right role to relaunch what at the time had become a nearly defunct acting career. She finally found it in a part that she determinedly pursued, the role of Sarah Tobias, the rape victim who uses the legal system to fight back against her rapists, in *The Accused* (Kaplan 1988). Her pursuit resulted in a critically acclaimed performance for which she won an Oscar and a Golden Globe and that established her indisputably as a major Hollywood star.

As Foster's determined campaign to get the role in *The Accused* suggests, she has worked in two important ways to build her career and to shape her image. She carefully selects and actively seeks out roles in accord with her personal career design, even if this means persuading producers and directors that she is right for the part, replacing another actress who was the filmmakers' first choice, and willingly taking a screen test to demonstrate her acting ability.[3] As her power has grown in Hollywood, she has also dropped out of films and rejected lucrative roles when she determined the part did not fit with her overall career plan.[4]

Foster's commitment to shaping her career through careful role choice stems not only from her mother's influence, but also from her attitude toward acting. She has said, "But I don't make movies for flashy, juicy performances. I have to find something in the story that's part of my progress, part of this little train I'm on. In order for me to spend three months on something, to understand it, it has to speak to me personally."[5] Yet Foster found that she could not completely control her career simply by choosing roles based on a personal connection with her characters. After she won her second Oscar in 1991 for her portrayal of FBI trainee Clarice Starling in *The Silence of the Lambs*, Foster did not use her clout within the industry to advance her acting career by moving into more lucrative projects, as she says she was advised (Chunovic, 122), but rather to move into producing and directing.

She engineered a three-year production deal with Polygram Filmed Entertainment that allowed her to establish her production company, Egg Pictures. Under its auspices, she has produced several films. She also moved into the director's chair, directing two films: *Little Man Tate* (1991) and *Home for the Holidays* (1995). Her most ambitious enterprise as a producer was *Nell* (Apted 1994), a star vehicle in which she played a wild child initiated painfully into civilization. This portrayal, for which Foster developed her socially isolated character's unique language, earned her a fourth Oscar nomination.

Although Foster's careful career management has had a major effect on the development of her career, this development has also been affected by another factor beyond her control. Foster's career has been plagued by a series of scandals, the most notorious of which was the assassination attempt on President Ronald Reagan by John Hinckley, Jr. in 1981. Hinckley claimed to have been led to this deed by a desire to impress Foster, with whom he had become obsessed after seeing her performance in *Taxi Driver*.[6] In addition to the Hinckley incident, Foster's sexually provocative roles following *Taxi Driver* and the publication of her seminude photos in *High Society*, a soft-core celebrity porn magazine,[7] seemed to tarnish her image severely.[8]

She managed to avoid career collapse, however, by systematically reconstructing her star persona. First of all, she composed an article entitled, rather self-pityingly, "Why Me?" that was published in *Esquire* shortly after the Hinckley incident. Characterizing herself as an unwilling victim of Hinckley's obsessive attentions, Foster described how, as an innocent college freshman, she was "skipping hand in hand across campus with my best friend" when she was devastated by the news of the assassination attempt. With one article, she transformed herself from an oversexualized teen movie "nymphet" whose provocative star persona motivated a Presidential assassination attempt into the pitiful victim of a deluded maniac:

> But I knew that there were two Jodie Fosters. There was one as large as the screen, a Technicolor vision with flowing blond hair and a self-assured smile. She was the woman they had all been watching. But the second Jodie was a vision only I knew. She was shrouded in bravado and wit and was, underneath, a creature crippled, without self-esteem, a frail and alienated being.[9]

Although Foster's career did not immediately recover, it was restored after her college graduation when she applied her "Why Me?" strategy to role selection. Foster reactivated her career in two ways. First, she adamantly refused to talk about the Hinckley affair in interviews, thus preventing the incident from overshadowing her acting performances. Second, she reenacted her role as victim in her choice of roles. It seems odd that someone who had been stalked by an obsessed madman would then accept parts in films such as *Mesmerized* (Laughlin 1986), *Five Corners*

(Bill 1988), *Backtrack* (Hopper 1989), and, finally, the career-restoring *The Accused* (Kaplan 1988), in which she repeatedly played victims of male obsession and violence.

Whether a deliberate strategy or an unconscious means of psychological release (given Foster's careful master plan for her career, one suspects the former), this role selection actually made perfect sense in terms of image reconstruction. Foster needed to shed her "nymphet" image, which had now taken on a negative association with male obsession and violence. There could be no better way to do this than to place herself in the filmic role of victim, showing, as *The Accused* does so effectively, that male obsession and violence against women are not the female victim's fault.

Foster's association with scandal unfortunately did not end with the Hinckley affair. Another incident occurred after the release of her second Oscar-winning film, *The Silence of the Lambs* (Demme 1991). As part of a protest against the film's portrayal of its serial killer as what some gay activists saw as an antigay stereotype, Foster's long-reputed homosexuality was finally "outed" when she was attacked in the gay press as a closeted lesbian willing to further her career by starring in an antigay film. Michaelangelo Signorile wrote in *Outweek*:

> Jodie Foster, time's up! If lesbianism is too sacred, too private, too infringing of your damned rights for you to discuss publicly, then the least you can do is refrain from making movies that insult this community. Is that too much to ask of you? You want to have your cake and eat it, too. No way sister (Kennedy, 174).

Rumors of Foster's lesbianism reach all the way back to her teenage years when at fifteen she was photographed while making a film in Rome with another young actress, Sydne Rome. When they were asked if they would mind being photographed walking with their arms around each other, Rome reputedly replied: "Since we're living in a climate of feminism, it's better to photograph two women together—the worst they can say is we're lesbians."[10] Foster was also rumored to have had affairs with her female costars Natassja Kinski in *The Hotel New Hampshire* and Kelly McGillis in *The Accused*, but never had the rumor and innuendo been so public as after *The Silence of the Lambs*. Michael Musto's "La Dolce Musto" column in the *Village Voice* published a poster that had been circulating in New York City proclaiming: "Absolutely Queer. Jodie Foster. Oscar Winner, Yale Graduate, Ex-Disney Moppet, Dyke."[11] Foster responded with even more reticence than she had demonstrated in response to the Hinckley affair. She simply resorted to a "no comment" strategy, and the protests subsided.

The next flurry of gossip occurred in 1997 when her brother, Buddy, published a tell-all unauthorized star biography, *Foster Child: an Intimate Biography of Jodie Foster by Her Brother*. In it, he not only discusses his suicide attempt and history of drug problems (as well as the teenage drug problems of another Foster sister) (116–118, 96), but also reveals sordid details of their childhood family life. According to *Foster Child*, their estranged father abandoned his pregnant wife and their four small children, only begrudgingly and infrequently paying child support (22). The devoted and caring mother, whom Jodie always presented in the most favorable light, according to Buddy, had actually precipitated her husband's desertion by having an affair with another woman (18). Buddy describes their mother as so unstable that she was given to hysterical fits and verbally abusive behavior toward her children (58–59). He characterizes Jodie as a spoiled child always favored by their mother and implies that she was taught at an early age to hate men (56–57). He claims that he found his sister to be a cold, uncaring person and that he always believed she was bisexual (181).

When asked for her response to the book, Foster's reaction was brief, but pointed. She said that she considered her brother to be a distant acquaintance whom she had seen as little as fifteen times in the past twenty years and who knew nothing about her personal life. According to Jodie, "This unauthorized biography consists simply of hazy recollections, fantasies, and borrowed press excerpts."[12]

A final gossip-worthy event emerged in 1998 when the unmarried Foster gave birth to a son and refused to identify his father. Rumors spread that Foster had been artificially inseminated, even that she had gone to a London sperm bank and requested a donor who was a certified genius.[1] She had a second son in 2001, again refusing to discuss his father's identity. Like the other scandals in Foster's life, her refusal to discuss her pregnancies has engendered rumors and innuendo, but it cannot be said to have profoundly damaged her career. After the birth of her first son, she even gave interviews to *Ladies Home Journal* concerning her views on motherhood, creating the image of the devoted traditional mother rather than of the unmarried, possibly lesbian, artificially inseminated single parent.[14]

Despite her attempts at career management, the unforeseen publicity from this series of personal scandals rendered the trajectory of Foster's career choppy and uneven. It moved haltingly through a series of four phases, each characterized by different levels of popularity and success, markedly different types of films and roles, and significant image shifts:

- an initial child actress phase
- a transitional phase between child and adult roles distinguished by a marked sexualization of her image
- a first adult phase characterized by victim-survivor roles
- a second adult period dominated by portrayals of female heroes

In the initial phase of her career (1972 to 1977), Foster, as a child actress, had recurring roles in television commercials, then television series, and finally in children's films, but she never achieved star status. In addition to her debut feature, *Napoleon and Samantha*, notable films in this period, many of them for Disney Productions, include *Tom Sawyer* (Taylor 1973), *Candleshoe* (Tokar 1977), and, as noted earlier, her first role in an adult film, *Alice Doesn't Live Here Anymore* (Scorsese 1974). In this phase, her image was largely created by a series of precocious tomboy roles and a reputation as an extremely bright, mature young actress.

In 1976, Foster's career moved into a transitional stage between child and adult roles (1976 to 1987) characterized, as noted previously, by an increasingly sexualized image, bigger budget films, and minor stardom. Her Academy Award-nominated performance in *Taxi Driver* (Scorsese 1976) initiated this phase, which subsequently included several other sexually provocative roles. With the notable exception of *Taxi Driver*, this period contained a series of box office failures. Foster's career moved into its first adult phase (1986 to 1989) when she was in college. This period was dominated by post-Hinckley victim–survivor roles and includes again numerous box office failures, such as *Mesmerized* (Laughlin 1986), *Five Corners* (Bill 1988), *Stealing Home* (Aldis 1988), and *Backtrack* (Hopper 1989), but culminates in her career-making, Academy Award-winning performance in *The Accused* (Kaplan 1988).

Foster's second Academy Award for *The Silence of the Lambs* (Demme 1991) initiated her second adult career phase. This period of her career, which extends to the present time, is characterized by major star status, her ability to headline big-budget Hollywood productions, a greater diversity of roles, substantial control of role choice, and the movement into producing and directing. In addition to the popularly successful and critically praised *The Silence of the Lambs*, notable films in this period include Foster's directorial debut, *Little Man Tate* (Foster 1991), *Sommersby* (Amiel 1993), *Maverick* (Donner 1994), *Nell* (Apted 1994), *Contact* (Zemeckis 1997), *Anna and the King* (Tennant 1999), *The Panic Room* (Fincher 2002) and *Flight Plan* (Schwentke, 2005). In this period, Foster seems to have moved her roles and her image very consciously in new directions, but with mixed results.

With the role of Clarice Starling in *The Silence of the Lambs*, Foster established herself as an incarnation of the female hero. In interviews at the time of the film's release and later in the audio commentary on the DVD version, she repeatedly describes Clarice as a mythical female hero. As she told reporters at a press conference after winning a Golden Globe for the role, "Mythically, in terms of the movies, I think it is the first time that women have really had access to that myth—to a real folklore connection to what a hero is" (Chunovic, 130). In her Oscar acceptance speech, she described Clarice not only as a mythical figure, but also as "an incredibly strong and beautiful feminist hero" (De Angelis, 86).[15]

The film roles that propelled Foster's career from one phase to another and brought her greatest critical accolades all combine character attributes from an earlier career phase with those representative of an emerging period. This is true of each of the crucial films in her career: *Taxi Driver*, *The Accused*, and *The Silence of the Lambs*. *Taxi Driver* added a sexual element to Foster's previously established tough girl persona, *The Accused* combined her already sexualized image with a victim–survivor dimension, and *The Silence of the Lambs* lifted her roles from victim–survivors to feminist heroes who are no longer victims, but instead place themselves in danger in order to save other women from victimization.

Throughout the most recent period of Foster's career, notably in *Contact*, *Anna and the King*, *The Panic Room*, and *Flight Plan*, she has embodied heroic female characters, but with considerably less critical and popular success. In addition, she has moved into more romantic roles (*Somersby*) and ones in which her character shows greater emotional vulnerability (*Nell*). As she approached her early forties, she began with *Little Man Tate*, *Anna and the King*, *The Panic Room*, and *Flight Plan* to move into the maternal roles traditionally allocated to ageing actresses. Foster's maternal roles, however, are combined with her earlier heroic persona, displacing her maternal figures from the conventional maternal melodrama and transporting them into contemporary drama (*Little Man Tate*), historical epic (*Anna and the King*), and thriller (*The Panic Room* and *Flight Plan*) formats. Foster's focus is never on the traditional stay-at-home mom, but on the heroic single mother who single handedly triumphs over adversity, whether it is economic hardship, foreign culture, home invasion, or airline terrorism.

Foster's films that fit into the preceding categories, however, have been relatively unsuccessful and have generated only mixed or negative reviews. In this period, Foster has also sought to demonstrate her versatility as an actress, accepting, for instance, her first role in a comedy opposite Mel Gibson in *Maverick*. This was an unusual role for Foster not only because she had never before done comedy, but also because she gave up star billing to Gibson, something she had not done since *The Accused* and has not done since.[16]

The Jodie Foster Star Image

Foster's image is composed of three basic categories of elements clustered around the qualities of privacy, courage, and intelligence. These categories are assemblages of components that interact at times to reinforce and at other times to contradict her screen roles. Over the course of her career, some elements have moved to the foreground and others have been masked or displaced in a complex interweaving of ingredients that allows Foster's image to remain exceptionally mutable and open to various reading possibilities.

Privacy: "… She Has Never Given the Slightest Hint"

More than any other contemporary actress, Foster has expressed a determination to keep her private life private. The precipitating cause of this determination has been tied to the scandals and flurries of gossip that have plagued her career, especially the Hinckley affair. Yet Foster's reticence to discuss her private life,[17] which has been described as demonstrating her "reserve rather than reclusiveness," is so unwavering that it has created wide speculation concerning her relationship with her family and her sexual orientation. When granting interviews, she is said to threaten to terminate the session immediately if either of two issues is discussed: John Hinckley or what has been loosely described as her "personal life," which actually seems to be a code word for her romantic relationships.

Although squelching rumors about her family situation and romances to a certain extent, Foster's well-publicized desire for privacy has also elevated several aspects of her personal life to an unusually prominent position in her image lexicon. The first is her relationship with her mother. In interviews, Foster has always been quite willing to discuss her mother's influence on the direction of her career, as well as their strong personal bond. This seeming forthrightness has, in fact, covered over a host of speculations about a troubled family background.

Against charges, especially in regard to her casting in *Taxi Driver*, that she was exploited in the tradition of Judy Garland by a greedy stage mother, Foster has always maintained that her mother, with whom she insists she has an extremely loving and tender relationship, always had her best interests in mind in directing her early career. In fact, Foster utilized her first Oscar acceptance speech to honor "most importantly" her mother, who, Foster touchingly proposed, "taught me that all my finger paintings were Picasso's and that I didn't have to be afraid. And mostly that cruelty might be very human, and it might be very cultural, but it's not acceptable" (Chunovic, 102). When she found playing a rape victim in *The Accused* emotionally draining, Foster says she called upon her mother to provide her with moral support on the set (De Angelis, 74). Repeatedly, she has described her mother as her best friend and has said that she hopes that her relationship with her own sons will be as close and loving as the one she has had with her mother (De Angelis, 99).

This enduring mother–daughter bond covers over a host of rumors of family dysfunction culminating in the publication of Foster's brother's tell-all book. Out of myriad stories of a troubled family life, it is Foster's estrangement from her father that has influenced her image most strongly. During her early years as a child actress, she was repeatedly asked about their relationship. Her reply was remarkably brusque and certainly can be interpreted as indicating troubled feelings:

> My parents were divorced when I was nine weeks old. They separated when I was minus two months. Sure, I've met him a few times. He remarried once and divorced again. It's not as if he's really my father. I try never to mention him. I wouldn't recognize him in the street if I saw him (Kennedy, 20).

This paternal estrangement is mentioned often in Foster's publicity and is emphasized by each of her unauthorized biographers. It is even said to have influenced her role selection, leading her repeatedly to play characters searching for father figures.[18]

The area of Foster's private life that is most closeted involves her sexual orientation. With no serious publicized heterosexual relationships, rumors of affairs with female costars, "close friendships with other women—such as film producer Renée Missell—the two wear matching bracelets,"[19] and tales of artificially inseminated pregnancies, Foster's reputed lesbianism seems more than groundless rumor. Yet, as Mike Walker explains in *The National Enquirer,*

> Jodie Foster does not act like she is gay. She really is a mystery woman. She is probably the most successful star at keeping her private life private .... In the gay community, however, they consider Jodie Foster to be one of them, but she has never given the slightest hint (Kennedy, 173).

Fitting into the tradition of sexually ambiguous Hollywood actresses extending back to Greta Garbo and Marlene Dietrich, Foster appears to have cloaked her sexual orientation under the cover of a desire for privacy and for the everyday lifestyle of a noncelebrity.

Foster's image fits well with Richard Dyer's conception that star images represent a combination of the ordinary and the extraordinary. In regard to her choice of lifestyle, Foster has repeatedly presented herself as unpretentious and down-to-earth. She is said to dislike the Hollywood life of glamour; to live in a rented house in Los Angeles, even though she owns a larger one in the valley; to prefer doing her own cooking, cleaning, and errands (Kennedy, 183–184); and to be devoted to her sons as "my priority and my focus."[20]

This image of the working actress trying to live a normal life and protect her privacy fits well with Foster's role selections, which include numerous working-class women, notably Dede Tate in *Little Man Tate* and Sarah Tobias in *The Accused*. These women are shown to be ordinary in their everyday existence, but exceptional in their courage and in the strength of their convictions. Linda Ruth Williams even proposes a "class agenda" underlying Foster's portrayals because repeatedly "her underclass figures are pitted against ambitious, professional, middle-class women." Williams also points out, however, that Foster's "position vis-a-vis class is far from straight forward" because she has also been described as "Hollywood's classiest actress, an intellectual patrician figure … driven by liberal sensibilities."

Courage: "The Only Thing I Know I Can't Play Is a Weak, Dizzy Woman"

Foster's penchant for playing ordinary women who end by becoming models of courage and heroism has spilled over into her image.[21] Although, as we have seen, she began her career playing tough little girls and then moved in her teen years into more sexualized parts, Foster always, even in her sexualized teen roles, portrayed determined, resilient characters exhibiting considerable inner strength. As Williams points out, although in her teen years, Foster "traded on her Californian golden-girl looks," she never became "bimbo fodder"; instead, in films from *Carny* in 1980 to *Backtrack* in 1989, she presented young adult "femininity as riven by dark desire rather than erotic availability." When her career moved into its victim–survivor phase, Foster noted that her roles could be seen as regressive:

> Someone said to me, "You call yourself a feminist and yet you play victims in movies." But can you tell me that being a victim is not part of womanhood? If I portray a victim, does that mean I'm not Wonder Woman? Well, I'm not trying to be. There are a lot of ugly

things in our history, as in black history—and the truth has to be told (Kennedy, 137).

Even as victims, Foster's characters are not simply passive female figures, but strong, self-directed women who, like Sarah Tobias in *The Accused*, struggle against their victimization. With *The Silence of the Lambs*, however, Foster moved definitively out of this victim phase and began to play heroic female figures. Within this category, we find:

- Dede Tate, a working class single mother devoted to her intellectually gifted son in *Little Man Tate*
- Ellie Arroway, a brilliant scientist determined to reach out to extra-terrestrial life in *Contact*
- Anna Leonowens in *Anna and the King*, a young widow who set off with her small child to teach in China in a time when women rarely undertook such perilous journeys
- Meg Altman in *The Panic Room*, a recently divorced yuppie mother who determinedly defends herself and her daughter from home invaders

These courageous characters, models of female heroism, have lent Foster's image a distinct air of exceptionality.

In spite of her timidity in refusing to confront rumors of her homosexuality, the image of Foster's personal life also partakes of this heroic image. From her years as a child performer, she has always been described as extremely self-confident and independent. Directors consistently characterized her as a remarkably mature, precocious, completely reliable child actress. When asked about her work in *Taxi Driver*, for instance, Martin Scorsese proposed:

> I never had any doubts [about her ability to handle the role of a teenage prostitute] …. She takes direction extremely well and has a natural craft, a natural capacity when acting, which is a delight. In one scene she plays with Robert De Niro, they're in a cafe together and she has to pour sugar on top of jam on her toast, and she does it in such a way that it is not only childish and natural but it is also sophisticated and sensual. She was the master of that scene (Kennedy, 41).

From her very first film, Foster's publicity touted her as tough and resilient. The story is told repeatedly in biographical profiles of her career that when shooting *Napoleon and Samantha* at the tender age of eight she was mauled by a lion. As Foster later described the incident, "He took me up by my hip, turned me sideways and started shaking me." After the trainer got the animal to release her, Foster explains that "there were two holes in my front and two in my back. So I got seventeen shots and had to eat broth and Jell-O." Nonplused by the incident, Foster explained her decision to return quickly to the set: "My mom left it up to me, but I think she felt it was smarter for me to go back—you know, to get back on the horse that bucked me" (Kennedy, 34). Combined with Foster's role choices, stories of this sort very early established her persona as one of strength and courage.

Her reaction to the Hinckley incident also contributed to this image. Rather than cringing in fear after learning that she had been stalked by a madman capable of murder,[22] Foster projected an image of quiet strength and composure. She not only wrote the article discussed earlier explaining her reaction to the incident, but also quickly granted an interview in which she further discussed the situation; later, she testified against Hinckley in a deposition for his trial. She even described her behavior in coping with the situation in courageous terms, "I played cowboy and got through it the best way I knew how" (De Angelis, 65).

Foster's relationships with her directors also support this image of strength and self-reliance. Once she reached major stardom, she demanded top billing on all her films. As film critic Roger Ebert, who has interviewed her repeatedly throughout her career, explains, "I think she is single mindedly determined not to become a female lead in male pictures, which is the career route that so many actresses are trapped by" (Chunovic, 174). Although she respects a director's control over a project and her relationships with her directors seem largely to be cordial, she is known for freely offering her suggestions for scene changes. In the commentary on the DVD version of *The Silence of the Lambs*, for instance, she explains that she contributed the idea for the opening sequence in which Clarice is seen running through an FBI training course.[23] Jonathan Kaplan, her director in *The Accused*, is reputed to have nicknamed her "Bossy Little Thing" because, as he explains, "… she was the first actress I've ever worked with who'd come up and tell me I was wrong about something that had nothing to do with her" (Kennedy, 137).

Foster not only requests script changes during shooting, but is also known for demanding alterations in her character before she will agree to accept a role. This was reputedly the case with *Sommersby*. Before accepting the role, she insisted that her character, Laurel, be rewritten to make her stronger. According to Foster, when she was shown the script, "I had reservations. I always do. I said, 'This is what I want, get it there and I'll do the movie.' The only thing I know I can't play is a weak, dizzy woman" (Kennedy, 179).

Foster's desire for control of her career and for power within the industry is said to have motivated her move in midcareer into producing and directing. As she explained when asked about her decision to establish her production company and move into directing, "The idea here is to have more control over my own creative destiny and over that of the material I am engaged with" (Kennedy, 194). Foster also has described her attraction to directing as a fascination with the power the director wields on the set. As she sees it, the actor is always at the service of the director, whose vision it is the actor's job to realize, but the director is the one "at the controls" (Kennedy, 165). She describes herself as thriving in the director's chair: "I love it. I like the stress of directing. I enjoy making decisions."[24] Diane Wiest, who costarred with Foster in her first directorial effort, *Little Man Tate*, found Foster's in-charge directorial style a bit overpowering. As she describes the experience,

> The downside of it for me is that first-time directors tend to be very controlling which makes me feel suffocated. We had some tension there. But if I were directing my first film, I'd want to be very controlling too. In the end I was glad for some of her strong-mindedness (Kennedy, 161).

Intelligence: "the Eleanor Roosevelt of Nineties Hollywood"

A final category of elements that predominate in Foster's star image centers around her intelligence and her acting talent. From an early age, Foster was reputed to be a precocious child. Her mother proposes that she "spoke full sentences when she was twelve months old, and you could reason with her. She taught herself to read at three …. At five she could go in cold and audition like an adult" (Chunovic, 2). Enrolled by her mother in the elite Le Lycee Francais, an exclusive private school in Los Angeles, she was a straight "A" student who became fluent in French and graduated as valedictorian. Upon graduation, she was accepted into Yale and graduated with honors in 1985.

Foster's publicity presents her not only as an academically brilliant but also as an exceptionally perceptive and intuitive actress. Even as a child, she was described as exceptionally gifted. Alan Parker, who directed her in *Bugsy Malone* when she was just thirteen years old, claims he was amazed at her extraordinary acting ability. An anecdote from the set tells of his having gone into her trailer with three pages of newly written complicated dialogue that she learned on the spot:

> I went to tell Jodie that I had rewritten the scene and to take her time learning the script and let me know when she was ready. She

took the script from me, read it through once and said, "I'm ready now." I didn't believe her and told her so. She said, "Try me," so I read the lines to her and she came back word perfect. Now that's total photographic recall. It's phenomenal and she has it all the time. What's more, she takes such an intelligent interest in the way the film is being made that if I had been run over by a bus I think she was probably the only person on the set able to take over as director (Kennedy, 45–46).

Reviewers have also been remarkably positive in their evaluations of Foster's acting performances. Even in films that received negative reviews over all, Foster's performances have been consistently lauded. As Williams points out, "Foster has been likened to America's *grandes dames*. One writer called her 'the Eleanor Roosevelt of Nineties Hollywood' and Bette Davis remarked, 'She's damn good. She's a young Bette Davis'" (Williams). Since she won her Oscars for *The Accused* and *The Silence of the Lambs*, this high level of acting recognition, accompanied by accolades for her extraordinary intelligence, has formed an essential component of Foster's image.

Approach to Acting: "I've Never Even Had an Acting Lesson"

Foster's reputation for extraordinary acting ability fits well with her often expressed self-conception as an "actress" rather than a "star"; however, it does not fit so well with her theories of acting. In fact, in interviews Foster has suggested that she views acting neither as a skilled profession, nor as a craft that can be taught. She has said that she sees acting as a "blue collar job" and herself as a "technician" (Chunovic, 92, 25). Having honed her skills on the job as a child performer and totally lacking in formal training, Foster in many ways epitomizes the Hollywood working actress. Although her brother claims in his book that the two of them took acting lessons as children and that Jodie in particular studied "cold reading" and The Method (83), Foster insists that she never took an acting lesson in her life, even when at Yale. Her attitude to actor training is decidedly antiacademic:

A while back I bought some acting books because I'd started feeling very insecure about not knowing the terminology …. So I looked at them, and I realized that most of it was common sense: if you're sitting at a table and it's cold, you're cold; or, if you're supposed to eat something, you actually eat it; if somebody's dead, you're upset. It's all about common sense and human behavior and paying attention. Ultimately, I think I did probably do a lot of the things that acting classes and acting schools teach, but to me, it was just the way it was supposed to be. I had grown up that way and didn't really know anything else.[25]

Given Foster's lack of formal training, it is perhaps not surprising that her expressed theories about acting seem unsystematic and contradictory. She ascribes to no established school or methodology. Her brother describes her approach as

> ... almost Zen-like. She is now completely the opposite of the Method actor. It takes her a mere second to get into character. She just relaxes and flows into it. I don't think it's something she could explain or teach to other people. I've heard her compare acting to archery, drawing comparisons to how archers can "become one with the target" (84).

This idea of inhabiting a role, becoming "one with the target," is one that Foster has advocated. She proposes that, because she is not a naturally expressive person, a role "has to speak to me personally" (Chunovic, 181). Although this description of personal involvement with a character seems inspired by Method terminology, Foster has, in fact, expressed complete disdain for Method acting. She staunchly proposes:

> I'm no Method actor. In fact I've never even had an acting lesson. If anything, what I do is by instinct. My method is just do what I think is right. I don't think you have to feel the character and research it for years. Maybe I would do research if I were playing Henry VIII, but otherwise no (Kennedy, 39).

Yet she has done considerable research for some of her roles. She spent a week at the Quantico FBI training center to prepare for *The Silence of the Lambs* and read scientific texts as background for her characterization of astronomer Ellie Arroway in *Contact*. However, Foster does not see acting as creating a lifelike character so much as constructing the fantasy of a character. For instance, when directing *Little Man Tate*, she gave this advice to child actor Adam Hann–Byrd: "Just pretend really well and then think about what that pretending looks like" (Kennedy, 157).

Foster is unique among the actresses that we are considering in that her acting career is entirely limited to films. Throughout her career, she has acted in only a single play, a small production while she was in college. She has expressed little interest in theatrical acting, not seeing it, as many other actors do, as a place where she might be able to hone her acting skills. According to Foster, film and theatrical acting are entirely different, and she feels comfortable only in one:

I think I would have a very hard time going back to the theater and not being lambasted by every critic around because they would have access to a first performance or a new performance. So much of what you do in theater is about learning things and making mistakes. And I think it would be very difficult for me to be able to make the kind[s] of mistakes you need to make.[26]

In the tradition of naturalistic film acting, Foster has always described herself as an instinctive actress. In interviews, she has often described acting as involving natural talent and unteachable skills:

I think it's something you're kind of born with. You know there are people who are very beautiful in real life, but they never look good in a picture. And then there are other people who can't help but take a good picture. I think I'm the latter. It may be something to do with confidence. It's not just being photogenic. It's more like instinct. It's instinct that tells you which way to put your body so that you'll look good. And I think I've always had it (Kennedy, 190).

Playwright and screenwriter John Patrick Shanley, who worked with Foster in *Five Corners*, proposed that the reason she denies the existence of acting methodology is because, being untrained, she does not really understand her acting technique: "She has a lot of technique which she doesn't like to talk about. When she walks on a set, it's obvious she's done a lot of preparation. She can do something extraordinarily natural and repeat it five times. It moves you" (Kennedy, 125). Jon Ameil, who directed her in *Sommersby*, describes her as very close to "the perfect acting machine." He sees the essence of her technique as the ability to move in and out of character easily and rapidly. For him, "Jodie combines all the technical facility of a child actor with the maturity of a really seasoned campaigner" (Kennedy, 181).

Ruby Rich calls Foster's technique "hyperrealism"—the ability to give her performances an air of authenticity and verisimilitude (8). At the same time, however, Foster's acting always gives the impression of being well thought out. She says that studying literature at Yale influenced her approach to acting because she realized that she could bring the critical abilities that she learned in her classes to her performances or, as she puts it, "incorporate and analyze literature in making movies" (Kennedy, 122). Williams even describes Foster's preparation for her roles as "critical interpretation" and her characterizations as "forensic." She proposes that

Foster starts with private textual analysis to produce three-dimensional emotional precision. Though she chides herself that

"I didn't end up having the personality to be a writer, to be a novelist," the performances that result from her readings are themselves a kind of text, undertaken to influence other people's lives and experiences in the same way that psychologists would or a novelist would.

Foster has said of her acting process:

I have a hard time describing what I do as an actor, but I realize as I've gotten older that my mind works much more like a director. So for me I appreciate the text, whether its a novel or a screenplay, and I try to interpret that with all of the different vocabularies at my disposal. So let's just say I was a prop man. Then I would say, you know, "I think these type[s] of glasses are the right type[s] of glasses this character would use for their martini." And as an actor I do the same thing .... I try to refer back to the text, to refer back to the screenplay and try to help the screenplay have a life of its own.[27]

Reviewers have also pointed out that Foster is especially effective in her use of carefully executed expressive close-ups. Anthony Hopkins, her costar in *The Silence of the Lambs*, describes her as a master of facial gesture: "She works with such economy. She doesn't do a thing, and yet you can see all the thoughts going through her eyes .... And I think that is the great skill of an actress like Jodie—it just shows on her face; she doesn't have to act it" (Chunovic, 126). Foster has characterized a certain type of close-up, one in which she begins by smiling and then allows her face to become pensive, as her acting trademark: "It's unconscious but I know I do it all the time. I think it emphasizes that anything you do or feel may have a double significance .... I love the written word but that kind of silent gesture is what tells most about working in film" (Chunovic, 115).

Foster also describes her acting methodology as eclectic:

You look at some tintypes, you wear a hoop skirt for a week, and it will come to you. Not that it's so easy. There is nothing worse than an actor who puts on a pair of breeches and speaks in the same bad California accent that he walked in with. But for me it's all a game. You use everything: a painting that you saw, something somebody said. Anything that works (De Angelis, 87).

She also strives for versatility: "My goal is longevity in this business and the plan is to accept roles that are different. If I did a comedy, I next did a drama. If I did an artsy film, I followed it with a down-to-earth film" (De Angelis, 128). Indeed, her acting choices have included a wide range of roles and genres from thrillers to social problem films, from romances to comedies. Paradoxically, however, although she strongly advocates careful role choice and an overall career design, she still views actors as essentially powerless within the larger filmmaking process. For Foster, the actor is completely in service to the director: "[If] the director feels one way and you feel another way, you always go with the director" (De Angelis, 93). It seems to have been largely because of this conviction that she moved into directing in midcareer. As a director, rather than a star, she seems to feel she can best realize her artistic vision.

Jodie Foster: Actress and Image

Although it is clear that Foster sees her acting and directing careers as means of artistic expression, it is difficult to say what her artistic vision is exactly and how it relates to the social significance of her star image. Academic critics looking at Foster's screen roles have overwhelmingly seen her as a progressive figure, even a feminist auteur. For instance, Christina Lane has characterized her as a "liminal figure" who calls into question the legitimacy of gender role dichotomies through her ambivalent sexual persona.[28] Unquestionably, feminist elements are present in many of Foster's film characterizations, and she is one of the few Hollywood actresses who has openly identified herself as a feminist. Her mother even attributed her daughter's career to the growth of the feminist movement:

> [Jodie] was never a traditional-looking girl. And I think that has a lot to do with her success. It was just at the beginning of women's liberation, and she kind of personified that in a child. She had a strength and uncoquettishness. Maybe it comes from being raised without a father to say, "Turn around and show Daddy how pretty you look" (Rich, 7).

There does seem to be a historical connection between the development of Foster's image and the movement within the larger society from victim to power feminism. On screen, Foster moved from playing rape victims to portraying female heroes and in her private life from being the object of John Hinckley's obsession to being listed as one of the most influential people in Hollywood. Just at the time when feminism was fending off criticism that it focused too much on women's victimization by men rather than on their success in "a man's world," Foster's image offered a model of female triumph over victimization. Rather than rendering the political personal and thereby defusing the social message that her image offered to her female fans, Foster actually rendered the personal political, converting her star image into a social statement about gender.

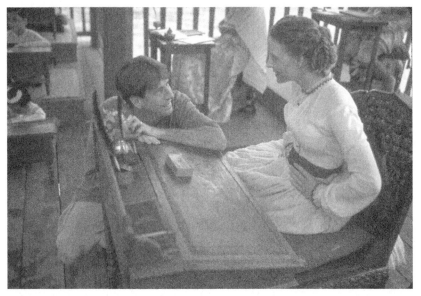

Figure 6.2 Jodie Foster being directed by Andy Tennant on the set of *Anna and the King.* Foster has always cultivated good relationships with her directors and has even said, "[If] the director feels one way and you feel another way, you always go with the director" (De Angelis, 93). (Reproduced with permission of Corbis.)

Thus, in many ways, Foster represents an anomic female star whose subversive image offers a real challenge to prevailing gender norms. She is not, however, a rebel working outside the established order, but, as she has said of her character in *The Silence of the Lambs*, someone who works for change within the established system ("Jodie Foster Looks Back"); she is not a revolutionary figure, but rather a reformer. Her image does not call into question existing gender norms by overtly attacking them, as a revolutionary figure would, but rather by seductively subverting them, charmingly calling them into question. She has said that, although she sees herself as a feminist, her films are not about that and, indeed, in a sense, this is true. Foster's determination to stay within the confines of the Hollywood system has prevented her from giving free reign to the anomic elements within her image.

Writing in 1991, B. Ruby Rich saw Foster as taking film portrayals of women in a completely new and decidedly progressive direction. She characterized Foster as on the brink of finally bringing a sense of "wholeness" to female screen characters by refusing to be the "locus of someone else's desire." According to Rich, Foster was just about to take "the biggest risk of all: the gamble to fuse an active female sexuality with an equally active female authority" (10). Yet, Foster's most recent films have not taken that risk. In what appears to be a reaction to reviewer's criticism of her acting as too distanced, her characterizations as needing more emotional vulnerability, and her romantic relationships with her leading men as lacking in chemistry, Foster abandoned the desexualized female heroes she played so effectively in *The Silence of the Lambs* and *Contact.*

She turned her attention instead to more conventionally feminine figures: an emotionally damaged young woman in *Nell*, romantic heroines in *Sommersby* and *Anna and the King*, and persecuted mothers in *The Panic Room* and *Flight Plan.* None of these performances has been particularly memorable, however, despite Foster's attempts to bring to these roles the same strength and courage associated with her earlier characterizations. The roles of a yuppie mother trapped in her apartment by home invaders in David Fincher's *The Panic Room* and a young widow whose daughter is abducted on a transatlantic flight in *Flight Plan* appear in particular to represent missteps in her career, seeming returns to her previous female victim–survivor roles. The films made respectable showings at the box office, although they definitely did not do as well as was expected, but Foster received some of the most negative reviews of her career. Her performances were seen as far too intense for the films' crudely generic subject matter. It was as if Foster thought she were in far more serious films, perhaps *The Accused* or *Silence of the Lambs,* rather than trapped in Fincher's and Schwentke's formulaic woman-in-peril plots. For some time, Foster has expressed an interest in starring in a biopic, which she would produce and perhaps direct, dealing with the life of the brilliant and notorious Nazi filmmaker Leni Riefenstahl. This project might provide a new stimulus for her career; however, it seems to be hopelessly stalled.

Like her acting roles, Foster's personal life has recently taken her into areas that mask the most progressive aspects of her image, what Christina Lane has called her "sexual liminality" (Lane, 149). Since the births of her two sons, she has refused to discuss, except in the most conventional terms, the unconventional family situation she has chosen to create. When asked about her relationship with her children, she reacts stereotypically, designating them her "priority" and her "focus," and suggesting that she now feels compelled to turn down any projects about which she does not feel "really passionate" because she wants to spend as much time with them as possible (Laddy 1999). Eager to express conventional maternal sentiments, she adamantly refuses to answer any questions about single motherhood, a role that challenges accepted gender norms.

Clearly, Foster's screen roles and her star image portray her as an extremely powerful, independent woman who threatens male control within the film industry and within society as a whole. Her move into directing seemed to solidify that image, but it has been notably less successful than anticipated. As a director, she has thus far failed to establish herself as an accomplished filmmaker, let alone as a feminist auteur. She has directed only two films, *Little Man Tate* (1991) and *Home for the Holidays* (1995), the former a modest success and the latter a definite disappointment. She has had plans to direct a third feature, *Flora Plum,* since 2001, but the project has been very slow in coming to fruition— especially because, in 2002 (ostensibly due to her family commitments), she closed Egg Pictures, the production company that she established in 1992. Thus, her directorial career has by no means been a remarkable success. She continues to produce, however, and has had some success in this capacity with the critically praised low-budget comedy, *The Dangerous Lives of Altar Boys* (Care 2002), in which she played a small supporting role as a one-legged nun.

As an established actress and a still promising director and producer, Foster is without question a major feminist force within an extremely male-dominated Hollywood system. Her career, in spite of some recent disappointments, remains a model of power feminism. She has fashioned her roles to create heroic female characters; built her image around her acting talent, rather than her beauty; carefully planned the progression of her career; and assumed ultimate control of that career by moving into producing and directing. Her initial success as a powerful female presence within the Hollywood system was encouraging, but the subsequent stalling of her career once she had finally attained a position of substantial influence within that system is disheartening. Foster's ultimate significance as a feminist star and filmmaker, however, still remains to be revealed.

References

1. Foster had a regular role in *The Courtship of Eddie's Father* (1970–1972) and starred in *Paper Moon* (1974), the television spin-off from the 1973 film starring Tatum O'Neil and her father Ryan.
2. Quoted in De Angelis, Therese. 2001. *Jodie Foster.* Philadelphia: Chelsea House, p. 54; hereafter cited in text.
3. She has said that she persuaded the filmmakers to cast her in, and took screen tests for, both of her major film successes, *The Accused* and *The Silence of the Lambs.* She also was willing to replace actresses originally cast or considered for the roles in *The Silence of the Lambs, Maverick, Anna and the King,* and *The Panic Room* (De Angelis, 72–73, 82, 88; "Nichole Kidman's Knee Injury Costs Her $10.5 Million" Internet Movie Data Base. <http://www.name/nm0000149/news>).
4. Most notably, she reportedly withdrew from *The Hot Zone* when she came to feel that her part was being minimized in favor of Robert Redford's

("Ridley Scott and Brother Tony Forged a Multi-Picture Deal," Angel Fire.com <http://www.angelfire.com/movies/ridleyscott/info/hotzone. txt>), and she rejected the role of Clarice Starling in *Hannibal*, the sequel to *The Silence of the Lambs* ("Foster Has No Stomach for *Hannibal*" Imbd. com <http://www.imdb.com/name/nm0000149/news>).

5. Quoted in Chunovic, Louis. 1995. *Jodie: A Biography*. Chicago: Contemporary Books, p. 122.

6. Kennedy, Philippa. 1995. *Jodie Foster: The Most Powerful Woman in Hollywood*. London: MacMillan, p. 174; hereafter cited in text.

7. Her mother had apparently allowed the photos to be taken of her then fifteen-year-old daughter as a way to promote her move into adult films (Foster, Buddy, and Leon Wagener. 1998. *Foster Child: An Intimate Biography of Jodie Foster by Her Brother*. New York: Signet, pp. 156–157).

8. For an example of the extremely condemnatory reactions to Foster's image at this point in her career, see Sinclair, Marianne. 1988. *Hollywood Lolitas*. London: Plexus, pp. 5, 15. Sinclair describes Foster as a "celluloid nymphet" and implies that she was exploited by her avaricious mother.

9. Foster, Jodie. 1982. "Why Me?" *Esquire*, December, http://www.jodiefoster. windygats.com/html/atricles/why_me.html.

10. "Jodie alla Romana." 1977. *People,* Dec. 12: np, Jodie Foster Clippings File, Margaret Herrick Library, Beverly Hills, CA.

11. Musto, Michael. 1991. "La Dolce Musto," *Village Voice*, April 16: np, Jodie Foster Clippings File, Margaret Herrick Library, Beverly Hills, CA.

12. "Jodie Foster Attacks Brother's Book." May 13, 1997. Mr. Showbiz.com, <http://www.mrshobiz.go.com/archive/news/Todays_Stories/970513/5_ 13_97_15foster.html>.

13. Murray, Iain. 1998. "It's All in the Gender, You Know." *Marketing Week* [London] 21(3) (March 19, 1998): 110.

14. Gerosa, Melina. 2000; 1995. "Fascinating Moms." *Ladies Home Journal* 117 (Jan. 2000): 88–91 and "Jodie Loses Her Cool." *Ladies Home Journal* 112 (Feb. 1995): 152–154.

15. Foster has never fully explained why she refused to accept the role of Clarice in *Hannibal* (Scott 2000), the sequel to *The Silence of the Lambs*, even though she had earlier expressed interest in participating in the project. She is said to have told an interviewer for the December 1999 issue of *W Magazine*, however, that she considered the character in the sequel to be a violation of what she saw as Clarice's heroic status in the original film: "I stand to make more money doing this sequel than I've ever made in my life. But who cares, if it betrays Clarice—who is a person, in some strange way, to me" ("Foster Says No to *Hannibal*," Nov. 8, 1999, Mr. Showbiz Online, <http://www. mrshowbiz.go.com/news/Todays_stories/991108/fosterhannibal110899. html>).

16. In her introduction to Burl Barer's book on the making of *Maverick* (Boston: Charles E. Tuttle Co., 1994), Foster explains that she had been looking for a comic role for a long time and that she felt Maverick would give her a perfect

entre to this unfamiliar genre because of Gibson and director Richard Donner's extensive comic experience (xv).

17. Williams, Linda Ruth. 2002. "Mother Courage." *Sight and Sound*, May 2002. British Film Institute Online, http://www.bfi.org.uk/sightandsound/2002_05/feature01_MotherCourage.html.

18. For instance, reviewers have noted the large number of father figures in her major films, such as *Taxi Driver, The Silence of the Lambs*, and *Contact*. Louis Chunovic also finds father figures in *Mesmerized* (Laughlin 1986), *Svengali* (Harvey, made-for-TV, 1983), and *Backtrack* (Hopper 1989), films that she made during her college years (83).

19. Brooks, Richard. 1997. "Lesbian Icon Jodie Still Won't Kiss and Tell." *The Observer* (London), May 4, 1997: np, Jodie Foster Clippings File, Margaret Herrick Library, Beverly Hills, CA.

20. Laddy, Tamar. 1999. "Women.com Interview: Jodie Foster Changing Focus." Women.com., December 1999, http://www.women.com/entertainment/interviews/foster/foster.html.

21. Examples of Foster's portrayals of courageous ordinary women include Linda in *Five Corners*, Sarah Tobias in *The Accused*, Clarice Starling in *The Silence of the Lambs*, Dede in *Little Man Tate*, and Laurel in *Sommersby*.

22. In the aftermath of the Hinckley incident, Foster was also pursued by a copycat stalker, Edward M. Richardson. When arrested by the police for possession of a loaded automatic, which he confessed he intended to use to shoot the President, he admitted that Foster had been his original target, but that he had seen her in a theater performance in New Haven and decided she was too pretty to shoot (Di Angelis, 62).

23. Commentary by Jonathan Demme, Jodie Foster, Anthony Hopkins, Ted Tally, and John Douglas, *Silence of the Lambs*, DVD (Criterion Edition), directed by Jonathan Demme (1991; Chicago, IL: Home Vision Entertainment, 1998).

24. Figgis, Mike, John Boorman, and Walter Donohue, eds., 2000. *Projections 10: Hollywood Film-Makers on Film-Making*. London: Faber & Faber, p. 50.

25. Quoted in Rich, B. Ruby. 1991. "Nobody's Handmaid." *Sight and Sound*, Dec. 1991: 7.

26. Quoted in Miller, Prairie. 2000. "*Anna and the King*: Jodie Foster Interview," Big Star.com <http://www.bigstar.com/features/index.cfm?fa=iv_contrib&id= 1005326.2.>.

27. "Jodie Foster Looks Back" (Interview with Foster), *Freaky Friday*, DVD, directed by Gary Nelson (1977; Burbank, CA: Walt Disney Video, 2004).

28. Lane, Christina. 1995. "The Liminal Iconography of Jodie Foster." *The Journal of Popular Film and Television* 22(4) (Winter): 149–153.

CHAPTER 7

Angela the Icon: Angela Bassett

Career Trajectory: God Is "the Greatest Casting Director and Agent There Is"

Although her career has had its peaks and nadirs, Angela Bassett is arguably Hollywood's most respected contemporary African-American actress. Although Halle Berry won the distinction of being the first black star to win the Academy Award for best actress, Bassett's career has much more longevity and is much more distinguished and accomplished overall. Her career trajectory, image configuration, and views on acting offer a interesting study of the difficult position of the black actress in the over-whelmingly white milieu of Hollywood filmmaking.

She is said to have a reputation in the industry as a tough negotiator and relentless worker[1]; however, Angela Bassett, like many contemporary actresses, is reluctant to acknowledge the control she has exerted over her career. Instead, in interviews she has repeatedly described her stardom as miraculously bestowed upon her by a benevolent deity. A deeply religious person, Bassett is an anomaly among contemporary stars in that she has openly proclaimed her strong religious faith and credited divine providence with bringing about her stardom. Describing her career as "charmed"[2] and God as "the greatest casting director and agent there is,"[3] Bassett told a reporter for the *Christian Science Monitor*, "I feel very humble. I'm grateful for my faith in God. I realize I have been blessed. It's not some kind of an accident, a lucky break I've tripped into. I believe God has favored me with these wonderful parts that are seen around the world."[4]

Whereas Bassett gives all the credit to God, her publicity attributes her stardom not only to the miraculous intervention of divine providence, but also to Bassett's relentless drive toward success. Born in Harlem in 1958, she and her younger sister were raised by their single mother in the projects of St. Petersburg, Florida, after Bassett's father abandoned the family. Bassett has repeatedly told interviewers that it was her mother who from an early age instilled in her an ambition to succeed in whatever career she determined to undertake. Bassett also emphasizes her mother's strong support of her educational goals. With this maternal guidance and the help of the federally funded Upward Bound Program, Basset won a full scholarship to Yale, where she completed her undergraduate work in African-American Studies and then entered the graduate program in the university's prestigious School of Drama.[5]

Press accounts single out as key to Bassett's career success the influence of black role models and mentors who instilled in her a strong confidence in her abilities and an unquenchable desire to succeed. Her first role model was clearly her mother, whom Bassett describes as having "an amazing influence on my life": "She's very dramatic, very determined. She told us when we were little, 'Be whatever you want to be, just be independent. Never be reliant on a man to take care of you.'"[6] Beyond her immediate family, Bassett has also spoken of two father figures, prominent in the black theatrical community, who were instrumental in developing her acting talents and ambitions: James Earl Jones and Lloyd Richards. In fact, Bassett says she first began to consider an acting career after seeing James Earl Jones perform the role of Lenny in *Of Mice and Men* at the Kennedy Center in Washington, D.C.

She has repeatedly told interviewers the story of this "devastating" experience, which occurred when she was just fifteen years old and on a trip funded by the Upward Bound Program: "I knew at that moment that I had to be involved in theater. I went back and started acting with the St. Petersburg community theater."[7] Bassett presents this experience as so crucial for her because an aspiring black actress at the time had so few role models. She has said that this lack of inspirational figures made her doubt the viability of an acting career for a black woman: "It didn't make sense for me to become an actress. There were so few role models for me on television or in film. It just didn't make sense because it just didn't seem like you could keep a roof over your head as a black actress" (FitzGerald). Although Bassett has never made the connection herself, her attraction to characters that represent icons of black womanhood perhaps stems from her early realization that she lacked black female role models in her life. She seems determined to provide them for others through her screen performances.

Another male figure who Bassett acknowledges has played a significant role in her rise to stardom is the prominent black theater director Lloyd Richards, who was the dean of the Yale School of Drama when Bassett attended. Bassett credits him with providing her with a sense of discipline and with casting her in her first two Broadway supporting roles in *Ma Rainey's Black Bottom* (1984 to 1985) and *Joe Turner's Come and Gone* (1988) (FitzGerald, 26). Both plays were written by another icon of black theater, August Wilson, who can be seen as a third inspirational figure for Bassett. In fact, although Bassett's promotional material does not accentuate this connection, her early involvement with black theater was crucial to the development of her career. After her graduation from Yale and before she went to New York to break into Broadway, she toured with the NEC (Negro Ensemble Company), one of the oldest theater groups in the U.S. dedicated to performing and promoting black theater. Bassett had also done her undergraduate thesis at Yale on the history of this prestigious acting troupe (FitzGerald, 30).

According to Bassett's account of her star trajectory, neither black theater nor Broadway theater could satisfy her driving ambition, and she set out in 1988 for Hollywood, giving herself only six months to find work: "If it didn't work out? I could go back home if I wanted. I could go to business school if I wanted, even with a drama degree. But it was something I needed to do."[8] Bassett describes her move to Hollywood as a direct result of her determination to be a star, which she says she realized early would not come easily to a black actress. She told one interviewer: "New York actors would say, 'I'm not going until they call.' It occurred to me they don't do that for black girls. ... I think I've got to go there and beat on the door ..."[9]

Bassett has, in fact, repeatedly commented on the fact that opportunities for black actresses are not at all equal to those for whites. For instance, when asked if black actresses are getting "the same kinds of opportunities as their white peers are getting," she replied, "Absolutely not! It's never between me and, say, Sandra Bullock. And yes, it's still a challenge to be paid commensurately. But I am being considered more often for things, so that's progress."[10] Although Bassett has openly criticized racial discrimination in the industry, her publicity material is also quick to point out that within just a month of her coming to Hollywood, she was able to secure a recurring role in a television series, *A Man Called Hawk*, and make her film debut in *F/X* (Mandel 1986).

Sadly, God's providence and Bassett's relentless drive for success have not always worked to her benefit, and one wonders if now that her career seems to have lost its momentum she still would proclaim, as she did after getting her break-out role in *What's Love Got to Do with It*, "Thank you, Lord, for seeing the whole picture."[11] The whole picture actually has not been very rosy. Bassett's career has moved through three distinct phases that seem at this moment to form a downhill course: (1) early supporting roles in theater, film, and television (1984 to 1992); (2) major star status (1994 to 1998); and, finally, (3) a precipitous decline back into supporting roles and television dramas (1999 to the present).

As noted earlier, Bassett's rise to stardom began with supporting performances in two Broadway productions with clear roots in black culture: August Wilson's *Joe Turner's Come and Gone* and *Ma Rainey's Black Bottom*. In the former, she played a devoted wife and mother and in the latter a sexual temptress. It is the interplay between these two stereotypical black female roles—the mother and the whore—that would become a constant in Bassett's career. As she moved into Hollywood films, the wife and mother roles quickly began to dominate. Her most important films in this period were *Boyz 'n the Hood* (Singleton 1991), *The Jacksons: An American Dream* (Arthur, TV miniseries, 1992), and *Malcolm X* (Lee 1992); in each film she played a mother figure. Bassett took these maternal roles that one critic described as "call[ing] mainly for pious brow-knitting and humbly downcast eyes" (Testino, 127) and made them inspirational icons of female strength and endurance.

In fact, all of Bassett's major roles are marked by her ability to convey a sense of strong black womanhood. It is exactly this quality that is said to have won Bassett her break-out role and engendered the performance that would lift her to major stardom in the mid-1990s. Portraying Tina Turner in the biopic *What's Love Got to Do with It* (Gibson 1993) was a role highly coveted by black Hollywood actresses, and Bassett only won it after subjecting herself to grueling auditions in a final competition against Halle Barry and Robin Givens. Playing Turner could be seen as not only challenging but also dangerous for a young actress. As Donald Bogle suggests, "Playing Tina was such a big, demanding role—one that could eat you up if you weren't a very strong, confident actress. But Angela ate it up" (quoted in Samuels). Her performance won her critical raves, an Academy Award nomination for best actress, and star status. Afterward, she is said to have been offered roles commanding a six-figure salary (FitzGerald, 45), yet her promotional material evidences some disagreement about the effects the Oscar nomination had on her career.

The nomination was historically significant because so few African-American actresses have been nominated for Academy awards.[12] Although Bassett's promotional material does recognize the importance of her gaining this recognition, Bassett would later tell interviewers that her expectations of what the nomination would do for her were never realized:

> I remember sitting at the Oscars and thinking, "This is great! This is the beginning of something big for me." But I didn't work again for another year and a half. I guess I was pretty naive to think it would be different—that it was just about the talent—particularly for someone who looks like me. You forget that sometimes (Samuels).

Later, Bassett openly denounced the Oscars as racist: "There's just not a great deal of diversity in the voting ranks for the Academy Awards, and that has a great deal to do with who wins. If 80% of those who vote are male and white and over 60 years old, that's not a lot of diversity."[13] Yet the Oscar nomination and the rave reviews for *What's Love Got to Do with It* did elevate Bassett to star status. She told one interviewer that when she got the role, she knew immediately that it would have an enormous impact on her career: "… they may hate me, they may crucify me, but at least they'll know who I am" (Testino).

It was not really until her next major film, *Waiting to Exhale* (Whitaker 1995), became a surprise Christmas box-office hit that her position as a major star was confirmed. Based on popular black novelist Terry McMillan's bestselling novel, *Waiting to Exhale* was intended as an ensemble piece showcasing the talents of a foursome of black actresses. Stealing the film from the other women, especially from Whitney Houston, who ostensibly had the lead role, Bassett gave an impassioned performance that reviewers felt gave just the right amount of dramatic and emotional weight to *Exhale*'s semicomic account of the romantic lives of four black, single, professional women. Repeatedly in interviews, Bassett characterized *Waiting to Exhale* as the key film in her career:

> Exhale was just so special. It was just such a seminal event. It was just so important. It was a breakout experience in terms of roles …. If you have just one of those fabulous moments in your career, then that is pretty amazing …. You always aspire to that but you're not always going to make it. That was my Mt. Everest. I might not climb Mt. Everest two, three, four, or ten times in my lifetime. But I can aspire to that and try to do good work.[14]

The decline from Mt. *Exhale* began almost immediately when Bassett agreed to star in the film version of Terri McMillan's follow-up to *Exhale*,

How Stella Got Her Groove Back (Sullivan 1998). The film was clearly conceived as a star vehicle for Bassett, and she was so eager to be in it that she postponed her wedding to accommodate a shooting delay said to be precipitated by script problems.[15] The delay may also have been caused by the fact that the film had problems getting the studio green light. It was finally approved only after the supporting role of Stella's best friend was expanded to accommodate Whoopi Goldberg's addition to the cast. This delay may testify to Hollywood's distrust of Bassett's star status or to their overarching reluctance to finance a star vehicle for a black female actress. Unfortunately, this distrust would turn out to be prophetic.

Stella would, in fact, become just as key a film in Bassett's career as *What's Love* or *Exhale*, but not at all in a positive sense. It represented a chance for Bassett to prove that she had the necessary qualities for continued stardom: beauty, acting range, and sex appeal. Each of these qualities was emphasized in the way the film's director, Kevin Rodney Sullivan, shot Bassett and by the promotional material surrounding the film's release. Sullivan shot Bassett as a star, lavishing attention in long shots on her taut, well-conditioned physique and in close-ups on her high cheekbones and glamorous looks. In addition, the film was promoted as containing scintillating love scenes in a May–December romance between Bassett as an "older" professional woman and Taye Diggs as the younger lover she meets on a Jamaican vacation.

Additionally, director Sullivan repeatedly described the film in interviews as providing Bassett with the opportunity "to play more of the notes than she's been allowed to play. More comedy" (Farr, 228). Upon its release, the film definitely did not live up to the box office expectations raised by its promotion as McMillan's follow-up to *Exhale* and the presence in its leading roles of two of the biggest black female Hollywood stars at the time. *Stella's* failure marks the beginning of the catastrophic decline of Bassett's career.

Critics were extremely harsh on the film, although Bassett's performance was not singled out as its major flaw. In fact, some reviewers even lauded her acting as the only saving grace in an otherwise dismal effort, characterized overall as a slow-moving glossy soap opera with a travel brochure quality and unbelievable characters. It was repeatedly compared unfavorably with *Waiting to Exhale*, which critics felt was much richer and more convincing. The lack of chemistry between Bassett and Taye Diggs was particularly singled out as a major flaw in the film, which was ultimately branded an escapist women's romantic fantasy that lacked romance. Bassett was not held primarily responsible for the film's failure, but she would never headline a film again.

Figure 7.1 Angela Bassett and Taye Diggs in a promotional still for *How Stella Got Her Groove Back* (Sullivan 1998), a film that was clearly conceived as a star vehicle for Bassett. The film was also promoted for its scintillating love scenes between Bassett and Diggs, but reviewers complained that their scenes together lacked sexual chemistry. (Reproduced with permission of Corbis.)

Although *Stella*'s reception seems to have precipitated Bassett's career decline, that decline actually began even before *Stella*'s 1998 release. The year that marks the beginning of the end of Bassett's rise to stardom was 1995. In that year, she played the female leads in three major films: *Waiting to Exhale, Strange Days* (Bigelow), and *A Vampire in Brooklyn* (Craven). Although *Exhale* was a huge success, the other two films were major disappointments, in spite of prominent directors and major male costars like Ralph Fiennes and Eddie Murphy. Although, again, Bassett's performances were not blamed for the films' failures and many critics saw her portrayal of a female action hero as one of the best aspects of an otherwise flawed *Strange Days*, her association with two box office flops, combined with *Stella*'s disappointing reception, stymied her career.

It was also in 1995 that Bassett decided to leave her agent of ten years and sign on with Ed Limato at the high-powered Hollywood agency ICM (International Creative Management). Bassett said she felt the move was necessary to solidify her star status: "I felt like I was in the major league and it was time to go to the majors" (Testino, 127). Limato's advice does not seem to have been of major league quality, however. It was after Bassett signed on with ICM that her role choice drew her farther and farther from her roots in black culture and more and more into supporting roles behind prominent white stars. She does not seem to have taken these parts because of their inherent value, but rather for the chance to work with stars of the caliber of Jodie Foster, Meryl Streep, and Robert De Niro. Yet this series of unmemorable minor roles in *Contact* (Zemmikis 1997) with Foster, *Music of the Heart* (Craven 1999) with Streep, and *The Score* (Oz 2001) with De Niro did nothing to enhance her career. The low point really came, however, with a starring role in the science fiction box office disaster *Supernova* (Hill 2000).

The decline of Bassett's career in the late 1990s can certainly be attributed to poor film choice, and it would be hard to dispute this conclusion. However, another answer involves her attraction to color-blind casting. What Bassett's involvement with ICM led her to do was to break from exactly what had precipitated her enormous career success: her portrayals of black female characters who resonated with the black community, offered strong role models to black and white female viewers, and testified to a strong black womanhood that seemed to triumph over all adversity. When she began to accept role after role that portrayed her merely as the love interest of or the supporting player behind a major white star, Bassett's career took a precipitous decline from which it has never been able to recover.

This is not to say that Bassett just sat back and watched her career disintegrate. In fact, she seems to have adopted three different strategies to revive her flagging stardom: she turned to theater, television, and independent films; returned to roles that provided strong female role models with resonance for black audiences; and looked to producing television dramas to gain more control of her role choice. Her most notable theater performance to date was Lady Macbeth opposite Alec Baldwin in the 1998 Public Theater production of the classic Shakespearean tragedy, directed by the prominent black director George C. Wolfe. In 2000, she also starred opposite Danny Glover in the film adaptation of Athol Fugard's classic South African drama *Boesman and Lena*. Shot on location in South Africa, the film was directed by John Berry, who had directed the play's first New York production in 1970 starring Ruby Dee and Basset's mentor, James Earl Jones.

Bassett not only looked to classic works, but also turned to television dramas and independent films to engineer a career rebirth. In her television performances, she seemed to return very deliberately to the types of roles upon which she had built her stardom: inspirational figures who provide strong role models for female viewers. In *Ruby's Bucket of Blood* (Werner 2001), a Showtime production that Bassett coproduced with executive producer Whoopi Goldberg, Bassett plays a fiercely independent saloon-keeper in the post-World War II rural South. A second notable television performance is her starring role as one of the great heroines of the civil rights movement in *The Rosa Parks Story* (Dash 2002), which she also executive produced.

In addition, Bassett played a prominent role in the ensemble cast of John Sayles's independent feature, *Sunshine State* (2002), a performance for which she won considerable critical praise. Her work for television also includes a recurring role as a CIA director in the popular television espionage series *Alias*. Now that she is in her midforties, an age at which all Hollywood actresses find it difficult to find roles, it is doubtful that Bassett will ever regain the level of stardom that she once briefly held. It is an indication of the racism that plagues the Hollywood film industry that the most respected black actress in contemporary Hollywood only maintains a very tenuous hold on stardom.

The Angela Bassett Image

Angela Bassett's star image is composed of two major image clusters: (1) beauty, glamour, sexuality, and physicality; and (2) iconic status as a role model and a figure of strong black womanhood. The apparent seamless complementarity of these different components masks the significant contradictions between Bassett's role as an image of black female strength and her status as a sex symbol.

Beauty, Glamour, Sexuality, Physicality:
"A Real Movie Star Presence"[16]

Much of Bassett's publicity emphasizes her physical attractiveness. She has been described, for instance, as a reincarnation of glamorous black female stars of the past. As one reporter described her as she arrived for an interview, "Trained at Yale's drama school, and blessed with regal cheekbones and flawless skin, Bassett radiated a cool that audiences hadn't seen from a black actress on the big screen since the days of Diana Ross, Diahann Carroll, and Cicely Tyson in the early 70s" (Samuels). There is, however, a clear difference between Bassett and these earlier black Hollywood stars, and this difference involves the darkness of her skin.

Although it is almost never mentioned in her publicity, Bassett's stardom represents a quite progressive step for Hollywood in that she is a dark-skinned, black-featured female star who is recognized for her beauty, something unheard of in the past and still extremely rare. In fact, one reporter maintains that promoters of *What's Love Got to Do with It* were so uncomfortable with the darkness of Bassett's skin and so fearful that this darkness would frighten away white viewers that they did not allow her face to be exhibited on posters for the film; instead, all that was shown was a black line drawing of an unidentifiable profile floating in a white space (Als, 135).

After *What's Love Got to Do with It*, what began to stand out in descriptions of Bassett's appearance was not her beauty, but her physicality, which was in turn associated with a strong sexual presence. This aspect of Bassett's image seems to have stemmed directly from her association with Tina Turner. In fact, before her portrayal of Turner, who was always associated with a muscular, aggressive female sexuality, Bassett was strongly identified with nurturing mother roles and not at all with sexual allure. The extensive physical training she undertook in order to play the Tina Turner role changed all that, and Bassett became indelibly associated with an aggressive sexual presence, symbolized in particular by her "famously taut and structured upper arms." Her muscular biceps, in fact, became so famous that she told an interviewer that a fan even approached her in the street wanting to feel her muscles (Farr, 228).

The combination of muscularity and beauty in Bassett's star persona, suggesting as it does that women can be both strong and beautiful, provides a progressive female image, yet Bassett's reported discomfort with this aspect of her persona undercuts this progressivity. It seems to reflect her fear that too much focus on her physicality could make her seem unfeminine and to support traditional notions that a woman who is athletic has somehow compromised her beauty.

In fact, as her career took a downturn, Bassett and her promoters seemed to have become quite concerned that this association was not working to Bassett's benefit. As a result, she began to play down associations of her image with physical strength. For instance, *How Stella Got Her Groove Back*'s fashion designer, Ruth E. Carter, commented that "Angela always plays these wonderful role models, but they're very tough and structured and suited and tailored. I thought it was time to reverse that. I wanted to do glamorous the whole time" (FitzGerald, 83). When asked how she maintains her muscularity, Bassett told an interviewer, "I run on the treadmill, lift weights and run but only as much and as often as is absolutely necessary. I find exercising a real drag. I'm really blessed because my genes give me a real head start" (Hobson 1998a).

As part of her promotional activities for *Sunshine State*, a film that she clearly hoped would revive her career, Bassett was described by one interviewer as having shed her previously cultivated tailored elegance and "cranked up her style to sizzling with a hot, sexy look for red-carpet events." She wore a low-cut floral-on-white silk Roberto Cavelli gown to the Essence Awards; a tight, cleavage-revealing gown by young black designer

C.D. Green to the Council of Fashion Designers Association Awards; and a low-cut, tiger-print Escada jumpsuit to the *Sunshine State* premier. When asked about the change in fashion style, she proposed that she was "breaking out a little of what's comfortable and easy" and cultivating a look that is "modern and fresh, and perhaps a little bit more feminine."[17] The nervousness that Bassett expresses about the incompatibility in her image lexicon between physical strength and feminine glamour reflects a general cultural uncertainty about contemporary muscular femininity.

The Role Model: Angela the Icon

The sexiness of the Bassett image fits uncomfortably with an even more prominent aspect of her star persona: her status as a role model and a symbol of black accomplishment. Terry McMillan, for instance, describes Bassett as having an "aura" that is "about dignity and pride" (Als, 132). Similarly, Bassett has characterized her life as about "being self-assured, confident, growing, continually growing."[18] She has said that because she knew from an early age that she would "be in the public eye" (FitzGerald, 21), she paid particular attention to her mother's advice always "to go for the quality, try to take the high road in life" (Testino, 127). When asked if she sees herself as a role model for her fans, she said,

> I do and they've told me so. I just worked in Florida [on *Sunshine State*] and I met someone who said, "I drove down from Georgia to meet you because I wanted to tell you that I was in a relationship like the one you had in *What's Love Got to Do with It* and seeing that movie helped me." I hear that a good deal.[19]

Although she realizes that she "[c]an't live for everyone. Can't represent all people," she feels that she can still "stand alone and attempt to stand for things that are truthful and good and right" (Farr, 228).

Some critics have seen Bassett as engaged in a "struggle to reinvent Hollywood's view of black women as something other than wisecracking or doleful martyrs, their hair stiff with brilliantine and the funk of subjugation" (Als, 132); others have criticized her as a symbol not of black womanhood per se, but of what Hollywood wants black women to be. One interviewer even proposed that Hollywood only supports Bassett because of the unintimidating nature of her blackness, which "doesn't threaten because Bassett's somewhat strident self-respect satisfies the industry's moral yearnings" because she is not a "loud ... menacing or haughty Negress ... not idiosyncratic" (Als, 132).

One side effect of Bassett's assimilation into white Hollywood has been this questioning of the depth of her identification as African American. In fact, in an interview she did with a black journalist for *The New Yorker*, she seemed determined to confirm her blackness by using black dialect and joking about it in a way that demonstrated her sensitivity to the double consciousness experienced by many successful black women, "Now, y'all *know* I can speak proper English. I'm educated. My mama would be shocked to hear me speaking in this down-home way to a journalist. But I'm so *comfy*" (Als, 132).

Press releases discussing Bassett's personal life definitely emphasize her success within the white Hollywood film establishment and her affluent lifestyle, which includes her "big, elegant house" and tan Mercedes convertible[20]; her perfect marriage to fellow actor Courtney B. Vance; and her strong religious beliefs. Bassett's "big, elegant house" is located in Hancock Park, east of Beverly Hills, a neighborhood infamous for its racial restrictions until Nat King Cole moved in and challenged them in the late 1940s (Testino, 125). Thus, Bassett lives in a neighborhood noted for its association with a black star who successfully broke down barriers preventing his assimilation into white Hollywood. Also held up as exemplary is Bassett's marriage to Vance, a television and film star in his own right best known for his role in the popular crime series *Law and Order: Criminal Intent*. Bassett, who waited until she was thirty-nine to marry, has described Vance as the image of perfect black manhood, who was attractive to her because he was

> ... such a gentleman with everyone. He was a man who gave of himself so quickly and easily. He did such kind things for people like walking my best friend's mother's dog. The more I watched Courtney around other people, the more I knew he was the kind of man I could get through rough patches with and that was really important for me (FitzGerald, 76).

She also clearly was attracted to Vance because of his religious faith. They first met when they were attending the Yale School of Drama and became friends, but their romance did not accelerate until Vance turned to religion after the suicide death of his father and was baptized into the Abyssinian Baptist Church (FitzGerald, 76). As noted earlier, Bassett, a devout Baptist who describes herself as "a person with great faith,"[21] is unique among stars in that she has very openly proclaimed her strong religious affiliation. When asked before her marriage who would be her perfect mate, she listed religious belief as her highest priority, "First and foremost, he has to be a man of God. It's important to me that we have that foundation in common, because I think we'd be able to weather any storms that come along." She added, however, that she did not feel that having a man was essential to make her happy because women should not "make men the center of [their] joy. I don't. I make God the center of my joy" (Bates).

Another important aspect of Bassett's image is her representation of strong black womanhood. She has freely embraced this role in her film performances and her personal life, saying that she inherited it from her mother: "I'm a strong black woman. My mother is a strong black woman. So are my grandmother and my great-grandmother and my aunt. If nothing else ever happened, I know that I'd keep working. And if it all went away tomorrow, I know that I'd endure" (FitzGerald, 97). Bassett holds her mother up as having given her a sense of independence and female power, and she explicitly connects that power with the roles she has chosen to play. For instance, when doing publicity interviews for *What's Love Got to Do with It*, she told the story of her mother's brief marriage to an abusive man: "She immediately annulled the marriage. After seven days—boom!—annulled. That's my example. You don't have to suffer in silence" (FitzGerald, 18). In another interview, she explained what she learned from her mother's reaction to the situation:

> It was disappointing, but it taught her daughters that you don't suffer a man to put his hand on you. She said, "Grown people don't hit grown people." I remember that. She may not, but I remember it. A man has never been able to hit me. And that's what I would teach my children (Colier).

Bassett's status as a role model for her female fans is such a dominant element in her image and so strongly supported by the roles she has chosen to play that it tends to permeate every aspect of her acting career.

Approach to Acting

Like Meryl Streep, Angela Bassett's Yale pedigree has gained her a reputation as a classically trained actress and a substantial amount of respect in the industry. Lawrence Fishburne in *What's Love Got to Do with It* and Whitney Houston in *Waiting to Exhale* claim that one reason they took their roles opposite Bassett was because of their admiration for her acting talent (FitzGerald, 43, 61). Donald Bogle has even compared her to the great Hollywood actresses of the past: "Bassett is like the old-style actresses. She very much reminds me of Joan Crawford and Bette Davis, women who commanded your attention in a film even when their mouths were closed" (Samuels). Bassett also resembles "the old-style actresses" of Hollywood's past in that she downplays her extensive training and portrays herself as a nontheoretical actress, someone who regards acting as just "hard, hard work" (Bates). She describes her approach to performance as, "I just come out of my trailer and do all that I can."[22]

Yet her publicity also emphasizes her devotion to acting as a craft rather than merely as a job, especially in terms of her techniques of characterization. Like Meryl Streep, Bassett gained significant stature in terms of acting reputation from her early association with theater. For instance, John Sayles, who directed her in *Sunshine State*, proposed: "Because of Angela's theater background, she has a strong command of the art form. She just keeps digging and digging into a character so you get every ounce" (Samuels).

Also like Streep, Basset has been praised for her chameleonesque ability to assume a character and to submerge herself completely in a role. She is often lauded for cultivating a "dignified, alert, and earnestly emotive screen presence ... [that] generate[s] audience sympathy (Als, 132). Her manager Doug Chapin has described her as having "the ability not only to portray emotions, which a lot of good actors have, but to have the audience experience them with her" (Als, 132). Bassett has said that one of the reasons she has no interest in playing evil characters is because one of her acting goals is to create characters who garner audience "compassion and sympathy ... I always want to do that."[23]

Indeed, Bassett's role choice has demonstrated not only her aversion to playing villainesses, but also her attraction to playing larger-than-life inspirational heroines modeled on real life iconic figures from black history. From Katherine Jackson in *The Jacksons: An American Dream*, Betty Shabazz in *Malcolm X*, and Tina Turner in *What's Love Got to Do with It* to Rosa Parks in *The Rosa Parks Story*, Bassett's career seems to have been built on her effective incarnation of female icons from the annals of black history. Her success in these characterizations is most often presented as stemming from her ability to present them as real people with whom audiences can identify.

Another reason why Bassett is so successful in these roles that does get mentioned very frequently in press releases is her willingness to take great pains to model these characterizations after the real historical figures upon which they are based and to construct them as models of female strength and heroism worthy of emulation. She has discussed in particular the advice she received from Tina Turner during the shooting of *What's Love Got to Do with It*. Turner apparently was a frequent visitor on the set who coached Bassett on how to do her make-up and to perform her dance routines, even giving Bassett her white linen Armani shirt to add verisimilitude to her performance of Turner's "I Might Have Been a Queen" musical number (FitzGerald, 42). Bassett credits Turner with giving her the stamina to withstand the grueling rehearsals and the emotional intensity of the role. She describes her first meeting with the rock star in inspirational terms:

> When I walked into the room, she immediately hugged me and told her manager that she thought I was beautiful. And then she started showing me some of the dance routines from her days with the Ikettes. ... Seeing her energy, her serious work ethic, and just how beautiful she really is up close was all the inspiration I needed to be able to take on anything. When I walked out of that room, I was flying on cloud nine and I knew I would give the part everything I had! (FitzGerald, 41).

Bassett has similarly credited Katherine Jackson with giving her "some points" in regard to her characterization in *The Jacksons: An American Dream* (FitzGerald, 37). She has also said that in constructing her role in *The Rosa Parks Story* she drew on her memories of an earlier meeting with Parks. According to Bassett, Parks came across as "a very reasonable and calm and reserved individual ... very kind and sweet," so unassuming that she never even took credit for the important role she played in the 1960s civil rights struggle. Bassett says that to play Parks, she had to alter her usual acting style:

> [Parks] is very different from a lot of characters that I've played that, perhaps, chew up the scenery a bit. I was trying to be truthful to Mrs. Parks even though [with] my own personal drama, I would want to be bigger than life. I was always trying to be honest to her and not trying to make it more dramatic than perhaps it needs to be.[24]

Additionally, Bassett's success in reincarnating historical figures seems to stem from her willingness to do extensive preparations to add a note of realism to her portrayals. Publicity at the time of the release of *What's Love Got to Do with It* emphasized the grueling ordeal Bassett went through to create the role. Just in preparing for the auditions, she hired a choreographer to work with her on the dance routines and studied hours of video recordings of Turner's performances to perfect her imitation of the rock star's movements and mannerisms (FitzGerald, 40). As Bassett describes the process, "They gave you six songs, including "Proud Mary" top to bottom. They gave you four or five scenes—young Tina, 1960s Tina, dragged down the hall and get a fractured left hand Tina. It was rough" (FitzGerald, 41). Bassett did fracture her hand during the auditions, but she also won the role.

Once the filming began, a whole new set of trials was involved. Bassett describes her preparation for the role as intensely physical:

> I had a dialect coach, a singing coach, a choreographer and a personal trainer for 30 days before the filming began. I lifted weights for two hours a day, six days a week and went on a high-protein, no-sweets diet—egg whites, tuna without mayo, vegetables—to get Tina's incredibly muscular physique. If I had had two months

Figure 7.2 Angela Bassett performing as Tina Turner in a scene from *What's Love Got to Do with It* (Gibson 1993). Bassett told reporters that lip-synching Turner's songs was extremely difficult because "she's very extemporaneous. You've got to know every inflection and every breath she takes" (Sturley, 86–87). (Reproduced with permission of Corbis.)

to prepare, I think I would've been able to enter a bodybuilding contest afterward. I have to admit, though, once filming began and I saw the results of all the hard work I'd put in, I was like, "Wow, this is great!"[25]

Not only was the filming grueling because of the necessary physical preparations, but also because the studio was anxious to get the film released to coincide with Turner's world tour. As a result, the cast and crew were forced to work twenty-hour days. Bassett told reporters that on several occasions she was ready to quit from sheer exhaustion. On one day she says she cried for seventeen hours straight because of the emotional nature of the role, and after she almost fell asleep at the wheel on the way to the studio, costar Lawrence Fishburne insisted that she be given a chauffeur (Als, 135). Bassett also told reporters that lip-synching Turner's songs was particularly difficult because "there were rough mixes and she's very extemporaneous. You've got to know every inflection and every breath she takes."[26]

The result of Bassett's arduous efforts won her rave reviews. She was widely praised for having completely transformed herself into Tina Turner. Roger Ebert's glowing review is representative: "Bassett's performance of the songs are so much in synch—not just lip-synch, but physically, and with personality and soul—that it always seems as if we're watching Tina at work" (FitzGerald, 43).

Throughout her career, critics have lauded Bassett for bringing emotional range and psychological depth to her characterizations. For instance, she portrays Katherine Jackson, Tina Turner, and Rosa Parks through a wide range of physical and emotional changes from their mid-teens to middle-age. As her *How Stella Got Her Groove Back* director Kevin Rodney Sullivan proposes

> Angela Bassett was perfect [for the role of Stella] because of her range and depth. She has a life force, a soul, a spirit that is very powerful. Stella represents a three-dimensional character—sexy, funny, powerful. In the past black female characters have been limited—typically one thing or the other—never all. If audiences could see more African-American females in multidimensional roles, it would be wonderful (FitzGerald, 83).

Yet Bassett's acting range can also be seen as decidedly limited, and this limitation may at least partially account for her career decline. High drama is clearly her forte, and in many ways her only forte. Early in her film career her acting became very strongly identified with the intensity of her performances. She even described herself as "so much the drama queen" (Altman) that the industry came to perceive her as "serious with a capital S" (FitzGerald, 81). Her attempts to solidify her stardom by branching out into comedy in *How Stella Got Her Groove Back* and *A Vampire in Brooklyn* failed miserably and substantially contributed to the decline of her career. Bassett came to be such an extremely type-cast actress that, when not playing *historical* role models, she was playing women who are role models in other ways.

Although her acting roles thus became perfectly integrated with her star persona, they also could be seen as somewhat repetitious and predictable. All of Bassett's major film roles in fact embody strong, competent, and clever heroines who provide inspiration for female viewers, especially black female viewers. Reviewers have described her characters repeatedly as "tough paragons" (Seymour, F7), "strong resilient women, unbroken by faithless men, violent abuse, and other woes" (Rader, 4), and "characters pitched into emotional free-fall who, somehow, survive the ordeal" (Seymour, F1).

Bassett has told interviewers that she is "attracted to characters who make the best of their situation, where they at some point wake up to their own life and take control of it. Perhaps it mirrors my own life."[27] She has also characterized her favorite roles as "the underdog, women who struggle" (Als, 134). Because they "suffer and fight," she believes they find "a type of dignity" and "triumph in the end, in their spirit, if not physically or materially. But where it really counts, in your spirit."[28] She singled out Tina Turner in *What's Love Got to Do with It* and Bernadine in *Waiting to Exhale* as her favorite roles because "I admire that Tina overcame her circumstances; she called upon her strength to overcome tremendous obstacles and eventually found her self-esteem. Bernadine did the same thing. They're both heroes" (Bates).

In interviews about her role opposite Robert De Niro in *The Score*, she talked about taking the part because she felt her character had strong character traits, but when she arrived in Montreal for shooting, she found that director Frank Oz had altered the character in ways that made her "weak and unfocused." Bassett said she immediately demanded that the character be restored to the one she had agreed to play (Churchill). Yet when asked if she enjoys playing strong heroines, she demurred somewhat, obviously afraid that her image would come across as too harsh: "Yes. That's the image that I like to put out there, and those are the parts I'm attracted to. But not iron-fist kind of strong, just self-assured. I'm nice too" (Morales).

Bassett's role in *The Score* demonstrates another aspect of her role choice: her attraction to breaking the color barrier. Perhaps as a counterpose to her frequent casting as black female icons, Bassett has actively sought out "nonrace roles" where she is cast in parts not necessarily intended for a black actress. She said that she took the role in *The Score* even though it was relatively small because "when I read the script, it was obvious my role hadn't been written for an African-American actress. She was just a woman and a human being. When a woman of color was cast, I was glad it was me" (Churchill).

She explained her attraction to her roles in *Strange Days* and *Supernova* in the same way: "But in the script, she isn't black or white. They just wanted me to play the role. We're all human, and I hope we keep on moving toward that. You know, I could be a black Italian" (Brady). As noted earlier, Bassett also played Lady Macbeth opposite Alec Baldwin in director George C. Wolfe's 1998 production of the Shakespeare play. Wolfe, who cast a number of black actors in parts in the play ordinarily played by whites, eloquently expressed the philosophy behind his casting choices:

> The opportunity to play all types of roles was hard won. Critics, producers, and writers are sometimes so rigid and literal in approaching what is about imagination, and heightened reality. They couldn't see beyond, "How can she be playing his sister if she's black and he's white?" Only when they saw that people weren't running screaming out of the theater did they come around. It's a wearing down process until you get to the point where you simply get the best possible actor for the role. We still have a long way to go, but we're getting there (FitzGerald, 87).

Bassett has openly expressed her conviction that her race has interfered with her casting in several prominent roles. As noted previously, she felt the same opportunities did not open up for her after she was nominated for an Academy Award as would have been available to a white actress. She also proposed that she lost several roles in major movies because producers did not think she would be a good box office attraction opposite a white leading man (Sterns). Breaking the Hollywood tradition of stars refusing to discuss with the press roles they did not get, Bassett revealed to one interviewer the story behind her failure to be cast opposite Sean Connery in the 1999 thriller *Entrapment* (Amiel):

> Sean told me he would love what our being in the film would mean across the board for black and white. I remember him saying how beautiful our skin would look next to each other's and how I was perfect. I left the meeting thinking, "It's mine." But a few weeks later, they cast a lesser-known actress [Katherine Zeta–Jones] at the time. I guess Hollywood wasn't as progressive

as Connery thought. I think I really could have added spice to that role (Samuels).

It is not only Bassett's color that has lost her roles, but perhaps also her strong feelings about not doing on-screen nudity. She has complained that in movie sex scenes: "It's always the woman's body, never the man's body. And if it's the man's body, it's someone you're not interested in seeing anyway" (Farr, 228). After *What's Love Got to Do with It*, she said she received nothing but what she describes as "booty call" scripts, which she adamantly refused to do. She holds up Meryl Streep as her model: "Film is forever. It's about putting something out there you can be proud of ten years later. I mean, Meryl Streep won Oscars without all that" (Samuels).

Although reviewers used the euphemism "a lack of chemistry" in describing Bassett's love scenes with Taye Diggs in *How Stella Got Her Groove Back*, it was more likely the film's lack of steamy sex scenes that bothered them and ultimately hurt the film at the box office. Bassett had originally agreed to use a body double in the film's sex scenes, but then had second thoughts, "I thought, people will still think, 'Oh, there's Angela's head, there's Angela's behind.' Next thing you know, you're walking down Larchmont and it'll be, 'Hey, gi-i-i-rl!'" Then, she agreed to do the scenes if she could choreograph them with the director. Not even feeling comfortable with this arrangement, however, she finally refused to do any nudity at all (Farr, 228).

Her remarks on Halle Berry's Oscar-winning role in *Monster's Ball*, which involved a graphic sex scene with Billy Bob Thornton, stirred some unfavorable publicity. In an interview, Bassett implied that the role in *Monster's Ball* was demeaning to black women and added, "I wasn't going to be a prostitute on film. I couldn't do that because it's such a stereotype about black women and sexuality" (Samuels). Her interviewer then went on to point out that several other black actresses had passed on *Monster's Ball*, ostensibly because of the required nudity, implying that Bassett had been offered the role. Later in the article, Bassett commented,

> I can't and don't begrudge Halle her success. It wasn't the role for me, but I told her she'd win and I told her to go get what was hers. Of course I want one, too. I would love to have an Oscar. But it has to be for something I can sleep with it at night (Samuels).

Press reports of the interview announced that Bassett had said she had turned down the role in *Monster's Ball*, which she never really said, and that she attacked Berry for having taken it. *Monster's Ball*'s producer Lee Daniels, who is also black, was then quoted as having characterized Bassett's comments as "completely incorrect." First of all, he said Bassett had never been offered Berry's role in the film. Then, he went on to paint her as disloyal to her race: "There are movies that I don't like, that are black that I would never go to, but I am publicly very supportive of my people, otherwise there is no structure, there is nothing."[29]

Although Bassett might see nude scenes as a bit *too* realistic, she strongly advocates a naturalistic approach to acting. Although her publicity often emphasizes her "classical training," she has always spoken of her acting techniques as entirely intuitive. For instance, when asked about her process in playing Bernadine in *Waiting to Exhale*, she said: "I just went in with my gut as opposed to building the role from the inside out. It was just a matter of taking that which you've observed and getting at the emotional essence as intuitively as you can" (Seymour, F1–F7).

On the other hand, she is often described as "something of a purist as an actress" (Sturley) and as having a "mannered cool technique" (Als, 132). Her *Stella* director Kevin Rodney Sullivan characterized her as "technically brilliant. You'd stage a scene and she'd make it better because she understood a shot" (Farr, 228). Yet Bassett, like so many other contemporary actresses, has played down the technical aspects of her process, associating her acting method with naturalism. For instance, she describes acting as "not doing the extraordinary. It's doing the ordinary extraordinarily well" (Thompson), and she characterizes the "mark of a true professional [as] being able to get up and do it, even though it's hard work, but you don't make it look like it's hard work" (FitzGerald, 25–26).

She singles out Lloyd Richards as the most important influence on her acting methodology because "He insisted that I be honest in the work, even if it was painful. He always told me, 'The audience doesn't want to see how hard you're working. Make it look honest and effortless'" (FitzGerald, 25). His patented advice to students was "Don't wave the yellow chicken!" Bassett says she took from this not to "telegraph too much to the audience. Let them do some of the work" (Seymour, F7). There is, however, an ostensiveness to Bassett's performances that belies her stated devotion to naturalism. There is a bigness to her acting style that reviewers have labeled her "trademark intensity" (FitzGerald, 81). She has even described herself as capable of "chew[ing] up the scenery a bit" (Holmes). George C. Wolfe says the first time he saw her on stage in *Antigone* the experience was so enthralling to him not because of the naturalism of her acting, but exactly because he could see the actress behind the performance:

> To this day I can recall the sensation of sitting in that cold, dark theater, watching Angela work. I remember being rendered powerless by the endless swirl of contradictions that was her performance: absolutely in control, yet the essence of vulnerability; sensual,

delicate, provocative … fierce! And what she was doing to that language—kissing and caressing it one minute and then spitting it out with haughty disdain the next (FitzGerald, 30).

Similarly, Kathryn Bigelow, who directed Bassett in *Strange Days*, commented:

She's one of the most talented actresses working in the business today. If you want Angela to dial a performance down, you just say so and she's right in the zone … [or] you just had to ask her to increase the volume and she'd go as far as you'd ever want to go (Testino, 129).

Like many screen actresses, Bassett often speaks in interviews about her continuing attraction to the theater:

That's were I started. That's the way I grew up. I remember when I used to audition for theatrical roles, and I could do anything! Jump on a fireplace, roll around, and shout. Whatever was needed. And that's such a wonderful difference from working in front of the camera, which is like working with a laser, as opposed to a scalpel, to get at a character (FitzGerald, 86).

For Bassett, the major attraction of the theater is clearly the opportunity for a more ostensive performance than is possible in film. As she said when she did *Macbeth*,

I hadn't been back to the stage in so long. I missed that intimate contact with a live audience, the way you get into the emotion of a character. In movies you're doing small moments again and again, building a scene. But there's something about the passion you bring to the stage, the way you have to be bigger on the stage and reach all the way to the back of the theater, and I could pull it back and shape it and do whatever I want with it (FitzGerald, 85).

She even says she was attracted to doing the film version of *Boesman and Lena* because it offered her the "opportunity to on film do theater work. There's a play and a character and an arc and a depth that is sometimes not readily found in some of the scripts that I read. It combined for me the best of both worlds" (Murphy).

The mixed nature of the critical response to Bassett's performance in *Macbeth* reflects the contemporary critical disdain for ostensive star acting, even on the stage where a mannered performance is much more accepted than in film. Positive reviews of Bassett's performance—notably, they are by female reviewers—describe her, for instance, as

Returning to the stage after having her triumphant way with Hollywood ... [and] tak[ing] her first Shakespearean role in her teeth and wrestl[ing] it to the ground. Leonine, fearsome, glamorous, yet earthy, Bassett's Lady Macbeth seems quite capable of taking the throne away from all competitors without having to raise a dagger (Linda Winer, quoted in FitzGerald, 86).

Another reviewer describes Bassett as having

The audience completely mesmerized as she goes mad—sleepwalking while talking of murder and continually and forcefully motioning to wash her hands, which could never be clean of the blood of those she forced Macbeth to slaughter. One had to feel pity for this evil character, who reaped the fate of her deeds (Linda Armstrong, quoted in FitzGerald, 86).

Male reviewers were much less generous, perhaps because they were much less approving of an actress with such a big ostensive style. They proposed that the details of her characterization would "go in and out of focus" and that she seemed "oddly impersonal in her long speeches." Jack Kroll's review was the most scathing: "As fiercely beautiful as a hawk in her leather dress, she enters in a paroxysm of overenunciation and florid gestures. Exhorting hubby to 'screw your courage to the sticking point,' she grabs his crotch to make the point stick. Ouch" (quoted in Stearns). This idea that Bassett takes ostensiveness a bit too far has led to criticism that her performances are extreme and consistently "over the top" (Stearns). One wonders, however, why these same objections have not been made about male stars like Al Pacino and Danny Glover, who also have very ostensive acting styles.

Interestingly, despite her often stated love for the theater, Bassett has not returned to the stage in any consistent fashion to revive her dwindling acting prospects. Instead, as noted earlier, she has turned to television producing and says she hopes eventually to direct. Her turn to television is not necessarily a rejection of film, but rather a response to the difficulties she says she has experienced breaking into film producing:

It's a lot easier for me to get a producing credit on TV than in feature films. In the feature film world I still am, as many actors are, the hired hand. It's a rarefied world. Tom Cruise, Julia Roberts, Mel Gibson, they're able to produce and star. That's not my world. But in television, because I have been the lead in features and I have name and face recognition, it's easier for me to go to the smaller screen on television and get a picture made and to also produce it.[30]

That her interest in television producing is motivated primarily by her desire to provide herself with good roles seems confirmed by the fact that she has starred in both of the made-for-television films that she has produced: *Ruby's Bucket of Blood* (2001) for Showtime and *The Rosa Parks Story* (Dash 2002) for CBS. She became involved in *Ruby's Bucket of Blood*, an adaptation of the Julie Hebert play, when its executive producer Whoopi Goldberg decided she did not want to star in the film and asked Bassett to replace her. Bassett found her duties as producer interesting and instructive: "Basically, it was just me suggesting things to the director, which he accepted, a little bit to my surprise. I'm also going into the editing room and seeing how all that's done" (FitzGerald, 95). She was also involved in casting (Keveney 2001), a role she would assume again when she became executive producer of *The Rosa Parks Story*.

For *Rosa Parks*, she not only chose her male costar, James Holmes, but worked to get the prominent African-American independent film director Julie Dash to direct. When asked if she was interested in moving from producing to directing in the future, she replied enthusiastically: "You bet. That's what I'm planning to do next. I'm looking at scripts and directing is the next step. I want the whole deal, baby!" (FitzGerald, 95). Yet, in another interview, she was decidedly more tentative:

> I'm thinking about directing, but I know it's a lot of work and I appreciate what directors do and I would like to be good at it. The opportunity has presented itself four to five times and I usually said no because of the script. At this time, I've got enough projects to work with (Morales).

Angela Bassett: Actress and Image

There are certainly many progressive components of Angela Bassett's image. As an African-American female star, she has broken many barriers. She is a dark-skinned black actress who has been successful in Hollywood and a glamorous black star who refuses to do nudity or to promote herself by means of an overly sexualized image; instead, she has consistently portrayed characters that are icons of strong black womanhood and has brought to life inspirational female figures from African-American history. Additionally, many of her films have been empowering for women. As Bassett has pointed out, with its strong message of female triumph over male dominance, *What's Love Got to Do with It* empowered many of its female viewers to break out of abusive spousal relationships. The novel and the film, *Waiting to Exhale*, have been seen as feminist texts, championing the importance of female friendship. *Strange Days* established Bassett as the first black female action hero of the 1990s, and *How Stella Got Her Groove Back* offered a rare screen portrayal of romance between a middle-aged woman and a much younger man.

All of these progressive aspects are thrown into question, however, by Bassett's failure to sustain her stardom beyond the height of her success in the mid-1990s. Several possible reasons for her career decline include racism in the industry, poor role choice, the hazards to a female star of refusing to do nudity, and the lack of good roles for actresses over forty. Sadly, the failure of a black star of Bassett's stature and talent to sustain a flourishing career does not paint a very attractive picture of the possibilities for African-American actresses in white, male-dominated Hollywood.

References

1. Testino, Mario. 1995. "Just You Wait If You Haven't Noticed Angela Bassett." *Harper's Bazaar* Oct.: 257, Angela Bassett Clippings File, Margaret Herrick Library, Beverly Hills, California; hereafter cited in text.
2. Hobson, Louis B. 1998. "All the Right Moves." *Calgary Sun* Aug. 30 <http://www.canoe.ca/jammoviesartistsB/bassett.html>; hereafter cited in text.
3. Samuels, Allison. 2002. "Angela's Fire." *Newsweek*, July 1, MSNBC Online, http://www.stacks.msnbc.com/news/771033.asp.
4. Churchill, Bonnie. 2001. "Actress 'Scores' with a String of Solid Roles." *Christian Science Monitor* 93(160) (July 13): 18.
5. FitzGerald, Dawn. 2002. *Angela Bassett*. Philadelphia: Chelsea House, pp. 22–25; hereafter cited in text.
6. Altman, Sheryl. "Angela Bassett: What's Age Got to Do with It?" Women.com. http://www.women.com/entertain/celeb/articles.
7. Hobson, Louis B. 1998. "Angela Bassett's Career Is Working Like a Charm." *Calgary Sun* Aug. 30, http://www.canoe.ca/jammoviesartistsB/bassett.html.
8. Seymour, Gene. 1995. "Stopping Just Long Enough to Exhale." *L.A. Times* Dec. 18: F7; hereafter cited in text.
9. Als, Hilton. 1996. "A Crossover Star." *The New Yorker,* April 29/May 6: 134; hereafter cited in text.
10. Bates, Karen Grigsby. 1995. "Angela Bassett Is Not a Diva!" *Essence* 26(8) (Dec.): 78–80. EBSCOhost Academic Search Premier. GALILEO. http://galileo.peachnet.edu.
11. Brady, James. 1995. "In Step with Angela Bassett." *Parade,* Sept. 24: np Angela Bassett Clippings File, Margaret Harrick Library Beverly Hills, CA.
12. Only two black actresses have won Oscars in the supporting actress category: Hattie McDaniel and Whoopi Goldberg. Dorothy Dandridge, Diana Ross, and Diahann Carroll were nominated for best actress before Bassett, but like Bassett, they did not win. Halle Barry was the first black actress to win the Oscar for best actress in 2001.
13. "Angela Bassett Brands the Oscars Racist." 2002. Internet Movie Data Base, Feb. 14, <http://www.imdb.com/name/nm000291/news>.

14. Kirkland, Bruce. 1998. "Acting Out a Fantasy." *Toronto Sun* Aug. 30, <http://www.canoe.ca/jammoviesartistsB/bassett.html>; hereafter cited in text.
15. Farr, Louise. 1998. "Angela's Assets." *W Magazine*. August: 228; hereafter cited in text.
16. Sullivan, Kevin Rodney, director of *How Stella Got Her Grove Back*, quoted in FitzGerald, Dawn. 2002. *Angela Bassett*. Philadelphia: Chelsea House, p. 83.
17. Carter, Kelly. 2002. "Angela Bassett, Fashion Chameleon." *USA Today* Sept. 31, <http://www.usatoday.com/life/2002/2002-06-21-bassett.html>; hereafter cited in text.
18. Collier, Aldore D. 1998. "'Stella' and Angela Bassett Get Their Groove Back (New Movie Imitates Life)." *Ebony* Sept., <htpp://www.findarticles.com/p/articles/mi_m1077/is_n11_v53/ai_21080616>; hereafter cited in text.
19. Morales, Wilson. 2001. "An Interview with Angela Bassett." July, Blackfilm.com, <http://www.blackfilm.com/20010/features/i-angelabassett.html>; hereafter cited in text.
20. Rader, Dotson. 2002. "'Don't Settle for Average.'" *Parade* Feb. 17: 4, Angela Bassett Clippings File, Margaret Herrick Library, Beverly Hills, CA.
21. Hobson, Louis B. 1997. "Bassett's Dogged Faith." *Calgary Sun* July 22, <http://www.canoe.ca/jammoviesartistsB/bassett.html>.
22. Thompson, Bob. 1997. "How Angela Found Her Groove." *Toronto Sun* July 15, <http://www.canoe.ca/jammoviesartistsB/bassett.html>; hereafter cited in text.
23. Stearns, David Patrick. 1998. "This Stormy 'Macbeth' Is Short of Bewitching." *USA Today*, March, 17:1D, EBSCOhost Academic Search, GALLILEO, <http://www.galileo.peachnet.edu>; hereafter cited in text.
24. Holmes II, Emory. 2002. "An Actress Gets to Portray an Icon." *Los Angeles Times* Feb. 22: np, Angela Bassett Clippings File, Margaret Herrick Library, Beverley Hills, CA; hereafter cited in text.
25. Gregory, Deborah. 1993. "Angela Bassett Plays Living Legend Tina Turner." *Essence*, 24(3) (July): 52.
26. Sturley, Teresa. 1993. "Angela Bassett: What's Love Got to Do With It?" *Interview* June: 86–87, Angela Bassett Clippings File, Margaret Herrick Library, Beverly Hills, CA; hereafter cited in text.
27. Keveney, Bill. 2001. "Angela Bassett Sings Out about Ruby and Rosa." *USA Today* Nov. 29, http://www.usatoday.com/life/2001/2001-11-29-bassett.htm.
28. Murphy, Ted. 2002. "Angela Bassett on Playing Lena." What's News Online, 31 Sept., <http.//www.baseline.hollywood.com/screen/whosnews/abassett.asp>; herafter cited in text.
29. "Ball Producer Reacts to Bassett's Charges." 2002. Internet Movie Data Base, June 28, 2002, <htttp://www.imdb.com/name/nm000291/news>.
30. Owen, Rob. 2002. "Television Preview: Actress Respects Rosa Parks' Reserve as Well as Her Strength." *Pittsburgh Post–Gazette* Online, Feb. 22, <http://www.post-gazette.com/tv/20020222fnp3.asp>.

CHAPTER 8

The First Lady of Miramax: Gwyneth Paltrow

Career Trajectory: The "It Girl" or Not?

If her publicity is to be believed, Gwyneth Paltrow is a Hollywood princess, the "It Girl," the most promising young American actress of the twenty-first century.[1] At the age of twenty-seven, she won Academy, Golden Globe, and Screen Actor's Guild Best Actress Awards for her performance in *Shakespeare in Love*, only her second starring role. Lavish praise has also consistently been bestowed upon her by her directors, who routinely describe her as one of the most gifted screen talents working in contemporary Hollywood. For instance, after working with her briefly when he cast her in a small role in her first film, *Hook* (1991), Steven Spielberg remarkably characterized her acting as "classical."[2]

At the same time, however, few major Hollywood stars' stardom has been challenged to the extent that Paltrow's has. A cult of rabid anti-Gwyneth fans has even arisen with a fan site on the Internet dedicated to debunking her image; they claim that Paltrow's stardom has been completely constructed by media hype, that her films do not in any way substantiate her reputation as a highly accomplished actress, and that she has been "anointed a star without being one."[3] Thus, Paltrow's star persona places

191

in the foreground the question of authenticity that critics have seen as so central to the concept of stardom: Is she a bona fide star and a promising young actress or simply a media-constructed celebrity with a reputation for remarkable acting talent that has been completely fabricated?

The trajectory of Paltrow's career does in many ways call into question the legitimacy of her claims to star status and acting achievement. First, there is the matter of her family background. She was born to parents with substantial notoriety within the Hollywood system: Blythe Danner, a highly respected stage and screen actress, and Bruce Paltrow, a television producer/director known primarily for his work on the critically acclaimed medical drama *St. Elsewhere*. An indifferent student, Paltrow apparently determined to pursue an acting career against her parents' wishes. As she describes her childhood,

> When I was little, I'd want to audition for a commercial, and they'd say, "Absolutely not!" Then, in dinner conversation with my mother, I'd say, "I want to be an actress." And she'd say, "No, you want to be an anthropologist or an art historian, don't you?" And I understand why—because it's painful, there's so much rejection in this business. It's awful.[4]

Although her mother may have wanted her daughter to be an academic success, Paltrow was never an impressive student. She had originally attended a progressive grammar school when her family lived in California. When they moved to New York and she was enrolled in Spence, an elite Upper East Side girl's prep school, Paltrow found the transition difficult. She even had to be tutored because, as she puts it, she was "totally at sea" and "would have found it easier to translate Hebrew" than to tackle Spence's challenging curriculum (Milano, 21). During her high school years, a time her mother describes as "tumultuous" (Milano, 25), Paltrow seems to have been a "party girl" who snuck out at night to go clubbing with her friends and showed little interest in her studies. Her grades and college entrance exam test scores were so low that she was denied admission to Vassar and Williams; she was reputedly only accepted into the University of California, Santa Barbara, because Michael Douglas, a close friend of her father, intervened on her behalf.[5]

Her college experience as an art history major at UC–Santa Barbara was short and unimpressive. She confesses she found college "such an inappropriate place for me to be," routinely missed classes to drive to Los Angeles for acting auditions (Milano, 26), and by the end of her second semester, "sort of gave up ... [and] was barely there" (Shnayerson). With her college career following such a disastrous course, her parents finally gave their imprimatur to her acting ambitions. In the summer after her freshman year at college, her mother arranged for her to be given a small role at the Williamstown Theater Festival in a production of *Picnic*, in which her mother starred. As Paltrow tells the story, after seeing her performance, her father came backstage so impressed with her acting ability that he told her he did not think she should return to school (Milano, 27).

Although Paltrow's parents claim that their daughter made her way into the business entirely on her own, their influence in the industry clearly helped to pave her way and may have been the primary factor in her early success. Camille Paglia rather unkindly has called Paltrow's rise to stardom "affirmative action for show-biz brats" (Braustein, 164), but with some justification. Certainly, a major reason why the legitimacy of Paltrow's stardom and acting ability has so often been questioned is because of the enormous impact influential Hollywood figures have had on her success. Even before she gave her approval to her daughter's career, Danner repeatedly found small parts for Paltrow at the prestigious Williamstown Festival, where Danner was a regular star performer. When she went to Los Angeles to seek work, Paltrow was taken on informally by talent agent Rich Kurtzman because of her family connections, even though his agency officially refused to accept the inexperienced actress as a client. Kurtzman opened the doors to the offices of key producers, directors, and casting agents for Paltrow in a way unheard of for an unknown young actress.[6]

In fact, throughout her career, Paltrow has benefited greatly from her insider status within the industry. As noted previously, family friend Steven Spielberg gave her her first role in *Hook*, and he did so without even seeing her act. Sydney Pollack, the noted producer and director and a friend of her father, cast her in her breakthrough film, *Flesh and Bone* (Kloves 1993). Brad Pitt, her future boyfriend, asked that she play his wife in *Seven*, and Michael Douglas, another of her father's close friends, specifically requested her for the role of his wife in *A Perfect Murder*, despite the twenty-year age difference between them.

Unquestionably, the crucial relationship in her career, however, is her association with Miramax studio executive Harvey Weinstein, who one could argue almost single handedly made Paltrow a star. The publicity account is that Weinstein saw Paltrow's performance in *Flesh and Bone* at the Toronto Film Festival and decided he had to work with her. According to Paltrow, "In the beginning of my career, everybody else seemed like a complete Hollywood phony, but Harvey handed me scripts and said, 'I want to work with you.' He's a real movie maker. I definitely have a lot of respect for him."[7]

Weinstein not only wanted to work with Paltrow, but he also set out to fashion her career in a way comparable to executives' control over contract players in the studio era.[8] Weinstein began by signing Paltrow to a two-film deal. She agreed to do *The Pallbearer* (Reeves 1996), an uninspired romantic comedy with David Schwimmer, the popular star of the television sitcom *Friends*, in order subsequently to be cast in the star-making lead role in *Emma* (McGrath 1996), a Jane Austen adaptation at a time when Austen films had become very hot Hollywood properties.

Weinstein then proceeded to cast Paltrow in some of Miramax's most promising projects: *Shakespeare in Love* (Madden 1998) in an Oscar-winning role; *The Talented Mr. Ripley* (1999) with the critically acclaimed director Anthony Minghella and two major male stars, Matt Damon and Jude Law; and *Bounce* (Roos 2000), a star vehicle for her and her sometime boyfriend, Ben Affleck. With considerable hyperbole, Weinstein has called her "one of the finest actresses in America and somebody I think about for every single movie" (Milano, 165).

In interviews, Paltrow has always played down the influence her parents and Weinstein have had on her career. For instance, like so many contemporary actresses, she has claimed that her role choice actually exhibits

> … no pattern. I'm not interested in that. The reason I'm doing this is me. It's not for the money, though I like the money. It's got nothing to do with fame, which is the great evil of mankind. Billing? Hype? What's the point? Who cares? Actors who are hung up on those things haven't been raised by people who love and support them. I was. So I don't have that Hollywood version of penis envy. For me, it's all about acting (Milano, 64).

She even proposes that she does not "really understand the concept of having a career, or what agents mean when they say they're building one for you. I just do things I think will be interesting and that have integrity."[9]

She claims to lack the drive "to be number one" that she sees in other actresses and says she views her career as a learning experience and not at all as a pathway to stardom (Milano, 185–186). She actually proposes that she found having Hollywood contacts to be a disadvantage:

> I think it's taken me a lot longer than it would have taken anybody else to achieve respect, because first there was my mother and people thought I was getting roles because of my parents. Then they said, "Oh, she gets parts because of her boyfriend [Brad Pitt]." You start to think, "Well, there must be a reason this is happening this way, and I'll just ride through it, and keep doing my work." At the end of the day, hopefully that will speak for itself (Milano, 115).

She also characterizes the benefits of her parents' influence as minimal:

> I think it helps you in the way that people are sort of curious to see
> if the progeny is at all interesting or magnetic or talented or—so
> I think it sort of gets you in the meeting quicker, but then for me
> personally I found it much more difficult in terms of …. I felt I had
> to prove myself much more than somebody else would have had to
> in my shoes, you know.[10]

In regard to Harvey Weinstein's impact on her career, Paltrow says, "He took a vested interest in offering me good projects he had, when nobody else would have"[11] and "when he sets his sights on you, you know, he offers you everything he has" (Lipton). Although she admits that he "gets all pissed off and bitter" when she works for anyone but Miramax,[12] she denies that he has controlled her career. According to Paltrow, her relationship with Weinstein has been plagued by their creative differences. She says he has always wanted her to make commercial movies, when she really wants to make artistic films (Hochman).

It seems fair to say that Weinstein has not been able to completely dominate Paltrow's career, which actually divides into three stages: her pre-Miramax, Miramax, and post-Miramax periods. In her pre-Miramax films, Paltrow was able to obtain only small parts in inconsequential films. Her breakthrough performance came in her first substantial supporting role in *Flesh and Bone* (Kloves 1993). Playing a hard-edged young criminal drifter, Paltrow won critical praise and was singled out as the only bright spot in an otherwise dreary film, which many reviewers felt she stole from its woefully miscast stars, Dennis Quaid and Meg Ryan. Yet her critical success in *Flesh and Bone* did not open the way to larger, more substantial parts. Subsequently, Paltrow repeatedly lost major roles to more experienced actresses, such as Julliette Lewis in Woody Allen's *Husbands and Wives* and Julia Ormond in *Legends of the Fall* (Snayerson). Her audition for the latter film did pay off, however, in that she caught the eye of its star, Brad Pitt, who would later recommend her to play the role of his wife in his next project, *Seven* (Fincher 1995).

Although her role in *Seven* was a small one, the film had two extremely important effects on her rise to stardom. First of all, during shooting, she began a two-year, highly publicized romance with Brad Pitt. The barrage of publicity surrounding their relationship suddenly made Paltrow a major celebrity and shaped her star image even before she had a starring film role. It set up a pattern that would be followed throughout her career. Her image has always been molded as much as, if not more so than, by what she has done in her personal life, as by the roles she has played on the screen.

Her role in *Seven* affected both her level of celebrity and her film persona. She was transformed from the "bad girl" character she played in *Flesh and Bone* to the sweet love interest, the perfect wife to Pitt's character in the film, and his adoring girlfriend in real life. This image of the sugar-sweet "good girl" has been one Paltrow has alternately cultivated and struggled against throughout her career.

Although Paltrow may in some sense want to divest herself of this "good girl" image, Harvey Weinstein has not been at all interested in assisting in this divestiture. In fact, as he directed her career into its second phase, her Miramax years, he strongly promoted Paltrow's "good girl" persona. Under Weinstein's watchful eye at Miramax, Paltrow made her two career-establishing films, *Emma* (McGrath 1996) and *Shakespeare in Love* (Madden 1998). Weinstein was said to be so taken with Paltrow that he gave her the role of Emma without even opening the audition process to other actresses and, shortly thereafter, bought the rights to *Shakespeare in Love* with her specifically in mind after it was dropped in development by Julia Roberts (Milano, 129). The two films solidified not only Paltrow's "good girl" image, but also her stardom. Building on her now established star status, Weinstein would cast Paltrow repeatedly as "good girl" characters in other major Miramax films, such as *The Talented Mr. Ripley* (Minghella 1999) and *Bounce* (Roos 2000).

The most controversial event in Paltrow's career was her Academy Award for best actress for her performance in *Shakespeare in Love*. Immediately after Paltrow won her award and the film took home seven Oscars in all, including best picture, rumors began to circulate that Miramax had essentially bought its awards through a multimillion-dollar advertising campaign aimed at Academy voters. Mark Urman, copresident of Lion's Gate Films proposed: "Look at what happened at the Oscars. The machinery Harvey puts in place is like a juggernaut. All predictions, all sense of logic and, in some instances, a sense of fairness are thrown out the window" (Milano, 178). Paltrow won her award over extremely stiff competition from Meryl Streep, Emily Watson, Cate Blanchett, and Fernanda Montenegro, any one of whom could be said to have given a performance with greater depth, range, and nuance than hers.

The idea that her Oscar was essentially bought by Weinstein's advertising campaign gains added credence if one considers Weinstein's earlier media blitz just prior to the release of *Emma*. Paltrow's publicist Stephen Huvane claims that in conjunction with Miramax he carefully constructed a magazine campaign to make Paltrow a star just before *Emma*'s release. Her photo was placed on the cover of *Vogue, US,* and *New York,* and she was featured in major articles in *Time* and *Newsweek*—all in the summer of 1996, just before *Emma*'s release. Huvane says he and the Miramax publicists calculated that, in order for *Emma* to succeed at the box office, Paltrow needed to be perceived as a major star, so they constructed her as one through a carefully orchestrated media blitz.[13]

In addition to her films for Miramax during this period, Paltrow did make films with other studios as well, seemingly trying to widen her range and break free from Weinstein's control. She always has characterized herself as interested in artistic, noncommercial films, which she calls her "little movies," and proposed that, throughout her career, she has tried to avoid "mega-movie stardom." According to Paltrow, being a star

> … ruins your life. You can't go anywhere. People get so posses-
> sive. They think they know you. They can only see you in one way.
> They pay you all these millions. If the movie doesn't have a huge
> opening weekend, it's your fault. What kind of pressure is that?
> Terrible. Hollywood's values are so screwed up (Milano, 111).

She turned down the part eventually played by Kate Winslet in *Titanic* (Cameron 1997) to do what she considered to be a more challenging role in the much smaller and very unsuccessful *Great Expectations* (Cuaron 1998) (Milano, 107). After *Titanic* was an enormous hit and *Great Expectations* failed miserably, Paltrow was asked if she regretted her decision:

> Are you insane? *Great Expectations* had great characters and a
> great script. *Titanic* has a ship. I just do what I want, and I don't
> really care what the repercussions are, or what people say. I make
> the movies that I like; sometimes it's some Warner Brothers thing,
> but more often than not its a little British movie that I'm going
> over to England to do (Milano, 90).

Following her artistic aspirations, she has made other films with impressive literary pedigrees: *Possession* (LaBute 2002), based on A.S. Byatt's critically acclaimed novel, and *Sylvia* (Jeffs 2003), a biopic of the poet Sylvia Plath. Unfortunately, the films' literary credentials assured neither their box office success nor a favorable critical reception.

In her interviews, Paltrow seems determined to portray Hollywood as distinctly not her thing. She describes her decision to do *A Perfect Murder* (Davis 1998), which she calls her "first big Hollywood movie," as "selling out" (Milano, 107) and complains that "[t]here wasn't anything to sink [her] teeth into" in the role (Clehane). In spite of her sometimes vigorous criticism of what she calls the "Hollywood blockbuster mentality," she also proposes: "Of course, I want to do some Hollywood films. I want to earn some money, after all" (Milano, 94). She then adds, "You won't see me in

Speed III or *Terminator IV* any time soon. I'd rather go and do some play for five weeks and learn something" (Milano, 94). Paltrow's friends, however, are not totally convinced of her self-positioning as an art film actress. She confessed to one interviewer, "My friends and I were talking and I was saying I do independent films. And they were like 'Oh, shut up! You're a cheesy fucking movie star!' I said, 'That's not true! I do art movies.'"[14]

Rather than looking for films that "pack 'em in at the mall" (Waxman), she says she seeks out "worthwhile" films (Lipton) that are "different, challenging," and have "something redeeming" about them.[15] As Michael Shnayerson has pointed out, she is one of only a handful of contemporary American actresses willing consistently to take the lower salary that independent and British films pay: $5 to 8 million per picture. Her favorite film to date is a small independent British production, *Sliding Doors* (Howitt 1998), which reviewers did not find appreciably different from the standard Hollywood romantic comedy, but about which Paltrow raves as if it were the most innovative cinematic achievement of the century:

> It's a low-budget film and it has an independent sensibility, in that it has its own ideas, its own rhythms, its own point of view. It has an edge. It doesn't pander to audience expectations or their intellectual shortcomings. If you trust the film, you will be rewarded. But you have to keep on your toes. It's rare when you come across a script that's that funny and that smart (Milano, 96–97).

Figure 8.1 Gwyneth Paltrow as Viola De Lesseps in *Shakespeare in Love* (Madden 1998), one of the "worthwhile" artistic films that Paltrow has said she seeks out (Lipton). Paltrow has described the role of Viola as her most challenging. (Reproduced with permission of Corbis.)

Similarly, in discussing *Shakespeare in Love*, which would seem to have a more substantial claim to artistic brilliance than *Sliding Doors*, Paltrow proposes, "But when you do a movie like *Shakespeare in Love*, you feel like an artist. It doesn't go as smoothly, it's all quirky and backwards, but it's artful. You feel like you're learning and discovering things, and you feel like you know why you do this job" (Milano, 159).

In spite of Paltrow's frequently expressed devotion to independent and artistic films, her film choices have often strayed beyond this realm. She even admits to making some very bad film selections "based on 'good' premises, 'this could get there'—and that's always the wrong way" ("Here and Now"). She says she did *Hush* (Darby 1998) to work with Jessica Lange and for the money.[16] The film was scathingly reviewed by critics and Paltrow's performance reviled. Paltrow confesses that she never bothered to see the final film, calling it "appalling." She says, "I know how bad it is. I was there."[17] Other missteps in her career include the previously mentioned *The Pallbearer*, in which her performance, like the film as a whole, was ridiculed by critics for lacking depth and interest; *Duets* (Paltrow 2000), an ensemble film directed by her father, which reviewers almost universally panned as a disjointed hodgepodge with a television sitcom sensibility; and *View from the Top* (Barreto 2003), a disastrously bad stewardess comedy.

Paltrow's role choice in her post-Miramax phase, as she has attempted to move away somewhat from Weinstein's control, reflects her desire to establish some range, rather than simply to remain typed in sugar-sweet "good girl" roles. She has repeatedly expressed a determination not "to get stuck doing the same thing" (Milano, 80) and expresses admiration for Julianne Moore who, according to Paltrow, has done so many different types of roles that audiences do not expect her to be a certain way on screen (Milano, 90). On the other hand, she has singled out Julia Roberts, whom she sees as hopelessly typecast, as an actress she would not wish to emulate:

> It's hard when you see an actor or actress you respect, like Julia Roberts, continuously being asked to play the same role because that's what the American people demand. Anytime anyone gets too comfortable with the way they perceive me, what I should do, or how I should behave in a movie, then it's time for me to reverse it in some way (Milano, 160).

In order to break her "good girl" typecasting, Paltrow has tried to supplement those types of roles with what she terms "darker parts that are more gritty" and comic turns (Milano, 80). For instance, she played a prostitute in *Hard Eight* (aka *Sydney*; Anderson 1996), a recently widowed mother of two in *Bounce,* a part that her director Don Roos described as bringing her "down to Wal-Mart reality,"[18] and a childlike Las Vegas showgirl in *Duets.* She also starred in the Farley Brothers' gross-out comedy *Shallow Hal* (2002), in which she assumed the double role of a man's dream image of his girlfriend and, donning a body suit, the grossly overweight girlfriend. Similarly, she played the "Goth" daughter in an extremely dysfunctional madcap family in the offbeat indie comedy, *The Royal Tannenbaums* (Anderson 2002).

Breaking her good girl image in yet another way, Paltrow has been quite willing to take roles that are sexually explicit. Although she says she turned down *Boogie Nights* (Anderson 1997) because her grandfather would have "flipped out totally" over the film's overt sexual content, she claims doing film nudity does not bother her at all. She says she does not seek it out, but she feels nudity is expected of actresses when they are "starting out" and is comfortable with it as long as it is integral to the plot and does not make her "feel degraded or that it's about [her] naked body." She explains further: "It's always been my decision. I think we're too uptight about nudity in this country anyway" (Lipton). In spite of these recent attempts to establish range in her characterizations, however, Paltrow's roles as the sweet good girl seem to have marked her image in ways that are indelible.

The Gwyneth Paltrow Image: "Gwynethness"[19]

The lexicon of Paltrow's star image is composed of four image clusters centered around the qualities of beauty, naiveté, class, and boyfriends.

"a Kind of Friendly Beauty"[20]

Most emphasized in Paltrow's publicity and promotional material is her great beauty. *People* magazine has repeatedly named her one of its fifty most beautiful people, and *Biography* has listed her as among the ten most beautiful women of the 1990s. Reviews of her films comment almost obsessively on her glamorous demeanor and photogenic characteristics. For instance, Richard Corliss in *Time* magazine proposes that she is able to demonstrate her star quality "not by screaming and cussing Method style but by radiating an unforced glamour that recalls Hollywood in its Golden Age" (Milano, 154). Calvin Klein, whose fashions she has contracted to wear off-screen, says, "To me Gwyneth Paltrow embodies the women of the 90s. It is not only that she is beautiful and sexy, but she also radiates a confidence and grace that is timeless" (Milano, 77). Her directors, too, have commented on her photogenic qualities. According to Douglas McGrath, her director in *Emma,*

She's ravishing to look at and photographs like a dream. Especially on film: she just takes the light and sends it back. Men adore her, and women love her but don't envy her. She has a beauty you can enjoy and not be threatened by because it's a kind of friendly beauty. She seems like a real person. She doesn't seem like a goddess (Milano, 77).

Friendly, glamorous, and/or timeless, Paltrow's looks are without question a major aspect of her image, an aspect that ties her to classic film actresses of the 1930s and 1940s.

Childlike Naivete: "This Almost Holly Golightly Thing"

Paltrow's "friendly beauty" is complemented by her childlike mannerisms and demeanor. Her directors repeatedly describe her as very girlish. Steven Kloves' characterization of her on the set of *Flesh and Bone* is typical: "She had this almost Holly Golightly thing. She used to say this one thing that would just kill me. She'd be in the middle of a conversation and she'd say, 'I'm just a girl.' It used to slay people. 'But then, I'm just a girl'" (Milano, 39). Her interview responses to questions regarding her relationship with her parents also display this childlike quality. For instance, she says of working with her mother, "In a way, it's the most wonderful thing that I ever could think of. Because it's my mommy, you know, and I learn so much from her" (Beals, 119). Directed by her father in *Duets*, she played a young woman with the mannerisms of a twelve-year-old who is desperately searching for a father to take care of her. Paltrow's comments about the experience of making the film are telling. She recounts an incident when she asked her "daddy" if she could take off early to go to a rock concert: "'Daddy, I want to go see Courtney's band [Courtney Love's rock band Hole]. Can I get out of work early?' And he was like 'Of course, you can.'"[21]

Paltrow's relationship with her father was always extraordinarily close and loving. After his death in 2002, she told one interviewer: "He was my whole life, embarrassingly."[22] He died suddenly while in Venice visiting her to celebrate her thirtieth birthday. His death left her so devastated that she pulled out of two film projects and was unable to work for six months. The development of her whirlwind romance with rock star Chris Martin has even been attributed to his "being there for her" as she slowly recovered from the devastating loss of her father. When Paltrow announced her pregnancy by Martin in 2003, she attributed her great joy at least partially to the child's connection with her father: "It's just so amazing to know that I'm going to have something new that will be a quarter my dad."[23]

Paltrow's naiveté also is apparent in her responses to interview questions; these have seemed extraordinarily jejune for a sophisticated private school-educated young woman who has grown up in New York City and now alternates between living in New York and London. One interviewer even dubbed her "Sandra Dee without the innocence" (Braustein). Her descriptions of her relationship with actor Brad Pitt particularly exhibit this little girl quality, which is perhaps not difficult to understand since he was thirty-one when they met and she just twenty. She told interviewers that Pitt called her his "angel, the light of [his] life,"[24] and she described their first meeting as if it were a high school romance. She said she began to develop a "crush" on Pitt on the *Seven* set and that he would later tell her that he fell in love with her at first sight. She further described how she initially held back from getting involved in the relationship because she was afraid he was just "one of those movie star boys" (Milano, 55).

Other interview responses are equally childlike. In response to being asked, as the star of *Emma*, about her thoughts on the Jane Austen novel upon which the film is based, she said, "I'm not a huge Jane Austen fan. I find her a little too chatty" (Milano, 79). Literary critics would be less than overwhelmed by this insight. When interviewed just after the release of *Shakespeare in Love*, she was asked what questions she would have for Shakespeare, and her answer was: "I would ask him to bathe. 'Cause you know how they were back then" (Milano, 182). Her comments on turning twenty-four were:

> I feel that is a woman's age. Twenty-three is still kind of on the border. To me, at twenty-three you can still really be a kid. I just mean in terms of a number, because obviously everybody is different. For example, if somebody said they were twenty-four, you'd know they would have to be a woman, right? (Milano, 93).

Then, when she turned twenty-five, she selected that age as a new turning point on her road to an illusive maturity: "Before twenty-five, it's sort of kid territory. It's like you can totally get away with kids' stuff before then, but at twenty-five you better get it together …. Now at twenty-five, it's like you've got to step up and be a grownup" (Milano, 118).

This child–woman sensibility spills over into her performances. For instance, Paltrow has described almost all of her films as "sweet." *Emma*, she said, is "just a sweet, sweet movie that I'm very proud of," just as *The Pallbearer* is "sweet," and *Sliding Doors* is "sweet, resonant, and smart" (Milano, 63, 67, 113). She repeatedly describes her characters as "sweet" as well. Even when she played a prostitute in *Hard Eight*, she characterized the character as "sweet, sad, and fucked-up" (Milano, 65) and when she was asked about her choice of a bubble-gum pink Ralph Lauren ball gown for the 1998 Oscar ceremony, she described her goal as "to look sweet" (Milano, 174).

Paltrow's sexualized child–woman persona, like Jodie Foster's, seems to have had one extremely undesirable effect, however. It attracted the attention of a celebrity stalker. In 2000, she was pursued by a deranged pizza deliveryman, who was finally arrested after he arrived at her parents' home, but only after he had sent her hundreds of letters, e-mails, and packages. At his trial, she testified again in a childlike manner that she was so traumatized by his harassment that she had nightmares.[25]

Class: "My Girl's Got Class"

One of the glaring contradictions within Paltrow's star image is that, although she is regarded in so much of her publicity as childlike, she is also seen as classy, sophisticated, and fashionable. Much of Paltrow's reputation as "the classiest young actress of her day" (Shnayerson) is drawn from her association with her mother, who is highly respected as a stage and screen actress. For example, in describing Paltrow, with whom he worked in *Seven*, Morgan Freeman proposes, "I have always been floored by her mother, Blythe Danner. And then here she comes. She's spellbinding. She has the gift" (Milano, 52).

The notion of Paltrow as gifted appears to have been initially promulgated by her mother, who regularly has regaled interviewers with stories of her daughter's precocious acting accomplishments as a child. For instance, Danner tells of a young naked Gwyneth at the tender age of three at a Williamstown Festival rehearsal session reciting Nina's "Men and Beasts" monologue from *The Seagull*, which she had reputedly picked up from watching her mother perform (Milano, 15). This idea of Paltrow as a naturally gifted actress who inherited her mother's remarkable talents has been taken up in Paltrow's publicity and by Paltrow herself, who has said, "I know I am an actress because my mother was an actress" (Milano, 17).

Paltrow's reputation for class comes not only from this notion of her inherited acting talent, but also from other sources. As a *Vanity Fair* publicist said when asked why the magazine had put Paltrow on its cover before she had established a successful film career, "People look at her and say, 'This is someone who has a lot of class, a lot of talent. She has a name, she's Brad Pitt's girlfriend—she's bound to go far. It puts her in a different class than a lot of other actresses'" (Milano, 63). Her association with Pitt, who Paltrow told interviewers liked to describe her with the words, "My girl's got class" (Milano, 61), definitely added to her cachet, but her reputation for class and sophistication also comes from her New York private school background and her fashion consciousness. As noted earlier, she has an agreement with Calvin Klein to wear his clothes off-screen, has served as guest editor for the women's fashion magazine *Marie Claire*, and has been described by Kate Betts, the editor of *Harper's Bazaar*, as "the style role model of her generation" (Clehene).

Paltrow has connected her love of fashion to her artistic temperament: "I am fascinated by all forms of expression, whether it's Cubist painting or dresses. I think fashion's a totally noble art form, the most immediate interpretation of where our culture is at the moment. Plus, c'mon I'm a girl" (Milano, 173). Her fashion image was exploited in *A Perfect Murder*, where her expensive wardrobe, with jewelry reputedly costing in the hundred thousands of dollars, was regarded by many critics as the only interesting aspect of her role. She has even parodied herself as a fashion icon in a cameo in the small independent film *Intern* (Lange 2000), which was written by one of her friends from Spence. While making *The Royal Tenenbaums*, she adopted a trendy "Goth" look, fashioned after her character in the film, and made a fashion statement in a black "Gothish" gown with a sheer ballerina top that caused many fashion critics to name her the worst dressed woman at the 2002 Academy Awards Ceremony. That her reputation for fashion sense could survive this disastrous fashion *faux pas* testifies to the strength of this element in her overall image lexicon.

Boyfriends: "I've Broken up with my Boyfriend, and it's Been on the Cover of People Twice"

More than any other factor, including her acting accomplishments, Paltrow's relationship with Brad Pitt, which was publicized as "a storybook romance,"[26] promoted her to celebrity status. Although she often complained about the intrusion of the paparazzi into their relationship, there can be no doubt that by being so open with the press and telling them so many of the intimate details of their life together, Paltrow actually encouraged, perhaps unwittingly, their intrusive behavior. She admits that:

> I brought it on myself. I contributed a lot to the media attention. I used to talk about everything. I'm not guarded at all. I've had to really learn to be. I used to tell everybody everything. It didn't occur to me not to. I said things about being in a relationship that felt wrong to me even as I was saying them. It wasn't about whether I wanted to say more. I was more concerned about hurting the reporter's feelings or coming off as being overly protective (Milano, 121).

Paltrow claims she was completely unprepared for the level of media attention afforded to her relationship with Pitt, whom *People* magazine had just named "the sexiest man alive" shortly before their involvement. Paltrow's openness with the press, the couple's very public pronouncements of affection, and their visibility at celebrity events worked to make them the celebrity couple of the mid-1990s. The publicity blitz culminated in a British tabloid's publication of nude photos of the couple taken while they were vacationing in the Caribbean. When these photos were eventually circulated on the Internet, Pitt became so furious at the intrusion into his privacy that he decided to sue for damages (Milano, 59). The media frenzy continued when Pitt and Paltrow announced their engagement and one of their guests sold photos taken at their engagement party to the tabloid *The Globe* (Seymanski).

If their engagement was big celebrity news, their breakup in 1997 was even bigger, exacerbated by the fact that neither of them would reveal to the press the reason for their split. This led to endless press speculation, ranging from rumors that one or the other had been unfaithful, had gotten cold feet about the marriage, or had decided that the other was not social enough.[27] Paltrow describes the strangeness of experiencing a romantic breakup while completely under the scrutiny of the press: "There's not a lot of people who can relate when you say, 'I've broken up with my boyfriend, and it's been on the cover of *People* twice.'"[28]

Although Paltrow strongly lamented the publicity blitz that surrounded her relationship with Pitt, just months after their highly publicized breakup, she began a very visible on-again–off-again relationship with another heartthrob actor, Ben Affleck. They were photographed together as a couple spending romantic weekends in Manhattan, kissing, and being interviewed at the Sundance film festival (Milano, 121). Paltrow has testified repeatedly to the importance boyfriends have had in her life. She spoke of her breakup with Pitt in highly melodramatic terms, "It really changed my life. When we split up, something changed, permanently, in me …. My heart sort of broke that day, and it will never be the same" (Shnayerson). About her need for a man, she asserted, "I've never been without a boyfriend for even a month. I've always had a boyfriend, and it was always serious. I'd always go from one serious relationship to another." She proposed after the collapse of the relationship with Pitt: "I thought it was time to get to know myself …. I need to spend time with myself" (Milano, 118). However, by the end of that summer, she was involved with Affleck.

When her relationship with Affleck broke up, she was again very circumspect, adamantly refusing to discuss the circumstances of their split, as she had with Pitt. Afterwards, she was rumored to be involved with her leading man in each of her films until she met British rock star Chris Martin at one of his band Coldplay's 2002 concerts. Perhaps having learned from the publicity surrounding her earlier romances, Paltrow and Martin have refused to reveal any intimate details about their relationship. She has explained to interviewers who ask about their plans that their attachment is "so sacred that I feel talking about it is just wrong, in every bone in my body" (Thomas, 2D). Yet she giddily announced her pregnancy on *The Tonight Show*, only to follow that public announcement with a secret wedding ceremony not attended by family members—not even her beloved mother.[29] The inconsistency of her attitude to celebrity gossip has only served to make her love life an even more tantalizing source of fan interest and an element of continuing importance in her star image.

An Image on the Brink of Self-Destrution:
The Instability of "Gwynethness"

The clash of elements in Paltrow's image lexicon renders it particularly unstable, seeming always to be on the verge of shattering. Paltrow's publicity positions her as a fantasy figure for young women, the "It Girl" who can "change the chemistry of a room just by entering it" (Stamler). Hailed by some critics as the classiest, most fashionable young actress of her generation, she is also reputed by others to be all hype, a totally media-constructed celebrity. The clash between these two interpretations of "Gwynethness" takes her image to the brink of dissolution. The persona of the sophisticated, glamorous, gifted actress cannot be easily reconciled with the image of the overhyped immature child, prone to romantic problems and ushered into stardom by her Hollywood connections.

Recently, Paltrow has added the element of devoted motherhood to her image. Since her daughter's birth, she has repeatedly affirmed her determination to prioritize over her film career her motherly relationship with her child, whom she and Martin inexplicably named Apple. In accord with the beauty component of her image, she has nevertheless signed on as "one of the new faces of Estee Lauder, the cosmetics giant." She says she signed the modeling contract because "It allows me to be with my daughter, which is what I want to do until some fantastic movie role comes along and makes me change my mind."[30] Thus, her image remains, as it always has been, plagued by inner tension, always on the threshold of self-destruction.

Approach to Acting

Amazingly, or perhaps not so amazingly in light of her promotion as a natural talent, Gwyneth Paltrow is almost completely lacking in formal training as an actress. Her publicity never even suggests that she contemplated majoring in drama when she was in college or taking acting classes after she left. When she determined to drop out of school, she simply went to Los Angeles, got a job as a waitress, and began to audition (Milano, 29). Paltrow has mentioned auditing a few acting classes with acting coach Larry Moss during this period, but she confesses, "I never really got into it. I just observed ..." (Shnayerson). Rather than refer to herself as untrained, Paltrow describes her acting technique as instinctive. When asked by her fellow actress, Jennifer Beals, whether she feels she has "a process," she replied, "Not at all. I'd feel much more secure if I could say, 'This is how I do it' .... So far, I've approached each thing so differently" (Beals, 120).

Her directors have always given this lack of training a positive spin. For instance, Peter Howitt, who directed her in *Sliding Doors*, described her as

> ... not a trained actress, and in many ways, I think that's one of her assets. She's incredibly instinctive. There were times in the first week when I thought she couldn't care less, because she didn't seem to be doing anything. Then I looked at the rushes and thought, "Fuck, it's brilliant. When did she do that?" (Milano, 98).

Similarly, her father has characterized her acting instincts as "so flawless it's mind-boggling" (Shnayerson). Much like Meryl Streep, Paltrow describes her process in religious terms:

> I just open myself to God, really. And that I have to match the frequency in my soul to the frequency of everything that's greater than me. And then I get out of my head and I just open and then it just comes through. But I always feel that I have to do all of the proper work before that. All of the thinking in order to get to a place where I can let go (Lipton).

When she describes the initial work that she does to get into a role, she speaks of it as natural and unplanned. She says her initial preparation consists of first reading the script to open herself up

> ... for any kind of instinctual impulse about the person because that to me is always more important than anything you can create in your mind. If I can feel some detail of that, that opens up everything .... If you ever get an instinct about anything, you know, it's always right and just stick with it (Lipton).

If her instincts fail her, she turns to more conventional script analysis: "… I look through the script for any information I can get on the person. What makes this person tick? What are they doing? What do they want? Why are they in this movie or this play?" (Lipton).

In lieu of actor training, Paltrow depended upon her mother's guidance, and her mother's influence seems to have been absolutely essential to her development as an actress. Paltrow's respect for her mother is enormous. When she won the Screen Actor's Guild Award for *Shakespeare in Love*, she took the opportunity to praise her mother as "the most brilliant, beautiful and profound actress I know" (Milano, 169). Paltrow describes how she always knew she wanted to be an actress "because my mother was an actress," and she tells how she "used to sit and watch her in the theater, just rehearsing, and it seemed so magical to me" (Milano, 17). According to Paltrow, "My mother probably could have been a bigger star than any woman of her generation. She's a brilliant woman. But she chose to stay home and be with the family …. She's not ambitious like that, and I just respect her so much for that" (Milano, 16). Respect her mother she might, but Paltrow has set out to accomplish what her mother did not, to attain the film stardom that her mother gave up.

Paltrow actually seems to have developed her love for acting by watching her mother's stage accomplishments. For example, she says, "I always knew

Figure 8.2 Gwyneth Paltrow discussing her role with producer Sydney Pollack on the set of *Sliding Doors*, which Paltrow has said is her favorite film. Pollack has described Paltrow as having the quality of "Gwynethness," "a kind of hypnotic thing that happens with real movie stars that makes it difficult not to watch them" (Milano, 39). (Reproduced with permission of Corbis.)

that I wanted to do what Mom did …. I would watch her dress up and become these other people, and she seemed so empowered."[31] Paltrow describes how she would love to go to the Williamstown Theater Festival, where her mother would perform almost every summer. Paltrow would "go to rehearsals with [her] mother and sit barefoot and cross-legged watching her work" (Milano, 23). Blythe Danner's most critically praised stage performance was her portrayal of Blanche DuBois in Tennessee Williams's *A Streetcar Named Desire*, which she performed at Williamstown in 1988 with Christopher Walken as Stanley Kowalski and Sigourney Weaver as Stella. Paltrow describes her experience at the play's opening night as an epiphany:

> I had never read the play or seen a rehearsal. I went to the opening night and sat with my father, and Mom was too much. I just saw her come completely apart in front of me. It was the most profound experience. It was the most powerful, moving thing I'd ever seen in my entire life. She was so extraordinary, so gifted. Afterward, when I went backstage in her dressing room, all I could do was weep. I held on to her and I cried and cried and cried (Milano, 22–23).

As noted previously, Paltrow's mother not only offered herself as a role model to her daughter, but also secured small parts for her at the Williamstown Festival. Finally, while in college, Paltrow got the opportunity to play the major role of Nina opposite her mother's Madame Arkadin in Chekhov's *The Seagull* at Williamstown. It was this performance that persuaded her father to grant her permission to leave school and seriously pursue an acting career. Although Paltrow definitely considers her mother her inspiration, she has shied away from imitating her. In fact, when she did *The Seagull*, she speaks of deliberately refusing to watch the tape of Danner's performance in the same role twenty years earlier for fear that "[i]f I came up here [to Williamstown] with her Nina in my head, it would take me twice as long to undo it and refind it myself."[32]

Amazingly, Danner has given Paltrow very little overt acting instruction. She says that the only thing she ever told Gwyneth about acting was to "embrace it," and Paltrow claims that she picked up acting tips from her mother more by "osmosis" than by discussing craft (Shnayerson). She also describes working with her mother as "instructive and tense" (Beals, 119). In fact, Danner's influence seems to have been most profound in inculcating into her daughter high artistic standards and a respect for the craft of acting. Danner says she told Gwenyth when her daughter first attained some success, "You must work very hard, don't ever coast. You're incredibly talented, you're very, very beautiful, and don't be seduced by all the extraneous stuff. Remember it's the work that's first" (Milano, 28). Danner seems always to have encouraged Paltrow to regard acting as an artistic medium. When her daughter won the Oscar for *Shakespeare in Love*, Danner said of her performance: "What I was most thrilled about was the work. Luminous ... unbelievable range ... amazing performance. I'm sorry to be bragging about my daughter" (Roberts).

In spite of her mother's accolades, Paltrow's lack of formal training seems to have left her insecure about her abilities and reluctant to discuss her craft openly. Repeatedly, she has told interviewers that she does not like to talk about acting and would prefer to discuss something else (Conniff). Her insecurities seem profound and have perhaps been exacerbated by reviewers' criticism of her performances as uneven and dependent on the guidance of her directors. For instance, she told Anthony Minghella, her director in *The Talented Mr. Ripley*, that she fears theater because it is seen as an opportunity to perfect one's technique and she does not feel she has any technique to perfect. Concerning her acting methods, she has said, "... if it's not real, it's gone. It eludes me. If I don't feel the magic, I'm lost" (Lipton). She also confesses to being afraid to watch the rushes of her film performances because "I can't watch myself with pleasure. Not yet" (Milano, 64). Paltrow has also said that she worries that "the more successful I get, the less people will think of me as an actress" (Milano, 113).

Although Paltrow is reluctant to discuss her acting technique, others have commented upon it extensively, especially in regard to her approach to characterization. Perhaps the most mentioned aspect of her acting is her ability to transform herself quickly into a character. Paul Thomas Anderson, who directed her in *Hard Eight*, comments: "She's always one of the actors who's fucking around and talking between takes, and then you call, 'Action,' and boom she's there" (Milano, 65). Paltrow has attributed her ability to "quick study" a scene to her extensive preparation for a role: "It's just the way I work. I know where I'm going and I don't need to start doing it until I'm doing it. I don't take my character home and I don't need to walk it around the set, either" (Connelly, 3).

Her father and Ben Affleck have characterized her as coming to the set with a minimum performance already worked out before shooting begins. Her father has spoken of his experience directing her in *Duets*: "She comes with a character so fully formed in her head that I kind of step back and marvel at what she has brought to it. The only thing I can liken it to is what it must feel like for a jockey to get on an incredible race horse."[33] Similarly, Affleck says of working with her in *Bounce*: "Whereas Gwyneth, you can't make her bad in a movie. She's already decided how she's going to execute the role" (Shnayerson). Comparing herself to Affleck, Paltrow says,

> He'll just do things that come to him. I'll do that, too, but I'm a little more studied. Not Method at all, but …. It's really important before I start to work that I have a sense of the inner life of a character, and I think he discovers it as he goes along (Shnayerson).

Paltrow's need for extensive individual preliminary preparation before shooting begins may stem from her conception of characterization as "truly so personal. It's a strange, absolutely wonderful and quirky job: You dress up. You recite lines. And you go deep into character without being sure what the outcome will be. Hopefully, you feel this terrific sensation when you and the character become one" (Milano, 115). As she describes her preparation,

> Well, it's very important to me to understand where this person is coming from in terms of the framework within which they hang their ideas, the way they see the world, the way things affect them or hurt their feelings, the physicality. And I feel that everything that one is is shaped by their life experience, what that might have been. I start to build it internally. You know. I take this kind of idea and I …. It feels like I start to put bones and muscles together. You know, and then one day, you know, I … the person's there. What's really terrible for me is it's only after about three or four days of filming that I realize who the person is. But that's O.K. People don't usually notice (Lipton).

Paltrow sees herself as "the architect" of the characters she plays and believes acting involves her "responsibility to create someone from the ground up" using some of her experiences. She also proposes that "it really gets fun for the actor when you take it away from yourself. When you get to play somebody who's different from yourself, you know, and you start to build that" (Lipton). She says, "I worry and I struggle early on with the creation of the character. How is this person going to emerge? How am I going to do this? But it's not so hard for me once it's really in my skin."[34] She also attributes her need to prepare a minimal performance before shooting to the particular demands of film acting. She describes film as a performance space in which the actor

> … can't fake it … you can't in any way not be absolutely there.

Perhaps because of her youth and her close student–mentor relationship with her mother, Paltrow approaches acting as a learning experience. She has taken parts in films, sometimes with disappointing results, simply because she wanted to work with an established, highly respected star. For instance, as noted before, she says she did *Hush* so that she could work with Jessica Lange:

> I really wanted to work with Jessica. She's so brilliantly talented and such a terrific woman, and in that way it was an excellent experience …. [I]t was such a great lesson to just be around her and watch her work. But it was just the silliest character. I mean it was *not* a character (Milano, 85).

She also says she accepted the lead female role in *A Perfect Murder* because she wanted to work with Michael Douglas and experience what it was like to do a "big studio movie like that" (Milano, 111). In fact, she seems to approach her career as part of a work in progress. She says of her reaction to watching herself act, "There's always, like, a moment that I'm pleased with, that I 'think' I got that right! But I don't generally like my work through a whole film" (Heller). She sees *Shakespeare in Love* as her most challenging role:

> I've never worked so hard on anything in my life …. I had to give everything I had intellectually, looking at the structure, doing the research. Emotionally, too, it was very demanding. Not only because I was dealing with research of the period, but also I had to keep everything straight about whether I was a boy or a girl. And to do *Romeo and Juliet*—there was a lot going on, it really kept me busy. I was using everything that I had and was so spent to the bone every day (Milano, 140).

Like most contemporary actresses, Paltrow does not subscribe to any one school of acting. Although she denies any connections with Method acting, her attempts to "go deep into character" seem to associate her with the Method tradition, and her mother has been categorized as a Method actress.[35] On the other hand, her affection for the stage and her careful preproduction planning of a "minimal performance" associate her with theatrical acting techniques. Her ability quickly to get into character and tendency to play herself in every role, even when in period dramas, such as *Shakespeare in Love* and *Emma,* place her firmly in the tradition of the Hollywood studio actress.

Critics characterize her acting style as possessing three qualities: a mastery of accents, photogenicity, and freshness. In accord with her self-presentation as an instinctive actress, Paltrow claims to have had a natural facility with accents since she was a child; early in her career, her convincing British accents in *Emma* and *Shakespeare in Love* led some critics to mistake her as English born. She admits, however, to working on her accents with an accent coach who, she says, corrects the mistakes her "natural ear for accents" misses (Milano, 132). Her directors praise her not so much for her mastery of accents, but rather for her photogenic star qualities, which Sydney Pollack has dubbed her "Gwynethness":

> There's a kind of hypnotic thing that happens with real movie stars that makes it difficult not to watch them, and she has that quality. You could say it in a million different ways. You could say she's waiflike. You could say she's gamine. You could say she's gorgeous. You could say all those things, and they would be true, but it's the particular mixture—and the nonspecificness—that makes her fascinating. We saw that in *Flesh and Bone*. As soon as she came on the screen, you thought, "who the hell is *that*?" (Milano, 39).

Similarly, Douglas McGrath, her director in *Emma*, says "she photographs like a dream—all the light goes to her on the set, and she seems to absorb it and then give it back," and Alfonso Cuarón, who directed her in *Great Expectations*, proposes that "cameras were invented to photograph Gwyneth. She turns to the camera and it's like, *Gulp!*" (Milano, 184). Clearly, her looks are crucial to Paltrow's image. Her directors describe her as photogenic and also as possessing an aura of freshness and spontaneity. As Don Roos, who directed her in *Bounce*, points out, "She does moments of comprehension and realization so freshly, you can actually see the thoughts on her face that she's having. To make that spontaneous is the hardest thing for an actress to do" (Shnayerson).

Although Paltrow has established her career almost exclusively in films and has confessed to a fear of doing theater, she also seems drawn to the stage, perhaps because of the influence of her mother, who is best known for her stage performances and seems to have conveyed to Paltrow the conventional notion that the craft of acting is best perfected on stage. Early in her career, Paltrow clearly chose film over theater acting. In fact, she took the role in *Flesh and Bone*, which would turn out to be her breakthrough film performance, over a featured part that she had been offered on Broadway in Wendy Wasserstein's *The Sisters Rosenzweig*.[36]

After winning the Academy Award for *Shakespeare in Love,* however, she received considerable praise for choosing art over popular entertainment by immediately turning to the stage. That summer, August 1999, she accepted the role of Rosalind in Shakespeare's *As You Like It* at the Williamstown Theater Festival. Although the production received only a lukewarm critical reception and she was upstaged by her costar Alessandro Nivola, who received the greatest accolades from reviewers, Paltrow did gain some attention for creating a "lovely" and "alluring"[37] Rosalind and for having a "striking physical presence" on stage, although several critics pointed out that her voice projection could have been stronger (Milano, 183). Rex Reed perhaps best described critical reaction to her performance:

> I was grateful for Ms. Paltrow's charm, but Rosalind is so close to the role she played in *Shakespeare in Love* and her performance is in so much the same vein, full of bounce and posturing, there isn't much of a stretch to observe. I admire her for wanting to polish her craft like her mother ... but I wish she had chosen a fresher vehicle with a different kind of challenge.[38]

It was not so much Paltrow's stage talent that was exalted at Williamstown, but rather her decision to do a stage production in the wake of her film success. As Williamstown Festival Director Michael Richard put it, "We pay nothing, compared to anybody. Everyone gets the same pay, same campus housing, same shared restrooms. It's to Gwyneth's great credit that she's got the world in the palm of her hand, she can do anything she wants, and she's actually doing what she wants, which is this" (Milano, 182).

On the other hand, reporters pointed out that, although Paltrow did act for scale and walked around Williamstown without make-up, she also got the star treatment at the festival by being allowed to stay in a festival board member's home, rather than in the standard dorm room, and being escorted around town by "a board big-wig or the festival producer."[39] Paltrow's experience at Williamstown seems to have instilled in her an ongoing dedication to stage work. In 2002, she decided to tackle the London stage, opening to generally positive reviews in playwright David Auburn's Pulitzer Prize-winning drama, *Proof,* at the Donner Playhouse under the direction of her *Shakespeare in Love* director John Madden.

Although Paltrow has said that theater is very important to her and that one of her professional goals is to do more stage acting in the next ten years (Stark), she also appreciates the craft of film acting. She has said that film and theater are "like apples and oranges" with film acting seeming

… so small and so specific, and I always feel like you have to be so on top of where you are, and it's very kind of intellectual for me in that every day before I go to work I have to think about what's going on in the story. You know, it's all out of order, and you really have to piece together an emotional journey, but from a very removed standpoint. Whereas, on stage, you sort of have to plot it all out beforehand, and the gun goes off and that's it, you know (Lipton).

That Paltrow has ventured to appear on the London stage, but only under the secure direction of her *Shakespeare in Love* director, suggests her dedication to yet insecurity about her craft, as well as her need for strong directorial guidance.

In fact, Paltrow seems always to cultivate a relationship of mutual admiration with her directors. As can be ascertained from some of the remarks quoted earlier, many of them praise her in such lavish terms that their comments seem ridiculous in their hyperbole. For instance, Steve Kloves, after directing her in *Flesh and Bone*, characterized her appeal as based on her "spontaneity and raw nerve … her mystery and unpredictability." He then went on to compare her to Steve McQueen, of all people (Milano, 37). In spite of her decidedly limited theater experience and complete lack of theater training, Douglas McGrath said that he cast her in *Emma* because he "knew [incorrectly] she had theater training, so she could carry herself. We had many actresses, big and small, who wanted this part. The minute she started the read-through, the very first line, I thought, 'Everything is going to be fine, she's going to be brilliant'" (Milano, 69).

Anthony Minghella lavished praise on her performance in *The Talented Mr. Ripley* although she had a rather small underwritten role. He claims she transformed herself effortlessly from the "sunny, generous, beautiful, aristocratic" person he feels audiences expect her to be on the screen to a "thwarted, brittle, febrile, new person. There are very few actresses that can make sense of that journey with the skill that she did" (Conniff). If her directors sing her praises, she graciously returns their compliments. As she has repeatedly emphasized in interviews, she has chosen to work primarily with young, promising directors because "there's this great enthusiasm when you work with first-time directors that you just don't get when you work with older guys." She also prefers writer–directors because she says, "They've written it, so they have a very clear perspective. They have a real vision about the material because it's been born out of them" (Milano, 160).

Her extremely close relationship with her directors and their overwhelming praise for her work has led some critics to label her a very director-dependent actress, who can glow with a good director, but whose performance is greatly reduced by a lesser one.[40] This director dependence, coupled with her youth, immaturity, and insecurity, makes her an unlikely candidate for categorization as an auteurist actress. In fact, her career demonstrates very clearly how difficult it is for a young actress, even one with inside Hollywood connections and a reputation for natural talent and great beauty, to establish herself as an auteur. Paltrow's work has been heavily influenced not only by her directors, but also by producer Harvey Weinstein's fashioning of her career through star vehicles and publicity hype.

Weinstein reputedly engineered her London stage debut in *Proof.* He is said to have bought the screen rights to the successful Broadway play expressly as a star vehicle for Paltrow and as a way for her to collaborate with Madden on a theater production first and then adapt the play to the screen afterwards, which is exactly what has happened.[41] The film with Paltrow in the lead role and Madden directing was released in 2005. When asked if she felt she might someday want to develop projects for herself, Paltrow replied, "It's so grown up to start developing material, don't you think? … I feel I need to do what's handed to me for a while, or seek out things that are already there. I have a lot to learn at this time. It would be scary to take responsibility for a movie getting made" (Beals, 120).

Even so, Paltrow has taken several steps to assume control of her career and to make a mark on the industry. She has repeatedly spoken of her support for small-budget independent films and seems genuinely, if not always too realistically, intent on establishing herself as an artistic, rather than a commercial, film actress. One small-budget film that she set out to defend with a crusader's zeal was *Hard Eight*, which she made in 1996 with first-time director John Paul Anderson. Originally titled *Sydney*, the project was a labor of love for writer–director Anderson. After spending years raising the money for the film and then having its release date repeatedly postponed, he was devastated when the studio insisted on significant cuts and a title change.

Paltrow, who had signed onto the production a year before it was finally shot, says it was a project with which she and her costars felt very connected. As she describes it, the film "was such a personal project for us, we were so emotionally involved and attached to it, it was just so hard to see it being pulled apart by the many people who didn't get it."[42] In support of Anderson's director's cut, Paltrow argued with studio executives and announced to the press: "If they don't release his version, I will be on a personal crusade to murder these people for the rest of my life" (Milano, 66). Anderson describes her in glowing terms: "She was so tough and so strong to stand up for me and help support me. She took her job to another level by being there for me in the editing process, by constantly supporting me and giving me advice on how to deal with the situation" (Strauss).

Paltrow's strong stand in regard to this project can be seen as an indication of a future auteurist activism on her part that may become more pronounced as she grows older and more secure about her position in the industry. On the other hand, it might merely be another indication of her extremely close and supportive relationships with her directors, to whose visions she fully submits.

Not only does Paltrow's auteurism remain unestablished, but also her acting ability. Reviewers have been very polarized in their assessments of her screen performances. Most praise her glowingly for her beauty, freshness, charm, and poise. This critical emphasis on physical presence, although positive on the surface, conceals an underlying doubt concerning the depth of her talent. Critics who do not focus on her looks point to serious flaws in her performances, involving a lack of depth, range, and character development; indeed, reviewers have labeled a number of her performances bland and uninteresting. One issue consistently raised is the failure of Paltrow's performances to rise to the level of the hype that has surrounded them.

Gwyneth Paltrow: Actress and Image

From a feminist perspective, the development of Gwyneth Paltrow's career and star persona would seem to be extremely regressive. She is in many ways a regression to the studio-controlled and -created actresses of the 1930s and 1940s. As Steven Kloves has described her, "In a sense, Paltrow is a throwback of the sort to make feminists cringe. The kind of girl who knows that self-deprecation will get her further, faster, than coming on strong, the kind of girl who knows her charms" (Shnayerson). Paltrow's career has also been very male directed, not only by Mirimax studio executive Harvey Weinstein, but also by her directors, who have always been male and upon whom she has been extremely dependent for guidance.

Her image, too, is strongly wedded to her romantic relationships with male film and rock stars, such as Brad Pitt, Ben Affleck, and Chris Martin. As Paltrow has described herself, she is "just a girl" and certainly not a figure of feminist self-determination. The major elements of her image—physical beauty, fashion, romance, and child-like innocence—perpetuate regressive female gender roles associated with female objectification, conspicuous consumption, male identification, and childishness. These qualities mark her strongly as a regressive fairly tale Hollywood princess for the twenty-first century twenty-something generation, an image hardly amenable to progressive feminist analysis.

Additionally, Paltrow seems to choose roles with no conception of the gender politics underlying them. Her film characters range wildly from feminist to antifeminist. Most of her films present women in love, dominated by their relationships with men, and demonstrating few heroic or female-affirming traits. Even when Paltrow is involved in a film that has feminist dimensions, she does not always recognize their significance. An example is *A Perfect Murder*, a contemporary remake of Alfred Hitchcock's *Dial M for Murder*, which Paltrow has repeatedly described in the most unfavorable turns as a big-budget Hollywood sellout.

What seems to have totally escaped her notice is the film's female-affirmative revision of its source. Even a cursory glance at *A Perfect Murder*'s revision of *Dial M for Murder*'s ending suggests the remake's progressive gender politics. The remake gives its conclusion a distinct note of female triumph and transforms the conventionally passive female victim played by Grace Kelly in the earlier version into an accomplished, self-assertive heroine. Perhaps because the film was not commercially successful or because she associates it with mainstream Hollywood, Paltrow viewed it very superficially, offhandedly condemning it as insubstantial.

Although regressive elements play the most prominent role in shaping Paltrow's image, one can still point to some progressive aspects. For instance, in spite of the strong emphasis placed on her looks, Paltrow has always emphasized her dedication to the craft of acting and to working to perfect her acting techniques. In interviews, she has consistently affirmed her determination to do worthwhile films and to be an actress, not just a Hollywood star. Although she may not always choose roles with an understanding of the gender politics that inform them, she has shown some appreciation for the messages that her films convey to women. Discussing her character in *Shakespeare in Love*, for instance, she has commented:

> She wasn't the traditional objectified muse. She brought out the best in him [Shakespeare] and was his partner. Who she was and what she represented to him brought out a whole creativity. It was a really interesting character for me because she was so strong, and so proactive in dressing as a boy to audition, and all of that. Even though the story is about him, she's an important element in the story. It's not your basic love-interest part (Milano, 157).

She was also eager to play the starring role in *Sylvia*, based on the life of Sylvia Plath, the famous poet and feminist icon of the 1950s.

Gwyneth Paltrow is without question a twenty-first century "It Girl," who in many ways represents a regression to the male-controlled and male-created female stars of the studio era, renowned for their beauty, childlike naiveté, and subservient manner, rather than for their acting ability. However, there is also a would-be actress concealed under this conventional movie star exterior. Only time will tell if this side of Gwyneth Paltrow will ever take control of her career and image.

References

1. She was named the "It Girl" by *Vanity Fair* in 1996 and included in a list of fourteen women who were deemed so highly in demand that they could be said to be on the "It List." (Bernard Stamler, "Separating 'Have Its' from 'Have It Nots,'" *New York Times,* 4 Sept. 2000: C6, Gwyneth Paltrow Clippings File, Billy Rose Theater Collection, New York City Public Library; hereafter cited in text.
2. Gandee, Charles. 1996. "The Luckiest Girl Alive." *Vogue.* <http://www.gwynethpaltrow.org/articles/GP_essay_vogue96.html>; hereafter cited in text.
3. Braustein, Peter. 1998. "Star Hazing." *Villiage Voice* (Oct. 20): 164, Gwyneth Paltrow Clippings File, Billy Rose Theater Collection, New York City Public Library; hereafter cited in text.
4. Milano, Valerie. 2000. *Gwyneth Paltrow.* Toronto: ECW Press, p. 15; hereafter cited in text.
5. Shnayerson, Michael. 2000. "Gwyneth Paltrow: The It Girl for the New Milenium." *Vanity Fair* (Aug.): 381, Gwyneth Paltrow Clippings File, Billy Rose Theater Collection, New York City; hereafter cited in text.
6. Waxman, Sharm. 1996. "A Star Is Born." *Washington Post,* <http://www.gwynethpaltrow.org/articles/GP_essay_washintonpost96.html> <http://; hereafter cited in text.
7. Hochman, David. 1999. "Love's Lady Talks." *Entertainment Weekly* (Jan.), <http://www.gwynethpaltrow.org/articles/GP_essay_ew99.html>; hereafter cited in text.
8. Clehane, Diane. 2000. "Beneath the Elegance." *Biography Magazine* (Oct.), <http://www.gwynethpaltrow.org/articles/GP_essay_biography00.html>; hereafter cited in text.
9. Beals, Jennifer. 1995. "Jennifer Beals Interviews Gwyneth Paltrow." *Interview* (Sept.): 120, Gwyneth Paltrow Clippings File. Margaret Herrick Library, Beverly Hills, CA; hereafter cited in text.
10. Lipton, James. 2001. Interview with Gwyneth Paltrow, *Inside the Actor's Studio,* Bravo Television, March 11; hereafter cited in text.
11. Dreher, Rod. "Gwyneth Speaks Out!" No source, Gwyneth Paltrow Clippings File, Billy Rose Theater Collection, New York City Public Library.
12. "Here and Now." 1998. *Los Angeles Times,* Sept. 15, <http://www.gwyneth-paltrow.org/articles/GP_essay_latimes98.html>; hereafter cited in text.
13. Pogrebin, Robin. 1996. "Behold! A Hot New Star! But Who Said It First?" *New York Times* (Aug. 12): D1, D3.
14. "Q&A with Gwyneth Paltrow." 1998. *E Online,* <http://www.eonline.celebs/Qa/Paltrow98/interview3.html>.

15. Stark, Susan. 2000. "Gwyneth Strives to Find Normalcy," *Detroit News* (Nov. 11), <http://www.gwynethpaltrow.org/articles/GP_essay_detroitnews.html>; hereafter cited in text.

16. Conelly, Sherryl. 1998. "Gwyneth Goes On." *New York Daily News* (April 19): extra 3; hereafter cited in text.

17. Morin, Rich. 2000. "Getting Over Gwyneth." *Harper's Bazaar* (Feb.): 218–222.

18. Stahl, Jerry. 2000. "The Talented Ms. Paltrow." *Elle Magazine* (Feb.). <http://gwynethpaltrow.org/articles/GP_essay_elle00.html>

19. The term was coined by Sydney Pollack, who directed Paltrow in *Flesh and Bone* (Milano, Valerie. 2000. *Gwyneth Paltrow*. Toronto: ECW Press, p. 39).

20. Douglas McGrath, who directed Paltrow in *Emma*, quoted in Milano, Valerie. 2000. *Gwyneth Paltrow*. Toronto: ECW Press, p. 77.

21. Conniff, Tamara. 2000. "Not a Dry Eye in the House." *Newsday* (Jan. 4): B2; hereafter cited in text.

22. Freydkin, Donna. 2003. "Will Pregnant Paltrow and Beau Wed?" *USA Today* (Dec. 5): Life Sec. 5E.

23. Thomas, Karen. 2004. "Paltrow, Martin's Baby Part of a 'Sacred Union.'" *USA Today* (Jan. 7): Life Sec. 2D; hereafter cited in text.

24. Clehene, Diane. 2000. "Gwyneth Paltrow," *Biography Magazine*, Jan. 2000. <http://www.gwynethpaltrow.org/articles/GP_essay_biography00.html>; hereafter cited in text.

25. "Paltrow Stalker Safe Behind Bars." 2001. Internet Movie Data Base, June 18, http://www.imdb.com/name/nm00005691/news.

26. Seymanski, Michael. "The Pitt Girl." Mr. Showbiz Online, <http://www.mrshowbiz.go.com/celebrities/interviews/314_1.html>; hereafter cited in text.

27. Gooden, Joan. 1997. "The Seven Deadly Sins Brought Them Together. Then They Discovered an Eighth." *The Observer* (July 27): 7, Gwyneth Paltrow Clippings File, Billy Rose Theater Collection, New York City Public Library.

28. Horyn, Cathy. 1997. "Gwyneth Bares All." *Harpers Bazaar* (Dec.), <htpp://www.gwynethpaltrow.org/articles/GP_essay_harpers97.html>.

29. "Paltrow and Martin Marry?" 2003. Internet Movie Data Base, Dec. 9, http://www.imdb.com/name/nm0000569/news.

30. Soriano, Cesay G. 2005. "Mommy and Model." *USA Today* (May 23): 1D.

31. Roberts, Cokie. 1999. "Like Mother, Like Daughter," *Life* 22(6) (May): 46–57. EBSCOhost Academic Search Premier, GALILEO, <http://galileo.peachnet.edu>.

32. Dullea, Georgia. 1994. "Not Entirely Out of Character." *New York Times* (Aug. 3): C7.

33. Wloszczyna, Susan. 2000. "Gwyneth Makes Room for Daddy," *USA Today* (Sept.), <http://www.gwynethpaltrow.org/articles/GP_essay_usatoday00.html>>; hereafter cited in text.

34. Heller, Karen. 2000. "Gwyneth Paltrow Plays Down Her Appearance in *Bounce*." *The Philadelphia Inquirer* (Nov. 16). EBSCOhost Academic Search Premier, GALILEO, <http://galileo.peachnet.edu>; hereafter cited in text.

35. For a discussion of Danner as a Method actress, see Steve Vineberg, *Method Actors: Three Generations of an Acting Style* (New York: Schirmer Books, 1994). Danner discusses her career and acting techniques in Jackson R. Bryer and Richard A. Davison, *The Actor's Art: Conversations with Contemporary Stage Performers* (New Brunswick, N.J.: Rutgers University Press, 2001), 40–54.

36. "Star Trak." 1998. *Miami Herald* (Feb.), <http://www.gwynethpaltrow.org/articles/GP_essay_miamiherald98.html>.

37. Lyons, Donald. 1999. "With Paltrow, Plenty to Like in 'As You Like It.'" *New York Post* (Aug. 10): 50–51.

38. Reed, Rex. 1999. "Gwyneth Goes to Summer School." *New York Observer* (Aug. 16): 29.

39. Feen, Gayle and Laura Raposa. 1999. "Gwyn's a Blythe Spirit at Fest." *Boston Herald* (Aug.) <http://www.gwynethpaltrow.org/articles/GP_essay_boston-herald99.html>.

40. Kauffman, Stanley. 2000. "Profane Rites." *New Republic* 223(24) (Dec. 1): 24–25.

41. "Paltrow's Tiny Play Leads to Movie Pay Day." 2002. Internet Movie Data Base, May 6, http://www.imdb.com/name/nm00005691/news.

42. Strauss, Bob. 1997. "Patience of Paltrow." *New York Daily News,* <http://www.gwynethpaltrow.org/articles/GP_essay_newyorkdailynews97.html>; hereafter cited in text.

CHAPTER **9**

Conclusion

Previous studies of Hollywood actresses have been limited to providing examinations of individual actresses and have rarely attempted to extrapolate from their findings what they tell us about the star–actress in general. This final chapter attempts to do just that. Although I realize that the study of five actresses is a limited endeavor and I certainly do not present my conclusions as exhaustive, I do think information on the careers, images, approaches to acting, and ideological significance of these five major Hollywood stars does reveal some very interesting things about the current state of female stardom.

Career

Every star whose career has been examined, except Jodie Foster, adamantly denies that she has had any substantial control of her career in spite of the existence of strong evidence to the contrary. These star–actresses portray their careers as a series of random events or the product of chance, magical circumstance, or divine providence. This denial seems to be a reflection of feminine modesty or societal prohibitions against women demonstrating business acumen, rather than an accurate reading of the state of events. Except for Gwyneth Paltrow, these actresses are not Galatea figures like the contract players of the studio era who were most often created and controlled by male Hollywood executives or directors. Paltrow's relationship with Harvey Weinstein is rather the exception than the general rule, and even she has attempted to assert her individuality by going against Weinstein's more commercial plans for her career and pursuing roles in independent films.

At the same time, however, most of these actresses have gone to great lengths to cultivate good relationships with their directors and with studio executives, and several have male mentors who have helped them in their careers. Even Susan Sarandon, who has been known as "difficult" in this regard, has been intimately involved with Louis Malle early in her career and Tim Robbins more recently, and both men have provided her with key roles that have greatly enhanced her stardom.

In spite of their denials, all of these star–actresses have demonstrated considerable control over the shaping of their careers, especially in terms of role choice. They all claim to have made the ultimate decisions about the roles they have played and these decisions have had a major impact on their stardom. In addition, Sarandon with *Bull Durham*, Foster with *The Accused*, and Bassett with *What's Love Got to Do with It* also very aggressively pursued key career-making roles, were willing to audition for them, and worked hard to persuade reluctant studio executives and directors that they were right for the parts. Many seem also to have turned down major big-budget films because they did not fit with the direction they wanted their careers to take. For instance, Foster refused to do the sequel to *The Silence of the Lambs* and Paltrow turned down *Titanic*.

Each actress' career seems to progress through a similar series of stages. Although somewhat different for each actress, the discovery stage in their careers, as presented in their star biographies, always seems to involve their active pursuit of stardom and their accession to acting success through natural talent. The belief in natural acting ability and the influence of luck on career advancement is central to the discovery sagas of each of these star–actresses—even Streep and Bassett, who are the most highly trained. This emphasis obscures the determination most of these women had to be stars. Sarandon continued to pursue her career despite many setbacks and a long circuitous route to ultimate stardom; while at Yale, Foster struggled to make a definite decision that acting was her career of choice, but once she made that decision she worked tirelessly to reshape her image through careful role choice; Streep and Bassett left budding careers on the New York stage because they were determined to become film stars, and Paltrow convinced her parents to let her drop out of college to go to Hollywood and seek acting jobs. These were women who in many ways acted to make their own luck.

In each actress's ascent to stardom, we see the crucial importance of certain key films. What seems essential is an initial "break-out film" that brings the actress significant critical attention, followed by a series of successes and especially by a major success that really affirms the star-actress's assent to the level of stardom. For instance, Streep had *The Deer Hunter* as a break-out film, *Sophie's Choice* as an affirming film, and then a series of subsequent successes. Foster had *Taxi Driver* as her break-out film, followed by two huge affirming films, *The Accused* and *Silence of the Lambs*. Paltrow had break-out success with *Flesh and Bone* and affirmation with *Emma* and *Shakespeare in Love*.

Actresses whose careers have faltered, like Sarandon and Bassett, have not been able to establish this pattern. Sarandon's risky role choice led her to follow up *Bull Durham* and *Thelma & Louise*, hugely successful films, with *Compromising Positions* and *Lorenzo's Oil*, films that did poorly at the box office. Bassett followed her break-out part in *What's Love Got to Do with It* and her stardom-affirming role in *Waiting to Exhale* with the failed star vehicle *How Stella Got Her Groove Back* and a succession of box office flops that caused the near collapse of her career.

Awards, but most importantly the Academy Award, represent another crucial factor in these actresses' rise to stardom. All have been nominated for Oscars at critical junctions in their careers, and the nomination has helped them break into stardom, affirm their star status, or weather a temporary career decline. Streep in particular has been able to establish a reputation for acting greatness largely based on her remarkable accumulation of awards and nominations. Sarandon's string of Academy Award nominations, beginning with *Thelma and Louise* in 1992, extending through *Lorenzo's Oil* in 1993 and *The Client* in 1995, and culminating in her win for *Dead Man Walking* in 1996 confirmed her continuing stardom at a time when most aging Hollywood actresses are struggling to keep their careers from totally disintegrating. Similarly, Foster's and Paltrow's stardom was propelled by Oscar wins in *The Accused* and *Silence of the Lambs* for Foster and *Shakespeare in Love* for Paltrow.

As Streep's stellar acting reputation demonstrates, one's status in the industry is also of crucial significance. Foster has worked hard to maintain good relationships with industry professionals and to be perceived as a dedicated professional, and Paltrow's mother Blythe Danner's status as a respected actress has helped her daughter build a reputation as a promising acting talent. On the other hand, Sarandon's rise to stardom was significantly delayed by her reputation for being "difficult." Although all of these actresses have been critical of the white, male-dominated Hollywood system, they have at the same time gone to great lengths to fit in with that system, even at times denying their own inclinations in order to do so. Streep has participated in the Hollywood social whirl that she and her husband strongly dislike; Sarandon has sold her sexuality and at times refrained from expressing her political beliefs; Foster has established herself as a team player and possibly kept her sexual orientation hidden; Bassett has taken supporting roles to white actors; and Paltrow has done commercial films against her more artistic inclinations. At the same time, they have all criticized the industry in major ways for discrimination against women, racism, or crass commercialism.

All of these actresses' careers also demonstrate a tendency to have peaks and nadirs. For instance, each actress has experienced a career decline due to family obligations, image changes, and age. Streep, Sarandon, and Foster have made career sacrifices for their families that have adversely affected their stardom and have experienced career declines as they advanced into their forties. Bassett's career is perhaps most illustrative of the many factors that can lead to career decline, including a series of box office failures, departure from type, failure of a star vehicle, moving into supporting roles, refusal to do nudity, agent changes, and industry racism.

Each actress has employed different strategies to resuscitate her sagging career. Streep and Sarandon have moved in their later careers into mother roles, Foster converted her image from the sexualized nymphet that resulted from her role in *Taxi Driver* and from gossip concerning the Hinckley incident to a heroic victim and then simply a female hero persona. Paltrow has worked to shed her good girl image and establish herself as an actress with considerable range.

One strategy that many of these actresses use to keep their careers alive even as they begin to age is to move into producing and directing. The transition to directing seems to be more difficult. Although Foster's directing debut was welcomed with great anticipation, her career as a director has only had moderate success. On the other hand, Sarandon, Foster, and Bassett have moved into producing, and each has made advances in this area. Although Sarandon's role as executive producer of *Stepmom* did not result in a narratively progressive film, it did furnish two major female stars, Sarandon and Julia Roberts, the rare opportunity of headlining in a major studio production. Foster has produced or executive produced a number of interesting small independent films, including *Waking the Dead* (Gordon 2000) and *The Dangerous Lives of Altar Boys* (Care 2002) and, for television, *The Baby Dance* (Anderson 1998). Additionally, Bassett's executive production of *The Rosa Parks Story* furnished her with one of her best recent acting opportunities.

Image

The concept of the star image seems very relevant to the careers of these actresses, who definitely emerge from their publicity and promotion as "characters in the drama of their own biographies." Many scholarly insights into the construction of star images seem applicable to a discussion of the image lexicons of these female stars. Their images are intertexual, polysemic, and contradictory. They seem to be shifting unstable combinations of progressive elements that challenge the status quo and regressive components that recuperate this progressivity for patriarchy. This combination of progressive and recuperative elements within the stars' images creates an ambiguous relationship between them and the existing social structure, which they seem to challenge as well as support.

Progressive elements that these stars' images seem to exhibit include the stars' reputations for acting talent, intelligence, and sociopolitical activism. Many of these star–actresses seem overtly through their role choice to offer themselves as role models and figures of inspiration for female fans, encouraging them to reject the victim's role and strive for heroism, courage, and success. Counterpoised against these positive elements are more regressive ones connected to traditional images of female stardom. Beauty and glamour are major aspects of each actress's image, and this beauty is always presented as entirely natural. What these actresses have done to construct and maintain their looks is rarely discussed, and when it is mentioned, it is common to argue against the constructed nature of their attractiveness. Streep and Sarandon have talked about their refusal to get face lifts, Bassett has attributed her muscular physique to heredity, and Paltrow is said to have inherited her beauty from her mother. Although fashion plays a role in each actress's image, Paltrow alone has established herself as a throwback to the clotheshorse stars of the studio era. Here, again, when Paltrow's connection to fashion is discussed, it is commonly in terms of her natural sense of class and fashion.

Yet the way physical beauty is embedded in these actresses' images is not always entirely regressive. Beauty and glamour are definitely components of Streep, Bassett, and Foster's images, but they have never been accented over their reputations as great actresses. As a dark-skinned black woman exalted for her stunning appearance, Bassett could also be said to take Hollywood glamour in a racially progressive direction. Although Sarandon's physical attractiveness has been more emphasized and more strongly associated with her sexuality than is the case for the other actresses, her sexual allure is still presented in a rather progressive manner, as stemming from her combination of sexuality with intelligence. Only Paltrow seems to be irremediably regressive in terms of the prominent role her perfect looks, fashion consciousness, and model's figure play in her star image.

The emphasis on motherhood in several of the stars' images is another recuperative element. Streep, Sarandon, Foster, and Paltrow have glorified motherhood at the expense of career goals. Every actress claims to have very willingly sacrificed career for family. In interviews, Streep has even reduced her acting career to the level of a hobby that keeps her from being ill-natured with her children. Paltrow, who recently gave birth to a daughter, has suggested that she may indefinitely put her career on hold to raise her child,[1] and Foster has made a sweeping reduction in her film work since the births of her children. Although each of these actresses can be seen as somewhat progressive in that none has really given up her career for her family, their descriptions of their devotion to motherhood always seem to involve its idealization at the expense of their career ambitions and their power within the film industry.

As it did for earlier female stars, romance plays a major role in the star images of all of these actresses. Like their devotion to family, it seems to function within their image lexicons to denigrate their positions as powerful professional women, demonstrate women's essential dependence on men, and posit long-term heterosexual monogamy as the source of ultimate female fulfillment. Their romantic lives have been major aspects of the promotion and publicity for all of these stars, except Foster; however, even in Foster's case, the highly publicized nature of her demand for privacy in her personal life brings the ambiguity of her sexuality and the mystery of her romantic inclinations to the foreground of her image. The romantic biographies of all the other actresses trace their quest for and eventual attainment of the perfect husband.

Streep overcame the tragic loss of her first love, John Cazale, to find perfect love in a marriage that has lasted for over thirty years with Don Gummer. Sarandon, who in her early career was notorious for her extensive list of love affairs with her fellow actors and directors, finally settled down into a perfect companionate relationship with her "true soul mate" Tim Robbins. In interviews, Bassett presented herself as always searching for the right man until the perfect love of her life, Courtney Vance, came along and swept her off her feet. Finally, Paltrow's highly publicized romances with a succession of actors after her high-profile breakup with Brad Pitt were presented as part of her search for a man who would truly care for and protect her, until she finally found just such a man in the rock star Chris Martin.

This focus on the quest for romance is indicative of another prominent aspect of these stars' images: their combination of the ordinary and the extraordinary. Richard Dyer's idea that this integration of the everyday and the exceptional is part of what holds the discordant elements of a star's image together seems very applicable to the images of these actresses. They are presented as extraordinary in their great beauty, glamour, natural acting talent, success, and the emotional intensity and heroism of the parts they play. However, they are also represented as just normal women who love their husbands and families, are devoted mothers, want normal and private personal lives, seek romantic love, and encounter personal problems in real life. As extraordinary ordinary women, they maintain their status as identification figures for their fans because they are, after all, just normal people with everyday desires and difficulties.

At the same time, however, they also serve as role models and hyper-semioticized charismatic figures who, through their exceptionality, offer fans compensation for what they lack and symbolic representations of what they hope for in their own lives. Streep offers her preeminent talent; Sarandon the possibility of being seen as sexy as well as intelligent; Foster a smart heroism; Bassett black courage, success, and triumph over adversity; and Paltrow the combination of beauty and talent. Significantly, the star images of these women do not present them as working professionals involved in the profession of acting, but as charismatic figures offering women paradigms of what they could be and want to be. The structured polysemy of their images offers women the possibility of being intelligent, successful, talented, strong, heroic, and independent, yet also beautiful, sexy, motherly, and romantically attractive to and protected by men. They offer their female fans what scholars have called numinosity, a sense of transcendent irrational significance that is difficult to resist.

That these star images involve the imaginary resolution of irresolvable contradictions seems clear, but what also emerges from an analysis of their components is the sense of instability and stability that characterizes them. Because they combine such disparate elements, star images always seem on the brink of self-destruction, yet in studying these stars over the course of their careers, it is remarkable how consistent and stable their images actually appear. Meryl Streep's acting reputation and motherly devotion dominate her image from beginning to end. Susan Sarandon begins as a sexual rebel, becomes a sexy–intelligent rebel, and ends a sexy older woman rebel known for her political activism. Foster moves from a precocious child star to a sexualized but tough teenager to a heroic survivor to a female hero.

Unstable images that do not hold to a central core do not bode well for a star's career. For instance, Bassett's career fell into decline when she ceased to play roles that offered iconic representations of strong black womanhood. Paltrow's inability to establish conclusively that she should be recognized not only for her looks but also for her acting talents has hurt her career.

Acting

Acting talent is a major part of the images of each of these actresses, and contrary to conceptions of stars as nonactors, these actresses are all quite articulate about their approaches to acting. Perhaps one reason why stars are not recognized for their acting ability is because they so often attempt to mystify their acting process. In some cases, this seems to represent an attempt to cover over their difficulty in explaining their technique, but it is amazing how often the actresses studied resorted in interviews to "the reverie approach" in describing their acting process. They also use this approach to contradict any tendency to see them as technical actresses, which is a term they seem to want to avoid at all costs. Streep describes acting in religious terms, whereas Sarandon, Foster, Bassett, and Paltrow insist they are instinctive or intuitive actresses.

In addition, all of the actresses are absolutely determined to present themselves as natural talents, not as highly trained professionals. The extent of their training is quite mixed, with Streep and Bassett gaining substantial prestige from their formal education at Yale, and Sarandon, Foster, and Paltrow presenting themselves as completely lacking in formal training of any sort. There seems to be a clear dichotomy among Hollywood actresses between those with formal training and those who seem to have gotten their training on the job. Neither, however, clearly has a distinct advantage.

Although a pedigree from Yale holds a certain amount of cachet for Streep and Bassett, their lack of training has not hurt Sarandon, Foster, or Paltrow. In fact, Foster even seems proud of her lack of training, describing acting as a common-sense endeavor that is not very difficult and labeling acting classes as nonsense. Yet among the actresses studied, she is only second to Streep in her reputation as a great actress. Sarandon similarly has characterized acting as "not very complicated" and has argued for the value of the type of on-the-job training she got working in soap operas—certainly not a prestigious acting venue. Paltrow seems never even to have considered formally studying acting in college or when she sought acting jobs in Hollywood. She has proposed that she learned how to act merely from watching her mother perform on stage.

Although there are wide disparities in the training these actresses received, none of them, even the most highly educated, ever seeks to emphasize her training. The great fear of being considered a technical actress has led to a strong emphasis on instinctive or natural acting talent. Streep regards her training as of mixed usefulness to her, and her publicity presents it as merely bringing out her natural talent. Sarandon definitely characterizes herself as an instinctive actress who prepares very little for a scene and dislikes rehearsal because she feels she can only really act when the cameras are rolling. Foster, Bassett, and Paltrow have also described themselves as working intuitively or instinctively.

Although many actors have greatly praised stage acting as the way to best perfect their craft and have denigrated film acting as less fulfilling and stimulating, this is not the case with the actresses studied here. Bassett and Streep, who started in theater, praise it as an exciting and technically challenging acting venue, but they never do so at the expense of film acting. Sarandon and Foster, who are primarily and, in Foster's case exclusively, film actresses, express no regrets about their lack of stage experience. Sarandon seemed to turn to the stage only when her early film career faltered and has never expressed a desire to return. Foster has professed a complete disinterest in the theater, seeing it as an entirely different acting medium from film and one in which she feels she would have to start all over in terms of her acting methods. Paltrow is somewhat in the middle on this issue. She has done some theater and speaks of it with high reverence, which clearly stems from her great admiration for her mother as a stage actress, but she never does so in a way that denigrates the quality of film acting.

Several of the actresses have made comparisons between film and stage acting in order to illuminate the craft involved in each form. They have described the differences much in the same terms used by critics and other actors. Stage acting is described as freer, more risky, and more reliant on technique, whereas film acting is seen as narrower, more microscopic, and more individual. Even Streep and Bassett, who praise stage acting the most, have made only brief forays back to the stage and have not forsaken film acting in any appreciable way to return to the theater. As Streep and Sarandon have pointed out, stage acting involves a far more grueling physical regimen and more time away from one's family than the medium of film, which, although the actresses do not mention it, is also considerably more lucrative.

The actresses' descriptions of their acting methodology show them to be very eclectic and hybrid in their techniques. They all define the primary job of acting as characterization, and when they talk about their acting, it is their methods of characterization that they discuss most fully.

Significantly, these methods always involve impersonation and never the personification that has commonly been associated with star acting. None of these actresses ever admits to playing herself on the screen, and Paltrow has even singled out Julia Roberts' career as one she does not want to emulate because she believes Roberts has been typecast in roles that seem to require her only to express her personality.

In spite of their rejection of personification as an acting mode, each actress plays roles that accord closely with her overall image and, as stars, they are inevitably perceived as bigger-than-life hypersemioticized figures. As a result, any one of them can be characterized as in a sense playing herself on screen. Streep plays highly emotional roles, Sarandon intelligent sexy women, Foster and Bassett female heroes, and Paltrow sweet young ingenues.

Yet this tendency toward personification is also combined with the methodology of impersonation. Although they very often pay roles closely related to their images, their techniques of characterization strongly reflect the idea that acting means creating a unique and different character in each role. They also gain a significant amount of prestige from trying to do just that, and every actress talks about wanting to achieve range and depth in her characterizations. Streep and Bassett have been praised for a chameleon-like ability to convert themselves into different characters and Sarandon describes acting as understanding the personalities of the characters one plays. Foster calls it pretending, and Paltrow has talked about going deeply into character and becoming one with the person she portrays. These actresses demonstrate clearly that star acting is really hybrid in its combination of impersonation and personification, as well as in its mix of star image, role, and actor. The star's type, the individualized character played, and the actor's craft must be evident to the audience. Star performances also mix the commercial with the artistic, box office attraction with personal charisma, and industry creation with individual expression.

In their descriptions of the process of preparing for a role, the actresses studied demonstrate a combination of techniques that differ significantly from actress to actress, demonstrating that no shared methodology exists among them. Streep talks about not liking to read the script too much, making a connection with the character, and entering a zone when performing, yet she also discusses shaping roles by imitating public figures, literary characters, or people she knows in her private life. Sarandon talks about being a "money actor" who can only perform when she is in front of the camera, and Foster and Paltrow describe themselves as getting quickly in and out of character. Foster and Paltrow also confess to not understanding their technique, yet Paltrow proposes that she always prepares a minimum performance before she arrives on the set, and Foster describes interpreting the script as a literary critic would.

In terms of their adherence to established acting traditions, these actresses are again eclectic. None subscribes to any one theoretical school, but they all seem in essence to hold to the tenets of naturalistic acting, describing acting in terms of verisimilitude, realism, and invisible technique. Streep talks of her need for a realistic context for her performances, Sarandon describes good acting as fresh and spontaneous, Foster characterizes it as common sense, and Bassett talks about the need to make one's acting look honest and effortless. All have also been praised for looking natural on the screen and making their characters seem real.

Although they do not necessarily recognize the exact source of their influences, Stanislavskian naturalism clearly has had a strong influence on each of them. As many scholars of acting have suggested, Stanislavski's ideas appear to have been so thoroughly absorbed into the practice of Hollywood acting that they are invisible and no longer recognized for what they are. Even if they do not use the argot of Stanislavski's system, these actresses still talk about employing acting methods that he advocated. They discuss the need to live the part by experiencing character emotions, to place themselves in the situations experienced by their characters, to employ scene analysis to uncover the subtext of a scene, and to attempt to construct a spontaneous introspective performance.

Ideas associated with The Method have also had an influence, although The Method seems to be universally rejected by these actresses and especially repudiated by Foster. In spite of scholars' claims that The Method was profoundly influential on Hollywood acting, it seems much less so than purely Stanislavskian ideas. These actresses feel that they achieve effective characterization not so much by substituting their emotions for those of the character, as The Method advocates, as by living the part by entering into the character's emotional life.

At the same time, however, all of them speak of drawing on their experiences to find the needed connection with their characters. They also make some reference to Method concepts such as being in the moment, listening to other actors, and the illusion of the first time. Method influence seems most pronounced, however, in the priority these actresses give to character psychology, the need for emotional truth in performance, the cathartic nature of the acting experience, acting as self-discovery, and the rejection of personification as an acting mode.

Naturalism's dominance is also seen in the strong disinclination these actresses and reviewers of their performances feel toward ostensive acting. In fact, critics have severely criticized several of them for being too mannered or showy in their acting style and have repeatedly praised others for their naturalness. Streep has often been accused of being a mannered, detached and aloof actress who "eats up the scenery" and whose use of accents and recurring mannerisms allows audiences to see too much of the actress behind the character. Similarly, Bassett has been criticized for being over the top, too big, too intense, and overly emotional in her performances, and this reputation seems to have hurt her career. The actresses who lack formal training fare better in this regard. Sarandon has been praised throughout her career for the reality she brings to her characters, Foster for being able to look natural in repeated takes, and Paltrow for the realistic sound of her British accent. The idea of ostensive acting seems to have become such a negative in Hollywood and to be so detrimental to an actress's reputation that each of these actresses tries to avoid it completely.

This dominance of naturalistic acting does not mean that these actresses are uninfluenced by the studio acting style. Their focus on preparing for a role by creating a model of their character and then rendering that model effectively in performance, of employing careful script analysis, of doing extensive preparation before coming to the set, and of mixing techniques with a "whatever works" attitude, as well as their photogenicity and tendencies toward personification, are inherited from studio performance. What does seem to distinguish them from earlier studio actresses is that their acting is less about their looks and more about their acting abilities. They also seem to have more influence in shaping their careers than did actresses under contract during the studio era.

The major trait that distinguishes these contemporary actresses from their predecessors, however, is the auteurist nature of their acting. Although every actress characterizes actors as the tools of their directors and Foster has even proposed that the only way to gain artistic control of a film is to go into directing, the creative input these actresses have had on their films does not totally support this characterization. Except for Paltrow, whose insecurity about her abilities and lack of training has led her to be very director dependent, all of these actresses are high-autonomy stars who have shaped their films in major ways. Streep and Sarandon seem to require almost no direction. Directors let Streep do what she wants to do with a role, and Sarandon has said that she prefers to be left alone to act and needs a director only to set the parameters for her performance and to give her advice when she asks for it.

None of these actresses seems to be just a tool under the control of her director; instead, each is actively involved in the creative process of filmmaking. Streep and Sarandon have even influenced the overall design of their films in significant ways. Streep has exercised auteurism throughout her career, influencing directorial decisions, even improvising or writing her lines, and reshaping characters through performance. Sarandon has exhibited her auteurism primarily through role choice. She has been very directed toward films that deal with political and social issues, but she has also reformulated characters without even consulting the director, suggested script changes, persuaded directors to change scenes she did not like, and initiated her own projects. Foster and Bassett, who have been less auteurist in their acting, have moved into producing and directing to gain more control. Even Gwyneth Paltrow, who has spoken of being afraid to have too much artistic input, has become involved in developing her projects and is reputed to have future plans to produce a Marlene Dietrich biopic in which she will star.[2]

Ideological Significance

It seems clear from all that has been said here that these actresses are much more than passive objects of desire or creations of the film industry, but what exactly they mean to their female fans remains somewhat ambiguous. It is extremely difficult to determine a star's ideological significance because audience studies have made a strong case for the active nature of fan response to film stars and for the wide range of possible interpretive possibilities. One can only suggest some of the potential reading positions that these stars' images offer to their fans. What we see in each star–actress's image lexicon is a mixture of progressive and regressive elements that allow fans wide possibilities for interpretation. In essence, the adage that stars are all things to all people is quite true. These actresses are perhaps stars because their images can be read in so many different ways, ranging from the progressive to the reactionary.

On the progressive side, in contrast to the traditional association of female stars with glamour and celebrity rather than acting accomplishment, each of the actresses studied has gained a substantial reputation for acting talent. Streep especially has been honored as a great actress, but each of the actresses has also been lauded for her acting talent. Additionally, they all have gained considerable power within the film industry and demonstrated significant control over the development of their careers and the construction of their images. None really can be seen as entirely the creation of the male-dominated film industry. They all have had creative input into their films, and Streep and Sarandon in particular can be considered auteurist actresses.

In addition, Sarandon, Foster, Bassett, and even Paltrow have taken active steps to put themselves in positions of greater power within the industry by moving into producing and, for Foster, into directing as well.

Additionally, each actress has put a progressive spin on her connection with Hollywood glamour by associating her status as a great beauty with a reputation for intelligence, acting talent, and artistic aspirations. Bassett has even broken color barriers in this regard.

These stars also have made progressive decisions in terms of role choice by starring in female-centered films, by taking the female characters they play beyond stereotype and conventionality to give them overtly or covertly feminist dimensions, and by adding a progressive slant to the screen representation of female sexuality. Additionally, Streep, Sarandon, Foster, and Bassett have called attention to sexism in the industry, and Bassett has attacked Hollywood for its racism. Several of these stars are known not only for their outspoken criticisms of the film industry, but also for their political and social activism. Streep and Sarandon have been willing in particular to use their celebrity to support various causes and to make political statements. This is not to say that these stars are overtly anomic actresses who have moved the representation of women on screen and the female star image in radically different directions. They do, however, have subversive dimensions to their careers and images that offer identities to women that are not totally in accord with the patriarchal status quo.

At the same time, the progressive elements associated with these female stars are mixed with regressive components that act to control and recuperate the stars' progressivity for the status quo. For instance, in spite of their great career success, power within the industry, and reputations for acting accomplishment, all of the star–actresses studied have taken pains to present themselves as traditional wives and mothers. They have discussed willingly sacrificing career for family, minimized the significance of their acting accomplishments, and taken roles that reinforce their connection to traditional motherhood.

None has declared herself a feminist, except Foster, who also tellingly has stated repeatedly that, although she sees herself as a feminist, her films are not about feminism. Sarandon has gone even further and denied any association with feminism for herself and her films. Streep, who has strongly criticized sexism in the industry, at the same time has not taken any steps to gain more power for herself as a producer or director, and, in spite of endless rumors, Foster has refused to make a definitive statement about her sexual orientation.

Although their role choices are often progressive, these stars have also played parts that represent conventional or even regressive female images. Streep and Bassett's highly emotional portrayals can be seen as contributing to the image of women as rightly confined to the world of feeling and sentimentality. The prominence of sexuality in Sarandon's image and her turn to mother roles in her later career can also be seen as regressive, as can Foster's penchant for female victim roles and Paltrow's string of innocent and not-too-smart ingenues. Several actresses' careers also have not lived up to expectations. Foster's directing accomplishments are much less than was initially anticipated, Bassett's career is in real trouble, and Paltrow has had a tendency to do embarrassing comedies. Her position as a Galatea figure to Harvey Weinstein and as a clotheshorse star makes her in many ways a regressive throwback to male-created and -controlled studio era star–actresses. Additionally, each of these stars can be seen as a victim of exploitation through industry sexism, racism, commercialism, and gossip.

In the final analysis, what do these star–actresses offer to their female fans? They clearly offer no overt challenge to the patriarchal status quo or to traditional views of women; however, as figures of resistance on a subversive level, their mixture of progressive and recuperative elements at least allows for the possibility that female fans can use the careers, images, and acting of these stars in positive ways. Their fans can choose selectively from among the various elements offered by these star–actresses to form female identities in accord with feminist ideals. In this way, Meryl Streep, Susan Sarandon, Jodie Foster, Angela Bassett, and Gwyneth Paltrow do offer a subversive challenge to male dominance and to the patriarchal status quo.

References

1. "Paltrow Gives Birth to a Baby Girl." 2002. Internet Movie Data Base, May 17, <http://www.imdb.com/name/nm00005691/news>.
2. "Paltrow to Play Dietrich." 2002. Internet Movie Data Base, May 17, <http://www.imdb.com/name/nm00005691/news>.

Bibliography

Affron, Charles. 1977. *Star Acting: Gish, Garbo, Davis.* New York: Dutton.

Amossy, Ruth. 1986. "Autobiographies of Movie Stars: Presentation of Self and its Strategies." *Poetics Today* 7(4): 673–703.

Austin, Thomas and Martin Barker, eds. 2003. *Contemporary Hollywood Stardom.* London: Arnold.

Barker, Martin. 2003. "Introduction." pp. 1–24 in *Contemporary Hollywood Stardom.* London: Arnold.

Baron, Cynthia. 1999. "Crafting Film Performances: Acting in the Hollywood Studio Era." pp. 31–45 in *Screen Acting,* eds. A. Lovell and P. Krämer. New York: Routledge.

Blair, Rhonda. 2002. "Reconsidering Stanislavsky: Feeling, Feminism, and the Actor." *Theatre Topics* 12(2) (Sept.): 177–190.

Bryer, Jackson R. and Richard A. Davison. 2001. *The Actor's Art: Conversations with Contemporary Stage Performers.* New Brunswick, N.J.: Rutgers University Press.

Butler, Jeremy. 1991. *Star Texts: Image and Performance in Film and Television.* Detroit: Wayne State University Press.

———. 1998. "The Star System and Hollywood." pp. 342–353 in *The Oxford Guide to Film Studies,* eds. J. Hill and P. C. Gibson. Oxford: Oxford University Press.

Cardillo, Burt, Harry Geduld, Ronald Gottesman, and Leigh Woods, eds. 1998. *Playing to the Camera: Film Actors Discuss Their Craft.* New Haven, Conn.: Yale University Press.

Carnicke, Sharon Marie. 1999. "Lee Strasberg's Paradox of the Actor." pp. 75–87 in *Screen Acting,* eds. A. Lovell and P. Krämer. New York: Routledge.

Chunovic, Louis. 1995. *Jodie: A Biography.* Chicago: Contemporary Books.

Clark, Danae. 1995. *Negotiating Hollywood: The Cultural Politics of Actors' Labor.* Minneapolis: University of Minnesota Press.

Damico, James. 1991. "Ingrid from Lorraine to Stromboli: Analyzing the Public's Perception of a Film Star." pp. 240–253 in *Star Texts: Image and Performance in Film and Television,* ed. J. Butler. Detroit: Wayne State University Press.

De Angelis, Therese. 2001. *Jodie Foster*. Philadelphia: Chelsea House.

DeCordova, Richard. 1991. "The Emergence of the Star System in America." pp. 17–29 in *Stardom: Industry of Desire*, ed. C. Gledhill. London: Routledge.

———. 1991. "Genre and Performance: An Overview." pp. 115–124 in *Star Texts: Image and Performance in Film and Television*, ed. J. Butler. Detroit: Wayne State University Press.

Dyer, Richard. 1979. *Stars*. London: British Film Institute.

———. 1986. *Heavenly Bodies: Film Stars and Society*. New York: St. Martin's Press.

———. 1991. "Charisma." pp. 57–59 in *Stardom: Industry of Desire*, ed. C. Gledhill. London: Routledge.

———. 1991. "Four Films by Lana Turner." pp. 214–239 in *Star Texts: Image and Performance in Film and Television*, ed. J. Butler. Detroit: Wayne State University Press.

Eckert, Charles. 1991. "Shirley Temple and the House of Rockefeller." pp. 184–202 in *Star Texts: Image and Performance in Film and Television*, ed. J. Butler. Detroit: Wayne State University Press.

Ellis, John. 1982. *Visible Fictions: Cinema: Television: Video*. London: Routledge.

———. 1991. "Stars as a Cinematic Phenomenon." p. 308 in *Star Texts: Image and Performance in Film and Television*, ed. J. Butler. Detroit: Wayne State University Press.

Figgis, Mike, John Boorman, and Walter Donohue, eds. 2000. *Projections 10: Hollywood Film-Makers on Film-Making*. London: Faber & Faber.

Fischer, Lucy. 1988. "*Sunset Boulevard*: Fading Stars." pp. 97–113 in *Women & Film*, ed., J. Todd. New York: Holmes & Meier.

———. 1989. *Shot/Countershot: Film Tradition and Women's Cinema*. Princeton: Princeton University Press.

———. 1991. *Imitation of Life* (Rutgers Films in Print). New Brunswick, N.J.: Rutgers.

———. 1999. "Sirk and the Figure of the Actress: *All I Desire*." *Film Criticism* 23(2–3) (Winter/Spring): 136–149.

———. 2003. *Designing Women. Cinema, Art Deco, & the Female Form*. New York: Columbia University Press.

———. 2004. "*Marlene*: Modernity, Mortality, and the Biopic." pp. 29–42 in *Stars: The Film Reader*, eds., L. Fischer and M. Landy. New York: Routledge.

Fischer, Lucy and Marcia Landy. 2004. *Stars: The Film Reader*. New York: Routledge.

FitzGerald, Dawn. 2002. *Angela Bassett*. Philadelphia: Chelsea House.

Foster, Buddy and Leon Wagener. 1998. *Foster Child: An Intimate Biography of Jodie Foster by Her Brother*. New York: Signet.

Gaines, Jane. 1990. "Costume and Narrative: How Dress Tells the Woman's Story." pp. 180–211 in *Fabrications: Costume and the Female Body*, eds., J. Gaines and C. Herzog. London and New York: Routledge.

———. 1990. "Introduction: Fabricating the Female Body." pp. 1–27 in *Fabrications: Costume and the Female Body*, eds., J. Gaines and C. Herzog. London and New York: Routledge.

Gaines, Jane and Charlotte Herzog, eds. 1990. *Fabrications: Costume and the Female Body*. London and New York: Routledge.

Geraghty, Christine. 2000. "Re-examining Stardom: Questions of Texts, Bodies, and Performance." pp. 183–201 in *Reinventing Film Studies*, eds., C. Gledhill and L. Williams. London: Arnold.

———. 2003. "Performing as a Lady and a Dame: Reflections on Acting and Genre." pp. 105–117 in *Contemporary Hollywood Stardom*, eds., T. Austin and M. Barker. London: Arnold.

Gledhill, Christine. 1991. "Introduction." pp. xiii–xx in *Stardom: Industry of Desire*, ed. C. Gledhill. London: Routledge.

———. 1991. "Signs of Melodrama." pp. 207–229 in *Stardom: Industry of Desire*, ed., C. Gledhill. New York: Routledge.

———. ed. 1991. *Stardom: Industry of Desire.* New York: Routledge.

Gledhill, Christine and Linda Williams, eds. 2000. *Reinventing Film Studies.* London: Arnold.

Griegers, Cathy. 1993. "*Thelma and Louise* and the Cultural Generation of the New Butch–Femme." pp. 129–141 in *Film Theory Goes to the Movies*, eds., J. Collins, H. Radner, and A. P. Collins. New York: Routledge.

Haskell, Molly. 1974. *From Reverence to Rape: The Treatment of Women in the Movies.* New York: Penguin.

Herzog, Charlotte Cornelia and Jane Marie Gaines. 1991. "'Puffed Sleeves before Tea-Time': Joan Crawford, Adrian, and Women Audiences." pp. 74–91 in *Stardom: Industry of Desire*, ed., C. Gledhill. New York: Routledge.

Higson, Andrew. 1991. "Film Acting and Independent Cinema." pp. 155–182 in *Star Texts: Image and Performance in Film and Television*, ed. J. Butler. Detroit: Wayne State University Press.

Hill, John and Pamela Church Gibson, eds. 1998. *The Oxford Guide to Film Studies.* Oxford: Oxford University Press.

Kennedy, Philippa. 1995. *Jodie Foster: The Most Powerful Woman in Hollywood.* London: MacMillan.

King, B. 1991. "Articulating Stardom." pp. 125–154 in *Star Texts: Image and Performance in Film and Television*, ed. J. Butler. Detroit: Wayne State University Press.

———. 2003. "Embodying an Elastic Self: The Parametrics of Contemporary Stardom." pp. 45–61 in *Contemporary Hollywood Stardom*, eds., T. Austin and M. Barker. London: Arnold.

Klaprat, Cathy. 1985. "The Star as Market Strategy: Bette Davis in Another Light." pp. 351–376 in *The American Film Industry*, ed. T. Balio. Madison: University of Wisconsin Press.

Knobloch, Susan. 1999. "Helen Shaver: Resistance through Artistry." pp. 106–125 in *Screen Acting*, eds. A. Lovell and P. Krämer. New York: Routledge.

Konijn, Elly A. 2000. *Acting Emotions.* Amsterdam: Amsterdam University Press.

Krämer, Peter. 2003. "'A Woman in a Male-Dominated World': Jodie Foster, Stardom, and 90s Hollywood." pp. 199–214 in *Contemporary Hollywood Stardom*, eds., T. Austin and M. Barker. London: Arnold.

Krasner, David, ed. 2000. *Method Acting Reconsidered: Theory, Practice, Future.* New York: St. Martin's Press.

Lacey, Joanne. 2003. "'A Galaxy of Stars to Guarantee Ratings': Made-for-Television Movies and the Female Star System." pp. 187–198 in *Contemporary Hollywood Stardom*, eds., T. Austin and M. Barker. London: Arnold.

Lane, Christina. 1995. "The Liminal Iconography of Jodie Foster." *The Journal of Popular Film and Television* 22(4) (Winter): 149–153.

Larue, Johanne and Carole Zucker. 1990. "James Dean: The Pose of Reality? *East of Eden* and the Method Performance." pp. 295–324 in *Making Visible the Invisible: An Anthology of Essays on Film Acting*, ed., C. Zucker. Metuchen, N.J.: Scarecrow Press.

Lovell, Alan. 1999. "Susan Sarandon: In Praise of Older Women." pp. 88–105 in *Screen Acting*, eds. A. Lovell and P. Kramer. New York: Routledge.

———. 2003. "I Went in Search of Deborah Kerr, Jodie Foster, and Julianne Moor but got Waylaid...." pp. 259–270 in *Contemporary Hollywood Stardom*, eds., T. Austin and M. Barker. London: Arnold.

Lovell, Alan and Peter Krämer. 1999. "Introduction." pp. 1–9 in *Screen Acting*, eds. A. Lovell and P. Krämer. New York: Routledge.

———, eds. 1999. *Screen Acting*. New York: Routledge.

Maltby, Richard. 2003. *Hollywood Cinema*. 2d ed. Malden, Mass.: Blackwell.

Maychick, Diane. 1984. *Meryl Streep: The Reluctant Superstar*. New York: St. Martin's Press.

McDonald, Paul. 1998. "Film Acting." pp. 30–35 in *The Oxford Guide to Film Studies*, eds. J. Hill and P. C. Gibson. Oxford: Oxford University Press.

———. 2000. *The Star System: Hollywood's Production of Popular Identities*. London: Wallflower Press.

———. 2003. "Stars in the Online Universe: Promotion, Nudity, Reverence." pp. 29–44 in *Contemporary Hollywood Stardom*, eds., T. Austin and M. Barker. London: Arnold.

Meyer, David. 1999. "Acting in Silent Film: Which Legacy of the Theater?" pp. 10–30 in *Screen Acting*, eds. A. Lovell and P. Krämer. New York: Routledge.

Meyer–Dinkgrafe, Daniel. 2001. *Approaches to Acting Past and Present*. London: Continuum.

Milano, Valerie. 2000. *Gwyneth Paltrow*. Toronto: ECW Press.

Mulvey, Laura. 1989. *Visual and Other Pleasures*. Bloomington, Ind.: Indiana University Press.

———. 1989. "Visual Pleasure and Narrative Cinema." pp. 14–26 in *Visual and Other Pleasures*, ed. L. Mulvey. Bloomington, Ind.: Indiana University Press.

Naremore, J. 1988. *Acting in the Cinema*. Berkeley: University of California Press.

Pearson, Roberta E. 1990. "O'er Step not the Modesty of Nature: A Semiotic Approach to Acting in the Griffith Biographs." pp. 1–27 in *Making Visible the Invisible: An Anthology of Essays on Film Acting*, ed., C. Zucker. Metuchen, N.J.: Scarecrow Press.

———. 1992. *Eloquent Gestures: The Transformation of Performance Style in the Griffith Biograph Films*. Berkeley, University of California Press.

Perkins, Tessa. 1991. "The Politics of Jane Fonda." pp. 237–250 in *Stardom: Industry of Desire*, ed. C. Gledhill. London: Routledge.

Pfaff, Eugene E., Jr. and Mark Emerson. 1987. *Meryl Streep: A Critical Biography.* Jefferson, N.C. and London: McFarland & Company.

Prince, Stephen and Wayne Hensley. 1992. "The Kuleshov Effect: Recreating the Classic Experiment." *Cinema Journal* 31(2) (Winter): 59–75.

Rich, B. Ruby. 1991. "Nobody's Handmaid." *Sight and Sound* (Dec.): 7–10.

Rosen, Marjorie. 1973. *Popcorn Venus: Women, Movies, and the American Dream.* New York: Coward, McCann, and Geoghegen.

Shapiro, Marc. 2001. *Susan Sarandon: Actress–Activist.* Amherst, N.Y.: Prometheus Books.

Shingler, Martin. 1999. "Bette Davis: Malevolence in Motion." pp. 46–58 in *Screen Acting*, eds. A. Lovell and P. Krämer. New York: Routledge.

Smurthwaite, Nick. 1984. *The Meryl Streep Story.* New York: Beaufort Books.

Stacey. Jackie. 1991. "Feminine Fascinations: Forms of Identification in Star–Audience Relations." pp. 141–163 in *Stardom: Industry of Desire*, ed. C. Gledhill. London: Routledge.

Staiger, Janet. 1991. "Seeing Stars." pp. 3–16 in *Stardom: Industry of Desire*, ed. C. Gledhill. London: Routledge.

Strasberg, Lee. 1991. "A Dream of Passion: The Development of the Method." pp. 42–50 in *Star Texts: Image and Performance in Film and Television*, ed. J. Butler. Detroit: Wayne State University Press.

Streep, Meryl. 1990. "When Women Were in the Movies." *Screen Actor* (Fall): 15–17.

Studlar, Gaylin. 1988. *In the Realm of Pleasure: Von Sternberg, Dietrich, and the Masochistic Aesthetic.* Urbana: University of Illinois Press.

———. 1990. "Masochism, Masquerade, and the Erotic Metamorphosis of Marlene Dietrich." pp. 229–249 in *Fabrications: Costume and the Female Body*, eds. J. Gaines and C. Herzog. London and New York: Routledge.

Thompson, John O. 1991. "Screen Acting and the Commutation Test." pp. 183–197 in *Stardom: Industry of Desire*, ed. C. Gledhill. London: Routledge.

Todd, Janet, ed. 1988. *Women & Film.* New York: Holmes & Meier.

Vilga, Edward. 1997. *Acting Now: Conversations on Craft and Career.* New Brunswick, N.J.: Rutgers University Press.

Vineberg, Steve. 1994. *Method Actors: Three Generations of an Acting Style.* New York: Schirmer Books.

Weiss, Andrea. 1991. "A Queer Feeling When I Look at You: Hollywood Stars and Lesbian Identity in the 1930s." pp. 283–299 in *Stardom: Industry of Desire*, ed. C. Gledhill. London: Routledge.

Wexman, Virginia Wright. 1991. "Kenesics and Film Acting: Humphrey Bogart in *The Maltese Falcon* and *The Big Sleep*." pp. 203–213 in *Star Texts: Image and Performance in Film and Television*, ed. J. Butler. Detroit: Wayne State University Press.

———. 1993. *Creating the Couple: Love, Marriage, and Hollywood Performance.* Princeton, N.J.: Princeton University Press.

White, Patricia. 1998. "Feminism and Film." pp. 117–131 in *The Oxford Guide to Film Studies*, eds. J. Hill and P. C. Gibson. Oxford: Oxford University Press.

Williams, Linda Ruth. 2002. "Mother Courage." *Sight and Sound* May. British Film Institute.Org. May 19, 2002. <htpp://www.bfi.org.uk/sightandsound/2002_05/feature01_MotherCourage.html>.

Wojcik, Pamela Robertson. 2004. *Movie Acting, The Film Reader.* New York: Routledge.

Woods, Leigh. 1998. "Introduction." pp. 1–13 in *Playing to the Camera: Film Actors Discuss Their Craft*, eds. B, Cardillo et al. New Haven, Conn.: Yale University Press.

Zucker, Carole. 1990. "'I Am Dietrich and Dietrich Is Me': An Investigation of Performance Style in *Morocco* and *Shanghai Express*." pp. 255–294 in *Making Visible the Invisible: An Anthology of Essays on Film Acting*, ed. C. Zucker. Metuchen, N.J.: Scarecrow Press.

———, ed. 1990. *Making Visible the Invisible: An Anthology of Essays on Film Acting.* Metuchen, N.J.: Scarecrow Press.

———. 1990. "Preface." pp. vii–xi in *Making Visible the Invisible: An Anthology of Essays on Film Acting*, ed. C. Zucker. Metuchen, N.J.: Scarecrow Press.

———. 1999. *In the Company of Actors: Reflections on the Craft of Acting.* New York: Routledge.

———. 2002. *Conversations with Actors on Film, Television, and Stage Performance.* Portsmouth, N.H.: Heinemann.

Index

Printed in Great Britain
by Amazon

64723837R00159